'Your book is the "really good book. Just one"
that Roger Butler would have wanted'
Sir Ian McKellen

'An engrossing, beautiful book about a chance encounter
and the unfolding story of a forgotten gay hero! Now, as
the rights of people are increasingly under threat, this
book is a reminder of the sacrifices that have been
made to achieve liberation'
Lord Michael Cashman

'Immersed as I have been in the twentieth-century campaign
for homosexual equality, I had never known about Roger
Butler, nor met anyone else who knew. What he did was
quite something, and that today we should be so surprised
that it was a shock bears witness to the revolution he
helped start. At times gripping, at times very personal,
this remains an important piece of objective history,
faithfully recorded and beautifully written'
**Matthew Parris, political writer, broadcaster
and former politician**

'Miraculous. *The Light of Day* reclaims a forgotten hero
of the struggle for queer civil rights in a story that is
a testament to courage, determination and love across
generations. Christopher Stephens and Louise Radnofsky
write with tenderness, power and scorching honesty.
I couldn't put it down'
**Will Tosh, author of *Straight Acting:
The Many Queer Lives of William Shakespeare***

'Searching, sad and quietly exhilarating, *The Light of Day* evokes British society's gay enlightenment through the prism of a single remarkable life. More than this, it tells a resonant story of youth, age and the possibilities of platonic love'
James Cahill, author of *Tiepolo Blue* and *The Violet Hour*

'More than a biography of a shamefully overlooked activist, *The Light of Day* paints a beautiful portrait of a friendship the gay reader will find instantly familiar and deeply moving. Tender, contemplative, wise, and funny, it fills the heart and then breaks it. Thanks to Christopher Stephens, Roger Butler is seen again'
AJ West, author of *The Betrayal of Thomas True* and *The Spirit Engineer*

'Shines a light on a forgotten milestone in LGBT history and a gay man of great courage who came out publicly in the press when homosexuality was still punishable in Britain by a maximum sentence of life imprisonment'
Peter Tatchell, LGBT+ campaigner

Christopher Stephens & Louise Radnofsky

The Light of Day

The first man to come out at
the dawn of gay liberation

HEADLINE
PRESS

First published in 2025 by Headline Press
An imprint of Headline Publishing Group Limited

1

Cataloguing in Publication Data is available from the British Library

Hardback ISBN: 978 1 0354 2152 7
Trade Paperback ISBN: 978 1 0354 2153 4

Typeset in Adobe Jenson by CC Book Production

Printed and bound in Great Britain by Clays Ltd, Elcograf S.p.A.

MIX
Paper | Supporting
responsible forestry
FSC® C104740

Headline Publishing Group Limited
An Hachette UK Company
Carmelite House
50 Victoria Embankment
London EC4Y 0DZ

The authorized representative in the EEA is Hachette Ireland,
8 Castlecourt Centre, Castleknock Road, Castleknock,
Dublin 15, D15 YF6A, Ireland (email: info@hbgi.ie)

www.headline.co.uk
www.hachette.co.uk

For anyone who's ever walked up to a bookshelf,
looking for something that will change their life.

'Homosexuality has quite a lot of good cards to play – it has been, and is, abominably treated, it is always a minority, it does no harm to anyone, etc. etc., – but they must be played in the light of day.'

Lionel Fielden to Roger Butler, 5th December 1960

Contents

PREFACE

The Pink Folder

I knew where it would be. It sat – no: was sitting (Roger hated that slip and regularly corrected me) – in the top drawer of the secretaire bookcase that dominated the drawing room at 41 Regent Street. A pink folder, waiting for me.

The glass upper portion of that bookcase, with its ogee curves – those 'lines of beauty' that Roger had explained when we read the Alan Hollinghurst novel together – framed a small, heavy bust of Napoleon, who seemed in that moment to be holding guard over its contents. I stared off Napoleon, opened the drawer, and there it was. Re-used (typical Roger) and a little frayed, the pink folder sat atop a neat pile of documents. Stuck to its front were two white labels, one in Braille, one typed:

```
In the event of my death this folder is to be
given to Christopher Stephens.
```

Roger had let slip during a bedtime conversation the previous August that he had been writing a one-sided letter

1

correspondence, addressed to me. This was a kind of diary, he explained, a record of the final years of his life. But he hadn't intended for me to know about it. Roger had wanted me to discover the letters at some future point, after his death. Until then, they would remain hidden in that folder, in that drawer, and further discussion would be off limits. I, of course, had wondered about those forbidden letters ever since.

I had been at Roger's bedside, in the hospice, as he drew his last breath on a cold January day in 2011. Hours later, when I let myself into the house that he had loved, standing in his hallway, I was consumed by a terrible mix of grief and relief. The ending of a life had also been the ending of weeks of watching my old friend die. In that heady mix of emotion, I was drawn to those letters. Perhaps they offered the promise of some stability, and a more attractive prospect than the grim round of telephone calls that lay ahead. Perhaps I had cried enough and wanted to hear Roger's voice again in some way. Perhaps it was no more profound than the desire to satisfy my curiosity.

So, sitting (yes, sitting) on Roger's deep red sofa, facing the small bay window onto Regent Street, I opened the pink folder. It contained four brown envelopes. True to form, Roger had labelled each and arranged them in date order. I began to read from the first.

30th May 2008

Sweetheart,
For the time being I've run out of subjects I want to write about for the occasional pieces

you've so indulgently endured and recorded for me. Nor do I have anyone to correspond with regularly these days, a la Lionel or Cobb,* but as I have this compulsion always to be writing something in my unoccupied moments, I've hit on the idea of writing a kind of open letter - or rather an ongoing letter - to you.

I'm not proposing to send it to you - you can read it when I've 'passed on' as the local kids always refer to the grim termination - or 'the distinguished thing' as Henry James called it. I'm beginning just after we've returned from our Nottingham weekend which I enjoyed so much - in truth more than I expected - not least, in fact chiefly, for being with you. I'm always content when I'm with you. It will at least be a record of my fluctuating thoughts and reflections.

I had the nerve when we were at Eastwood Hall to break the ice at last and tell you that I long for us to sleep together sometimes - as I said 'just for cuddles and company'. I've always yearned for us to share a bed occasionally, partly for the cosy intimacy and partly because there's such a lot I want to talk about and for that you can't beat being tucked up snugly in the dark - what's called pillow talk when

---

* Broadcaster and writer Lionel Fielden (1896–1974); historian and memoirist Richard Cobb (1917–1996). Roger sustained lengthy correspondences with both.

```
Cabinet ministers tell state secrets to their
mistresses.
    Well, sweetheart, enough of all this for now.
    All my love.
    Roger
```

I stopped.

I was a student when I first met Roger in 2003 and began visiting his home each Tuesday evening, initially as a favour to a friend. Every week, we would spend a couple of hours reading together those things that Roger's blindness prevented him from seeing. However unlikely it seemed to my college friends at the time, my visits had quickly become more than this and I formed a close friendship with this man, fifty years my senior – one which became increasingly close (and increasingly complicated) as the years passed.

Reading together was always at the centre of our relationship but by the time Roger wrote this letter, I'd also been regularly spending my days at Roger's house: afternoons helping him with small household tasks, followed by long evenings of eating, drinking, reading, talking. I would often stay overnight, escaping to a world that felt wholly apart from the hectic college life I left behind me each time I set off on my journey to Regent Street.

In the years leading up to my meeting him, Roger had become more and more isolated, to the point that he rarely left his home. But, as he came to enjoy my company and to trust me to care for him, Roger grew more ambitious. He began to ask if I would guide him into unfamiliar territory: in Oxford – to new restaurants, the city's parks and gardens, shopping – and for short trips out of town. Small things for many people, these were transformative for Roger.

This first letter, though, corresponded with the period when (in Roger's telling of it) I had left him.

By 2008, I had finished my studies at Oxford and was trying to build a life for myself – finding a job, entering what we thought of as the 'real world' in London. My visits were now less regular and made from further afield. They also became more intense. I was no longer a reliable presence, which Roger felt keenly. His health was declining. He was frailer, more vulnerable and again cut off from the world he had only recently started to rediscover. I visited Regent Street as often as I could and did what I thought would help, but I struggled to anticipate Roger's practical needs and couldn't give him the time and attention that would satisfy his loneliness. Upset by my distance, Roger began to talk to me more about what he wanted for me and from me. So long as I remained in London, I understood, there could never be enough time, never enough care available for him.

That passing remark about sharing a bed possessed, by the time I read it in 2011, a crushing weight: years of hopes and expectations, of feeling that I had never really been for Roger what he had wanted me to be, never really done what he wanted me to do. Reading it immediately caused me to question how I had acted towards him in those final few years. Why had I pulled away from the life he wanted to create for me in Oxford? Why had I left this man who needed so much from me?

Flicking through the rest of the folder, I could see that Roger had added new letters and the occasional memento whenever the mood struck, marking each typed page with a date. Some of the thin, white sheets of paper onto which he had written using his electric typewriter were clipped to receipts from dinners, tickets for museums, postcards of the historic houses we had visited. He even included the notes I'd sent him more latterly on cheap stationery from the hotels I'd been staying in while travelling for work. All this built up to more than just a lengthy one-sided correspondence: it was an archive of our shared life.

In the weeks and months that followed, I tried to read more from the first envelope. I made slow progress. The letters Roger had placed in there weren't the mere narration of what had happened; they were concerned as much with how events – and my actions, my decisions – had made him feel. Roger described, with brutal honesty, his experience of our relationship. The times we had spent with one another and the times we were apart – when he wished I was with him, but I was not. How I had pleased him. How I had upset him. How I had helped him. How I had hurt him. How my being increasingly far away from him made him anxious, concerned for both our futures, and regretful about the loss of what he had hoped might be.

Each letter cut into me as I read. In the best of circumstances, it is hard to see your life, your relationship to a person, written out in stark detail from the viewpoint of the other. When that person has died and any chance to do better has gone with them, it is devastating.

And then came a letter where Roger asked me to help.

```
All being well there's one thing I want you
to do for me posthumously - I want you to
```

6

```
take charge of all my letters and scribblings.
I'm afraid I've accumulated rather a lot over
the years. I've left instructions that all
this stuff is to be handed over to you. The
scribblings particularly I want you to have (all
those random pieces in binders) for reasons you
can understand. I may pass them over to you
myself nearer the time if I get the chance.
Many of them, though by no means all, you're
already familiar with - you from whom no
secrets are hid (or not many). What you do with
any of this stuff will be entirely up to you -
it will be immaterial to me by then.
    All my love sweet boy.
```

Up to me, perhaps, but I knew Roger well enough to hear this as an instruction.

During our years of reading together, Roger and I had worked our way through all kinds of materials. Initially, these were books or articles which caught Roger's imagination, suited his mood and which sounded interesting to me. More rarely, I suggested something I thought we might both enjoy (I was normally wrong). But as we grew to know one another better, our most important reading projects involved texts that Roger himself had written.

Diaries, essays, memoirs, biography: the letters and scribblings Roger was asking me to take were in fact banks of material he had created over decades of his life. We had read them together over countless hours in Roger's home, often with a cassette tape recorder whirring in the background so Roger could listen again to them alone without the assistance of a reader. Often, he would make small changes to his work and we'd re-read them, several times over, until he was satisfied. For me, this was an education in Roger Butler: lessons spread over years, learned through Roger's accounts of his past and interpreted through the lens of knowing him increasingly well in the present. And by 2008, we were reading very little else. Now, in these letters he had left for me, Roger was asking me to make use of that education. More than once, he turned the screw:

```
I very much want you to have (in due course)
as many of my goods and chattels - furniture,
books, various curios etc - as you would like
and which I think you would appreciate as I
do. And particularly I want you to take all my
personal papers for reasons you well understand.
```

I did understand. Those many hours of reading and recording together so much of what Roger had written weren't just an act of nostalgia (for him) and education (for me). He intended his work to be his legacy, to be passed on as a complete entity which described his life as the centre-point of a personal commentary on the people and the events which shaped him and the world around him. The experience of growing up gay in post-war Britain, of becoming blind during his early thirties, of Oxford University in the 1970s, his time with eccentric socialites, passionate biographies of his closest friends . . . all this, he believed, could be turned into something that people should want to read.

Roger prized writing above any other talent. On Christmas Eve of 1973, pondering what his future might hold, Roger confessed to his old friend Lionel Fielden that he had only one small hope for himself:

```
I don't really have any ambitions. Except
perhaps to write one really good book. Just
one.
```

A published book, he believed, would be anyone's greatest achievement, and the friends Roger kept in the years that followed reflected this – most of them writers in one way or another. Several of them – successful authors – had read Roger's work and encouraged him to shape it for a wider audience. He had dreamed of publishing his memoirs, I knew, but it had never happened. This was one of his greatest regrets.

It took very little time after us meeting for Roger to become certain about what I should and could do with my life, if I worked hard enough: be an academic, and be one in Oxford. When I left for London not having taken that path, Roger's ambition developed: finish my first academic book and then return to live with him at Regent Street and carry on a writing career, working from the study on the second floor of his house. On all those fronts, I had failed Roger, just as I had failed to give him the time and the care he needed from me in his final years.

Reading his unsent letters, I realised with total clarity that, as his life neared its end, Roger's final ambition for me had become wrapped up in his own. This was my task: to do what Roger himself had found impossible and tell his story, the story we

9

had read together and discussed in such detail. This was a story, spread across thousands of pages, which I had now inherited.

I stopped again.

I didn't open the second, third or fourth envelopes in the pink folder, and later, when the dozens of boxes of Roger's writings arrived at my London home after the sale of 41 Regent Street, I left them unopened, too. I told myself I was hiding from Roger's last request because the years that followed were just too busy. But, as time passed it started to feel inevitable that I would fail Roger yet again. Once more, I had stepped away from what he wanted from me and for me. Roger's story would go untold.

As I went about continuing to build my life in London, Roger surrounded me. With his furniture in every room of my house and his art on my walls, I would read his books, eat with his cutlery, pour gin from his decanter. I even used up his many unopened boxes of tissues (Roger planned ahead). Wrapped up by so much of him, I often wondered how Roger would rate the life I was now living, assess what I had achieved. Success or failure? His boxes of writing remained closed, yes, but I had done other things – I had managed, finally, to publish. In 2015, I dedicated my first book to his memory. Perhaps that was enough.

A year later I found myself – suddenly, somewhat unexpectedly – encountering the prospect of a baby. Louise, a friend since we were both college LGB reps (no T, no + in those days) at Oxford, was now living in Washington DC's gay village with her partner. She called me in the summer of 2016 to ask if I would help her and Stacey have a child. With a certain amount of cheerleading from my mother (who happened to be sitting with me when Louise rang), I didn't really hesitate.

We had discussed this in theory, on holiday in the years before, but we were unprepared for the reality of actually making a baby. In DC, we encountered a slew of paperwork, experienced several physical indignities and spent an extraordinary amount of time in dreary clinics and the offices of lawyers and licensed clinical social workers. During all that lingering and wondering about the oddities of this process, we had plenty of opportunity to talk, and particularly to talk about the future. Probably it was this which made me bring up Roger, in one of those bored moments in a waiting area, to ask Louise what she thought.

Louise – a journalist – would, I hoped, be able to help me find a way to tell Roger's story. She could lift me out from underneath what had come to feel like the impossible burden of Roger's expectation and perhaps help me to emerge with a story that others would be eager to hear. She could also let me down gently – free me? – if she concluded there was nothing in those boxes beyond the personal interest project of an old man. I asked whether she might help. This could be another project in which we shared. She agreed.

Back in England, I dug out thousands of pages: archive boxes stuffed with memoirs, files bursting with sheets of typed diaries, shoe boxes and large metal chests stacked with letters and photograph albums, and countless small envelopes filled with picture negatives and newspaper clippings. I used Roger's cassette player to listen to hours of recordings (stopped in my tracks the first few times I encountered my own voice and Roger's) and found ways of deciphering the Braille on Roger's labels identifying the content of some old audio spools. I catalogued it all, digitised what I could and sent it across the Atlantic, reading each line as I did. After Lucy was born, Louise began reading, too: something to look forward to, she said, when setting her alarm for 3am feeds.

Many of Roger's papers spoke of ordinary experiences, from childhood to old age. These were filled with the quotidian: petty complaints, gossip, musings about politics and philosophy of an unremarkable kind, concerns about finances and health. Louise was impressed that Roger had painstakingly created all this material that he himself was unable to read. It was clear to her that he had considered his own life important enough to document, which had to count for something. But what did it mean for anyone else?

Then she saw it.

Some way through the account of his earlier years, Roger described arriving in London fresh from school, book-shopping on the Charing Cross Road on a Saturday afternoon and picking up a paperback about homosexuality that revealed to him who he truly was. This might have been a description of Louise as a teenager in the 1990s – going in to London to browse on the same street, for the same material, for the same reason. As she read, it struck her that there was probably a teenager doing that exact thing, in that same place, on that very day. It was a common queer experience, except Roger's moment on the Charing Cross Road was lived out in a dangerously different context, at a time when male homosexuality was criminalised.

Roger and I had read together about his moment of discovery and about where it had led him: an underground gay social world of private clubs and bars, queer house parties, and brief encounters with sexual liberation under the continual threat of arrest. He hadn't shared with me, though, many of the details he described in these memoirs – of the days when Roger threw himself into the most nascent of gay rights activism. Now, Louise and I began to learn the real extent of his involvement in the battle.

Buried in the material was the tale of how Roger had become one of the very first volunteers in the newly formed Homosexual Law Reform Society – his brave journey to its earliest headquarters in 1958 as a young man of 23 and his determination to support the cause in every way he could. Reading all this unearthed a memory of being told that Roger had written to some newspapers arguing for the decriminalisation of homosexuality, but this letter was nowhere to be found. Roger had apparently copied and saved *every* letter he wrote apart from this one – it wasn't in the memoirs, nor was it in those many boxes of his papers. So I began to look through archives of the major journals of his day. Finally, in a compendium of the *Spectator*'s letter pages, I saw Roger's name on a letter dated 3rd June 1960.

In front of me was something far bolder than anything I'd imagined. Roger wasn't just making an argument for law reform; he had voluntarily and publicly identified himself as a homosexual in order to do so. Seven years before the law changed to permit sex between men, Roger signed his name at the bottom of a letter, telling the entire country that he was an unashamed member of this reviled, criminal group.

```
SIR,—We are homosexuals and we are writing
because we feel strongly that insufficient is
being done to enlighten public opinion on a
topic which has for too long been shunned . . .
```

Every historical description of the years before 1967 that I had read painted a picture of secrecy, of hiding, blackmail, terror and shame. Known homosexuals were systematically targeted by the police. Those who were marginally luckier still faced harassment, eviction, unemployment, disownment. Anonymity was essential – a matter of survival. And yet here was Roger Butler, an unknown 25-year-old estate agent from Banbury, apparently willing to jeopardise everything by revealing himself as a gay man.

As I carried on reading back issues of the *Spectator* and the *New Statesman* (where the letter had also been printed), I saw that Roger's letter had influenced public debate about homosexuality for months. I also found, in an obscure corner of the British Library, testimony from another campaigner of this period, Patrick Trevor-Roper, talking about Roger. Speaking as part of an oral history project to document the lives of people involved in the law reform movement, Patrick declared Roger's letter to be a milestone on the road towards the legalisation of homosexuality.[1] For a brief period, Roger was the most important gay rights activist in the country.

Why hadn't I known this before? Why hadn't Roger's published declaration become central to histories of the gay rights movement? Why weren't his words widely heralded in the gay community, plastered on badges, coffee mugs and t-shirts?

The closest to a recognition of his contribution I could find was in the same oral history archive in the British Library, which included a recording of an interview with Roger made in 1990.[2] Here, at last, was someone expressing curiosity about what he had done. But even this underlined the extent to which Roger had been forgotten. The interviewer had never planned to speak with Roger, and indeed had never heard of him until Trevor-Roper suggested she seek him out at the end of his interview. The audio file could only be obtained by special request, and then had to be listened to inside a designated, members-only reading room. After this, I found just three short descriptions of Roger's letter in academic texts.[3]

This became frustrating. Far from being celebrated, Roger seemed to have been relegated to the margins of the history of the gay rights movement. It seemed to Louise and me that by voluntarily and very publicly declaring himself to be gay, and especially by doing this as a political act to challenge anti-gay laws, he had done something entirely new: Roger had come out.

By the 1970s, the Gay Liberation Front was espousing the need for people to identify themselves as gay – to come out – both to shed their own shame and to claim their rightful place in society. It remained a core tactic of campaigning groups in the 1980s and 1990s, based on the theory that if straight people were aware that they knew gay people, they might be less willing to deny them rights. But the GLF did not invent the idea. Roger, acting entirely on his own, compelled by nobody else, had arrived at it in 1960, and had come out for exactly the same reason.

Was he the first to do so? We ticked through a roster of the famous homosexuals we had been raised to know who might lay claim to have come out before 1960 in order to challenge laws that criminalised homosexuality. Each of these great names fell short in some way. Some had been open only in private circles, avoiding wider declarations and sometimes explicitly denying the truth when pushed. Others had written on the subject but were anonymous or ambiguous. A handful had been direct and open about themselves in public forums, but only after their sexuality had already been revealed outside of their private circles through some form of compulsion. We kept looking. We keep looking. We still haven't found any man, well-known or obscure, who came out before Roger Butler in order to change the law.

But Roger has been completely forgotten for it.

Why? That is the story of his later life. Roger's insecurities and his shyness contributed, but it was his failing sight, which left Roger completely blind by the middle of the 1960s, that pushed him into the shadows and left him out of the history books. By the time homosexuality was decriminalised, Roger was just one more person who used to be involved in the Homosexual Law Reform Society. He had become preoccupied with surviving in a world not designed for blind people like him. The leaders of the reform movement had lost touch with Roger and were themselves quickly eclipsed by the radical activists of the Gay Liberation Front in the early 1970s. And as Roger moved into a different world, he fell out of sight of the chroniclers of the gay rights movement, too. Here was another reason that Roger's story needed to be told, we realised. It was disability and marginalisation that wiped Roger from the records of gay emancipation.

We had found our story: the unique, important truth of Roger's life which his colossal writing efforts and all that time he had spent immersing me in his past had saved for future generations.

Despite this happy realisation, I felt a new regret. Why hadn't I known this truth about Roger already? He had told me so much about his younger life in London, so why hadn't I asked more about what he had done in the law reform movement? Why hadn't I played interviewer to him when I had the chance? Why hadn't I found out about his work that had made it possible for me to live my life as I now do?

When I came to read his diaries from the rest of the 1960s, I saw that Roger had looked back on meeting another pioneer of the gay rights movement, Peter Wildeblood, with similar regret. The two men met at a party in 1962, but Roger was unable to report much at all about his hero. I was frustrated with his failure to ask more, but then I realised that I had behaved in exactly the same way with Roger myself. When I met him, I was about the same age as Roger had been when he met Wildeblood. He'd asked nothing; I'd asked nothing. Shyness of youth, perhaps. Perhaps just shyness – I'm not sure either of us improved much with age.

Roger loved to collect quotations that spoke to his experience. Typed onto a small slip of paper, placed among his memoirs, he had copied this assertion by Alexander Herzen:

```
In order to write one's reminiscences it is
not at all necessary to be a great man or a
notorious criminal, nor a celebrated artist, nor
a statesman. It is quite enough to be simply a
human being, to have something to tell and not
merely to desire to tell it but at least have
some little ability to do so.⁴
```

Roger had something to tell, the desire to tell it and more than some little ability to do so. His story is that of a quiet revolutionary, one who deserves a place among the giants of the gay rights movement but who has been overlooked. This story is a missing piece in our understanding of how we as gay people won the rights and freedoms we now have – how and why laws and attitudes changed. It's my story, and it's Louise's story, and it's the story of a teenager walking up to a bookshelf today, on the Charing Cross Road or anywhere else, looking to read the thing that will change their life.

Roger had many ambitions for me, for him and for the two of us. In the end, he couldn't achieve all he wanted and I couldn't achieve all he wanted for me. I still wonder whether the decisions I made in my life with Roger were the right ones, even as my experience continues to repeat the lesson that there are rarely right and wrong choices. Perhaps, though, in telling Roger's story I can make one right choice – to fulfil his last wish. In following his final instruction, I can (I hope) be some version of what he wanted me to be.

Lucca, June 2023

CHAPTER 1

Becoming a Homosexual

'It was one of these moments of revelation . . . one of those road to Damascus things'[1]

In the pale sunshine of the spring of 1957, Roger Brian Butler was sitting on a bench in Leicester Square, devouring the book he had just discovered, and which was about to change his life.

He had found it in a display of new paperbacks, set out in piles on a table in front of a parade of bookshops on London's Charing Cross Road. One of the Penguin publications, with the familiar white and orange cover, had caught his attention. Its title, in elegant, bold, black typography, was *Against the Law*, but it was the author's name, Peter Wildeblood, that caused him to look more closely.

Roger's life in London had, so far, been sedate, unremarkable. He enjoyed the freedom of a young man in a large city without commitments or expectation, and found some fulfilment in his job at a high-end estate agency. But a typical Saturday afternoon browsing bookshops was as much an event as anything else he had done or seen to write home about. In this moment, the elusive Something Interesting that Roger had come to the city to find (though perhaps not to write home about) had presented itself.

The description on the cover of *Against the Law* triggered Roger's memory of news headlines he had seen as an 18-year-old. Early in 1954, Peter Wildeblood had been one of a trio of men convicted and sent to prison for gross indecency and 'conspiracy to incite certain male persons to commit serious offences with male persons' under Section 11 of the 1885 Criminal Law Amendment Act. This 'Labouchere Amendment' criminalised all sexual acts between men, in public or private, extending laws against 'buggery', which dated back in English law as far as 1533.* The prosecution of Wildeblood along with Lord Montagu of Beaulieu and Michael Pitt-Rivers had been a high-profile scandal splashed across the newspapers, including the one where Wildeblood had been a star reporter. After his release, Wildeblood had nothing to lose and decided to lay himself bare, offer his own narrative, and expose the demeaning and cruel treatment he had received.

'Prompted by no precise impulse except an unaccountable curiosity,' Roger recalled, he bought the book for three shillings and sixpence and took it across to one of the seats in the square. He tore through most of it in the next two hours, until the strain on his eyes from reading caused him to stop. *Against the Law* proved to be nothing short of a revelation – about himself.

---

* Lesbians were never criminalised in the UK.

Becoming a Homosexual

Wildeblood, a seasoned writer and journalist, wrote in a fluent and engaging style, offering a highly charged personal apologia at the peak of his indignation immediately after exiting prison . . . it was a natural and appropriate book for its time, and on that afternoon in Leicester Square, its effect on me was electric.

Oblivious to the passers by and the continuous traffic, it suddenly dawned on me that everything Wildeblood was saying about himself and homosexuality fitted my situation exactly.

It seems extraordinary that I could have reached the age of 22 without recognising this, but so it was. Or perhaps it was - and this is more likely the case - that an awareness of my true nature had been growing inside me for some time but it took Wildeblood's book and his defiant exposition to make me face up to the same reality and spell out unequivocally to myself the uncomfortable truth, 'I am a homosexual.'

I remember feeling no sense of shock, no surprise even, more a sense of relief at knowing exactly where I stood. I simply had never looked at myself so starkly.

It might seem odd that Roger, or anyone, would identify with Wildeblood after reading his searing account of state-sanctioned

21

blackmail and the degrading, abusive treatment he experienced. But in the thick cloak of silence around homosexuality in 1950s England, criminal proceedings against gay men served as one of the few public acknowledgements that they existed. Cases where gay men had been exposed for having participated in homosexual acts were part of the currency of the lower-brow British newspapers, with shocking tales – often located in public toilets and involving trickery by the police – that nurtured readers' fears and fantasies. And these readers included many queer people growing up in the middle part of the twentieth century, Roger among them:

No one who has grown up since 1960 can really
appreciate what a dark age it was before then,
in that pre-Lady Chatterley era, for sexual
knowledge and awareness. Despite more than
half a century of Freud and psycho-analysis –
and more recently Kinsey – for most of my
generation, the whole subject was still as
guiltily veiled as those proverbial Victorian
piano legs.
   I had heard of men called 'pansies', although
I don't recall ever actually seeing one.
Then, of course, there were the vicars and
scoutmasters who regularly got reported in *The
News of the World*.

Wildeblood's is not quite as chilling a tale as it might initially sound – because after he had been convicted and his story had become the property of the police, the judiciary and the press, he made the choice to retell it on his own terms. And in Wildeblood's version, alongside the account of his mistreatment, he articulated a personal identity that Roger could recognise and claim:

> I am attracted towards men, in the way in which most men are attracted towards women. I am aware that many people, luckier than myself, will read this statement with incredulity and perhaps with derision; but it is the simple truth . . . If it was possible for me to become like them I should do so; and nothing would be easier for me than to assume a superficial normality, get married and perhaps have a family. This would, however, be at best dishonest . . . The truth is that an adult man who has chosen a homosexual way of life has done so because he knows that no other course is open to him. It is easy to preach chastity when you are not obliged to practise it yourself, and it must be remembered that, to a homosexual, there is nothing intrinsically shameful or sinful in his condition. Everywhere he goes, he sees other men like himself, forbidden by the law to give any physical expression to their desires. It is not surprising that he should seek a partner among them, so that together they may build a shelter against the hostile world.[2]

A statement of this kind in 1950s Britain was a radical affirmation for homosexuals – a validation of the very existence of gay men and a proposition that they were on an equal moral footing to the heterosexual majority.

The 1954 prosecutions of Wildeblood, Montagu and Pitt-Rivers triggered a brief but important demonstration of public sympathy. This emerged partly in response to the tactics deployed against them, especially the use of information from two RAF servicemen, who had been induced to provide incriminating evidence with the promise of immunity from prosecution. Their testimony was supplemented by letters written by Wildeblood to one of the servicemen. Discomfort with these methods may have been exacerbated by deference to the high social positions which Montagu and Pitt-Rivers enjoyed. More importantly, it was clear to a titillated population that this was not a case of molestation, or even public sex. There was a sense, Roger later concluded, that the state had overreached.

```
This trial had been the most sensational of
its kind since that of Oscar Wilde, not least
because of this distasteful method employed by
the prosecution to obtain convictions. It was
also seen to be a deliberately high publicity
case as part of an intensive anti-homosexual
campaign then being pursued by the police and
the Home Secretary.*
```

Walking onto the street as he left court, sentenced to eighteen months in prison, Wildeblood was faced by a crowd of people. He feared yet one more indignity. Instead, to his amazement,

---

* David Maxwell Fyfe (1900–67), later Viscount Kilmuir, was Home Secretary in the Conservative government 1951–4.

they had gathered to jeer the police and the witnesses who had spoken against him, and to call words of encouragement to the convicted criminals. Later, when he returned home after prison, his neighbours welcomed him and told him they were glad to see him back: 'We read all about it in the papers, and we thought it was a rotten shame.'[3]

Some of the political elite shared the sentiments of the crowd and Wildeblood's neighbours, and 'the Montagu affair' helped push the Conservative government of the time to establish the Departmental Committee on Homosexual Offences and Prostitution, soon known as the 'Wolfenden Committee' after its chairman, Sir John Wolfenden. The committee was given the task of reconsidering the laws prohibiting homosexual activity. Wildeblood himself would give evidence to it, describing his time in prison, the nature of his homosexuality and his views about the moral neutrality of same-sex sex. To both his readers and the committee, he was talking openly in a way that had never been done before:

Fear is a terrible emotion; it is like a black frost which blights and stunts all the other qualities of a man. If half a million men, who are good citizens in every other respect, are to remain under this perpetual shadow, I believe that Society itself will be the ultimate loser. The right which I claim for myself, and for those like me, is the right to choose the person whom I love.[4]

Roger was inspired. He finally knew who he was, and a few years later he would build on Wildeblood's calm articulations about homosexuality to make an even bolder declaration of his own.

Roger fled to London years before his revelatory moment in Leicester Square, late in 1952, while still 17. Because of his poor sight he had been rejected from National Service after leaving school, cutting off the escape route open to most boys of his age. He was an only child and close to his parents, but he knew he couldn't stay one more day than was absolutely necessary in the sleepy Oxfordshire countryside where he spent his adolescence in the immediate aftermath of the Second World War.

```
I had to get away from the God-forsaken little
town where I had spent the last eight years and
which held no interest and no future for me. It
was slowly suffocating me. London had to be the
answer.
```

Roger's life had in fact begun in London, but he and his parents left the city to escape the Blitz, moving to the Cotswolds village of Bampton. At the end of 1940, his father, Eric, was drafted into the RAF, and Roger and his mother, Doris, relocated to nearby Oxford and stayed there until his father was demobbed a year after the end of the war. Roger's father took a minor managerial role in the market town of Banbury and there Roger passed the 11-plus exam that took him to a local grammar school. Self-conscious in the ugly, metal-framed glasses that only partially corrected his weak vision, Roger always felt like an outsider. Nevertheless, it was at school in Banbury that Roger had his early experiences of sexual attraction and sexual activity. The first time was with George.*

He being lively and outgoing, we gravitated towards each other during our first term and became each other's best friend for a couple of years. During the first school summer holiday, George went away for a week to some kind of summer camp - the sort of thing I never went in for - where he shared a tent with two or three older boys. When he returned home, he came rushing round to see me brimming with the most amazing information. Apart from all the extremely interesting biological details, which were only of academic value at that time, apparently there was also something immediately relevant that one could do. By way of illustration George lay on my bed, pulled down his shorts and proceeded to demonstrate. I watched this with fascination.

At the end of the garden of the house where George lived was a solid brick-built garage above which was a low, dusty loft with bare boards and a small round window. It was the perfect den for small boys, well away from the house and quite safe from intrusion.

He wasn't bad looking I now realise, in a

* This and some other names have been changed for reasons of privacy.

small, sharp-featured impish way, but this meant
nothing to me then. I wasn't conscious of being
physically attracted to him. Our indulgences
were purely carnal.

Then there was Jack – 'the first great crush of my life'.
Roger's life was changed by the confidence with which he
grasped several of the most important opportunities presented
to him. He spoke often of 'flooks' and fairy godmothers,
strange strokes of luck with the air of destinies, and benevolent patrons he ultimately sought to emulate. But when it
came to sex and love, his defining experiences were almost
always those where opportunities were missed — and this
started with Jack.

It was, as it naturally is in such cases,
his combination of good looks and engaging
personality that captivated me. He was handsome
even at that age when features are still
unformed - wide-set eyes, high cheekbones,
small, delicate nose, fair but not blond hair.
Equally, it was his winning personality and
sunny disposition that appealed: he was good
natured, uncomplicated, uninhibited, easy-
going, one of those enviable types popular with
everyone. In short, just about everything I
believed I was not. He was my ideal type and I
idolised him throughout our school days.
    Needless to say, then, it was a torment for

me to hear it rumoured at one stage that he and two or three others had taken to gathering in George's loft-den. I lived in a total agony of jealousy and envy at being excluded.

I yearned to feel Jack's arms around me. And once – just once – it seemed as if this might have come to pass, during one of our school trips to the swimming baths. We were in the changing room and it was the only occasion I was ever alone with Jack. He was naked, standing on a slatted bench and we chatted idly while he dried himself with a towel. Then a silence fell between us and he stared at me very intently – I can see his eyes now – with that enquiring look which clearly says, 'Well, shall we?'. If I had been less timid I would have seized the moment: we could have slipped into one of the cubicles and for two minutes I would have been in heaven. But I let the moment slip and shortly afterwards some boys came noisily in and my chance of heaven was lost forever.

At the time, Roger was oblivious to the idea that he might have a particular reason to be frustrated with life in the provinces. What he had done and felt at school, he believed, was just boyish fun, nothing more. Because, seemingly, nothing else was possible. But even if he did not understand that his compulsion to get to London was one shared with generations of gay men, he knew there was something he was desperate to escape: 'the loneliness, the sheer bloody loneliness' he felt living with his parents, however much he loved them.

> I suppose I must have come across the word
> homosexuality but it had never registered
> as having any relevance to me. Like road
> accidents, it was something that happened
> to other people. It was hardly a topic that
> cropped up in casual conversation at home . . .
> It never occurred to me that my feelings for
> Jack might signify something deeper. If it had
> ever been put to me, for instance, that two
> men could be in love with each other and live
> together in a form of unholy matrimony, I would
> have thought this grotesque and probably been
> shocked.

With his small clutch of unimpressive exam results, there weren't many career paths open to Roger, but going to London offered a liberation, whatever his prospects. He couldn't just wait any longer for something interesting to happen in Banbury. He replied to four job advertisements in the *Telegraph* and took a position offered by Sam Waller of Waller and Way, making his haphazard entry into estate agency work.

Leaning on his parents for financial support, Roger took a room in West Hampstead without seeing it. It was 'a dingy little Victorian terrace in a back street, a landlady with watery eyes and a crumpled, harassed, featureless face' – and he immediately regretted his decision. Three months later, severe food poisoning from his landlady's cooking drove him out to a more expensive room in Belsize Park. It would be several more years – after a brief spell working in the House of Commons library, and then a move to a younger and more fashionable estate agency in Mayfair – before he was able to afford the rent for his first independent flat.

Despite the paltry salary, Roger had a lucky break with Waller and Way, letting furnished flats and houses in central London to a varied clientele, 'exotic, even'.

```
The telephone would ring and it might be Mrs
Syrie Maugham, deaf and irascible; or it might
be the more relaxed American tones of, say,
Robert Mitchum or Raquel Welch; or it might be
the fruity Russian baritone of Baroness Moura
Budberg, who was said to have included Gorky
and H.G. Wells among her lovers. There was also,
for instance, a certain historical interest in
walking round to Berkeley Square to see the
once magnificent but now aged and rather dowdy
Marchioness Curzon of Kedleston.
```

Meagre as his own initial circumstances might be, Roger could finally loose himself from the bonds of rural living: 'At last I was free to do whatever I chose, which chiefly meant being out and about seeing what life had to offer.' Still, in his early years in London, Roger had no social life of which to speak and initially made no real friends in town. When he connected with a former schoolmate, Michael, after bumping into him outside the

Royal Festival Hall, they branched out a little, but even that was limited to gentle, bourgeois activity: attending classical concerts and plays at a time when half a crown would get you into the gallery for almost any performance in London.

Roger pushed himself to grapple with contemporary music and theatre, watching Stravinsky conduct and seeing the first London production of *Waiting for Godot*, but deep down he knew that he was still somehow missing out.

```
 The truth was, although I couldn't quite have
put it into words at the time, like any young
man at that age, I was painfully in need of
a real relationship - intimate, emotional,
intense, exclusive and of course sexual. Looking
back, I can recognise this yearning perfectly
well for what it was - quite naturally I
desperately wanted to have an affair with some
very undefined partner. But how was this to be
achieved?

 I was aware that London must be full of
opportunities and dubious temptations on all
sides but I was quite oblivious of them because
I wasn't actively looking for them - or, more
likely perhaps, didn't recognise them when they
stared me in the face. If ever there was an
innocent loose in London it was me in those
days.
```

Until the bench in Leicester Square.

In a time when so many men could live their whole lives without recognising or accepting their true nature, Roger was thankful that reading Wildeblood's book jolted him into understanding his sexuality, 'belatedly, but not too late'.

A few years later, in October 1962, Roger had the opportunity to tell Wildeblood just how important his book had been to him. Roger had become a close friend of John and Venetia Newall, a respectable and wealthy couple whose philanthropic activity focused fleetingly on the campaign for the decriminalisation of homosexuality. After two years of that work, they decided to turn their attention to other issues and threw a small party.

There were only about a dozen people at the soiree. Roger, suffering from a bug of some kind, very nearly missed it, but he was delighted when he arrived to find himself in a group peppered with some of the big names of the law reform movement. He started chatting with a few familiar faces but couldn't help but be distracted by Peter Wildeblood across the room, talking to his hosts.

Venetia, who knew Roger well, ushered him over to join their conversation. Facing his hero for the first time, Roger was surprised by how tall and lean Wildeblood was, his pale, angular face betraying a rapid progression into middle age. Wildeblood exchanged a polite greeting with the young man but Roger found himself completely star struck, able only to smile in return and utter a few words of greeting:

```
My tongue-tied awkwardness prevented me from
being able to tell him, as I so wanted to, what
a profound effect his book had had on my life,
```

both when I read it and in the years which
followed.

Had he been able to speak, Roger might have told Wildeblood
how the clarity of mind he gained in Leicester Square had
prompted him to throw himself into the task of reading
everything he could about homosexuality and homosexuals. It
was a journey that had taken him into every seedy little Soho
bookshop he could find, rummaging nervously through the
shelves in search of anything available, from studies like the
Kinsey Report to a smattering of gay-themed novels like James
Baldwin's *Giovanni's Room* and Mary Renault's *The Charioteer*.
Roger bought everything he could afford.

Roger's Charing Cross Road adventures had given him a new
window into the world he had been seeking, but the view was
a partial one:

> Everything was so shrouded in obfuscation in
> those days that there was very little to go
> on. Even in the wider world there was virtually
> no open discussion of the subject except in
> the kind of progressive circles unknown to me.
> Books, radio, theatre, films were all heavily
> censored. We were still in the age when the
> establishment knew best, protecting us from the
> unseemly and possibly subversive influences.

Even in this environment, though, Roger's efforts didn't go
unrewarded. Barely a month after reading *Against the Law*,

he was presented with a chance to expand on his theoretical knowledge. And this time – unlike with Jack – he did not baulk.

Roger had taken to dropping into a local pub – attracted, he could now acknowledge, by the good-looking Irish assistant manager. The regulars included a 19-year-old off-duty policeman, easily identified by the dark blue shirt and black tie he wore under an innocuous jacket. Roger got into a tentative conversation with this man one evening as they stood at the bar and they rapidly formed an intense friendship, spending all their free time together. For a few enchanted weeks, they went around London, their relationship erotically charged but doggedly chaste, before Bryan abruptly decided the police force was not for him and resigned to join the RAF.

On his final evening in London, half a dozen of Bryan's colleagues gathered at the pub for a farewell drink. Roger was feeling both dismayed at losing his friend and nervous at being incongruously included in a group of policemen. As the group dispersed, Roger was left alone – not with Bryan but with one of the others. The next thing he remembered was finding himself, apparently without a word being said or anything proposed, in his own bed with a naked policeman.

```
The room is dark except for the dim glow from
the street lamp outside. This is the first
time I've ever actually been in bed with anyone
and being such a novice I've very little idea
what to expect. But it's very exciting, this
passionate love making, more so than I could
ever have imagined.
```

It was not lost on Roger that his first real sexual encounter and the most illegal thing he had ever done was with a police officer. He could imagine a ludicrous scene in which this person – could he plausibly call him his lover? – jumped out of bed, donned his policeman's helmet and arrested him for complicity in an act of gross indecency.

```
Absurd this might seem but in reality not so
far removed from the degrading practice whereby
young policemen were sent into public urinals
to display their penises in order to entrap the
unwary. I never asked Bryan or my friend of the
night if this had ever been among their duties,
but I'm inclined to give them the benefit of
the doubt. In any case, however, I came through
this initiation into the arms of the law
without acquiring a criminal record.
```

It was thrilling, Roger concluded, but it went nowhere further, and marked no kind of breakthrough into the gay world, which by now he knew must be out there, somewhere. He continued to long for more. A year later he would find it, at the end of a brisk, cold walk from Angel tube station, at the heart of a new group fighting to change the law.

Oxford, 2000

My own coming out was, characteristically, planned.

I arrived at Oxford University to read theology in the autumn term ('Michaelmas', I quickly learned to say) of 2000, determined that I would start as I intended to go on. This meant, more than anything, being openly gay. Old Christopher – the me of school, of rural Wiltshire, the vicar's son – would immediately pass, I had decided, into a New Christopher, who would live the fuller life I had been imagining since the age of 14, when I first understood why I was different.

The year before I went to university, the world seemed to be shifting. On television, *Queer as Folk* offered frank, exciting depictions of gay people actually being gay in the bars and clubs (and bedrooms) of Manchester. Jack, still in high school, had kissed Ethan in the idyllic teenage dream of *Dawson's Creek*, which was no less exciting for its innocence. I walked into my new college – Christ Church – with half a millennium of history breathing down on me from its unfinished gothic arches, ready for everything to change.

Outside the college walls, a new Labour government had lifted the ban on gay people serving in the military, but there was still a national battle raging over whether to lower the age of consent for gay sex from 18 to 16, as it had long been for heterosexuals. This saga had run for two years already. The House of Commons voted repeatedly in favour of equalisation, only to be blocked by the House of Lords, cheered on by a tabloid campaign to 'save' the nation's sons.

My family hadn't thought twice about bringing gay people into our lives, at a time when acceptance couldn't be taken for granted. They helped me understand that being gay didn't have to mean conforming to popular, diminutive stereotypes that still tended to dominate in the media. I also understood that it wasn't something bad. Like a lot of the world outside my home, though, school was never a safe environment.

I had always been certain I could never come out there, where 'gay' was a common insult, one of the worst. I heard it regularly, along with 'queer' and some of the more detailed and imaginative synonyms for homosexual. I did everything I could to distance myself, physically and mentally, from what became regular taunts from other boys, with occasional violence casually thrown into the mix. I was a homosexual, I was gay – I knew it, they knew it – but I vowed never to say it and I came to hate the words. To a degree, I still shy away from them. After so many years of pretending to find queerness as repulsive as my peers did, in order to survive, I can feel myself involuntarily flinching at having to own the label.

University could be different, and I determined that I would be an honest, authentic version of myself as soon as I got there.

Oxford, 2000

As I prepared for my A levels and planned for this new future, however, the news stands were still filled with headlines debating the proposed change to the age of consent – questioning whether I really had the ability to know who I was and if I should be allowed to make the choices heterosexual teenagers took freely. Commentators offered opinions that homosexuality was contagious – that any change to the law would be licence for sexual predators and the inevitable corruption of confused minors who, given a few more years, would naturally turn out to be straight. The reason not to equalise the ages of consent for straight and for gay people, they argued, was that the ramifications of gay sex were just so much more serious. Nobody in good conscience could allow teenagers who could be saved to instead be pulled along the wrong path. The law was protecting them.

Just like those boys at school, here were politicians proudly claiming a moral disgust at me – and it wasn't clear if I, as an 18-year-old, was to be considered pathetic or vile, or perhaps both.

But within a few days of arriving at Christ Church, I had been gathered up by Rebecca, the LGB rep, who took me to meet other gay people in college and showed me that university would be nothing like school. In an instant, I was welcomed into a group whose members were happy and willing to take me under their wings. They told me who I should know and where I should go, and made a point of holding my hand (literally as much as metaphorically) as I took my first steps into their gay world. Political and social hostility could be locked firmly outside the gates of our college, and I was encouraged to be and to do everything I wanted.

Meeting so many gay people, all at once, was transformative. For the first time, I felt how it was to be part of a tribe: a group pulled together by this common denominator. Here, finally, were my people. And for someone who had been isolated by his secrets for so many years, the relief and the joy of that – the feeling of safety that it offered – was thrilling. We were drawn together by shared experiences and the labels we claimed for ourselves, and I emerged with friends of a new kind, friends with whom I could be completely myself. And, like a symbolic shrug of acceptance from the world outside my new bubble, by Christmas, finally the age of consent had been equalised.

During the winter vacation, I decided to tell my parents: I was gay and I had a boyfriend, Tom.

My mother said her only fear was that I'd be treated differently: 'Won't things be difficult for you?' she asked. 'Won't life be harder, people treat you badly?'

I paused and thought. 'No,' I replied. 'I really think my life will be better.'

This wasn't my way of softening the blow. In that moment, I was in no doubt that coming out at Oxford had been the right choice and even, in that place and at the end of the year 2000, that being gay was in some ways an advantage. When that first year at college came to an end, I was elected LGB rep. Next year, it would be my turn to gather up the new gays.

It was another college's LGB rep, Toni, who first asked me if I would like to join a termly gathering of 'the like-minded' (code in Oxford for gay men). These were formal, black-tie dinners, organised by a self-selecting group of established academics, which took place in one of the university's heavily panelled and ornately carved Senior Common Rooms. Reserved normally only for Fellows of the college, they would be decorated, for the night, with the finest silver in Oxford – and some of its prettiest men.

I had some apprehension at first. I knew about another covert group of Oxbridge gays whose dining society we called 'breakfast and blowjobs', which I'd done my best to avoid. But this was a gathering of a very different order and any fears I had of not fitting in quickly faded. The pleasures were many, of course, in those rarefied rooms, but this was an encouraging, supportive group focused on good conversation and a happy conviviality. The longer-standing members offered guidance – academic and everything else – and, for the first time for people in their position, listened to me and encouraged me to think in new ways. Those dinners became a highlight of the term – and my introduction to Roger Butler.

One of the academics at the dinners was Nick, a Fellow at The Queen's College, who for many years had been one of a number of people who regularly visited Roger at his home. These visitors would read aloud the various things Roger couldn't access without a sighted person, or which he preferred to tackle in company – everything from his bank statements to novels and lengthy historical tomes.

In 2003, Nick was planning for a sabbatical year in New York and asked if I would fill in for him. He had been Roger's only gay reader for some time, at least as far as I could tell, and, if I was interested, it would be my job to continue that role while he was away. Roger had a retinue of what he called his North Oxford Ladies, Nick told me, who were dependable when it came to helping Roger work through his daily post, sort out his bills and read through the latest book reviews. But there were some things he suspected these genteel women would rather not read.

When I returned to Oxford to begin my Master's degree, I found a note in my pigeonhole in the porter's lodge, typewritten on a small, white piece of card.

3.10.03

```
Dear Christopher,
    Nick Bamforth rang me yesterday to say you
might be willing to do a little reading for
me sometimes. I shall be delighted if you can.
May I suggest that you pop over here whenever
you can spare the time so that we can have a
sociable drink and a general chat and hopefully
sort out some arrangement that will suit us
both. Do give me a ring when you have a moment
so that we can fix a time.
    Yours,
    Roger
```

Roger's telephone number was printed onto an address label and stuck to the top of the card, so I called soon after. We fixed a time the following Thursday evening. 'Cross the Magdalen Bridge and take the Iffley Road,' Roger advised, 'then, when you pass the university sports ground, look out for James Street. Take a left, then a right and you'll find Regent Street.' When I arrived, I was to lock my bicycle in front of the house, inside the low brick garden wall.

Oxford, 2000

Until that evening, I had spent very little time in East Oxford (why bother, when everything seems to be inside your quadrangle?) and so that first cycle ride, made before the days of iPhones and their maps, relied on the notes I took from our conversation:

Iffley

James

Regent

I left Christ Church and the bells were ringing the hour from the city's ancient towers as I rode up the Iffley Road, past the famous sports ground (which I had never visited) where Roger Bannister ran his sub-four minute mile, and cut north into the grid of terraced streets which lay behind. There were many lefts and rights to choose from and I was running late when, finally, I rushed around a corner and spotted a sign for Regent Street in the dim evening light.

After winning a short battle with the thick rosemary bush that dominated the space where bicycles were meant to stand (perhaps Roger couldn't see this obstacle?), I stood back and looked up at the house. Unlike many nearby, it still featured its original wooden sash windows. Handsome, I thought (horrid plate glass, Roger later encouraged me to think). In truth, 41 Regent Street was a standard Victorian terraced house in an unremarkable street, in a shabby part of town. Roger's home looked neat and well kept, but the houses around it were obviously inhabited by large numbers of students and treated accordingly. Windows rotted, bins were scattered, nasty metal handrails were nailed into walls.

The building I faced was almost completely dark, the dimmest of lamp light barely visible through a crack in thick, white curtains shielding the room behind the front bay window. Roger, he had made a point of saying, would greet me at his door only when the bell had been rung twice: the indication that his visitor was a known person, friend not foe. I did as I had been instructed.

A few seconds later, the house illuminated. Windows on every floor shone brightly as Roger switched the place on, eventually unchaining the glass-panelled front door (an ugly twentieth-century addition) and half opening it. In front of me was a slim, dark-haired man of around my own height (generously, five feet ten) and – I guessed – somewhere north of 60 (it would take years for Roger to tell me his age). He looked towards me with clouded, still eyes, framed by an inexpressive but gentle face. 'Hello?' he asked, a little uncertainly.

I paused for a moment, unsure exactly what the etiquette might be at the door of someone who cannot see his caller, but three years of being an Oxford undergraduate had taught me to be bold in the face of social uncertainty. 'Hello, Roger,' I beamed loudly and clearly at him, in the crisp tone which by then I'd picked up at Christ Church. 'It's Christopher – lovely to meet you!'

I was invited in.

Roger was dressed in beige, loosely fitting clothes, which, I came to learn, were his standard for days at home. I never did ask who had chosen them with him, or for him – it felt like too barbed a question. I assumed they were recommended by someone else and chosen for comfort over style. Roger himself had a keen aesthetic sensibility: strong, slightly condescending opinions on how things, and people, should look. Photographs of his younger self show a very different wardrobe, and on my study desk, in a thin silver frame, I keep a picture of him as I know he would prefer to be remembered. There he sits, languidly, on a folding chair, dressed handsomely for a garden party in a cream linen jacket, a thin knitted tie, trousers with a neat centre crease and stylish Oxford lace-ups, expertly polished to a shine.

In contrast to the clothes he had on that night, Roger's home was a thing of beauty. Stepping into his drawing room from a narrow hallway felt like I had moved miles from the street outside. The space had been designed to feel as close to a Regency country house in style as its size and architecture could sustain. Roger loved old country houses and when he bought his home in the early 1970s, he later told me, he recruited the aristocratic wife of the Warden of Wadham College to help him create as fine an interior as they could.

Together they had transformed what otherwise risked being a dingy Victorian building. The walls were intelligently dressed with fine paintings and etchings, many of which held clues to the stories of Roger's life. Some were works by his friends, whose names I would later come to know well; some showed places or objects that Roger most loved; some were old family portraits, the fixed stares of Butlers and Ives looking down on the culmination of their union. Other pictures, I learned, were historically important: early prints from *Punch*, Hogarth etchings of *A Rake's Progress*, framed letters of monarchs past and Oxford Movement leaders, and even what Roger called his 'fake Canaletto' – an intriguing copy of a Venetian scene, glazed to look (somewhat unsuccessfully) like the original.

45

Under the pictures, dark wooden furniture punctuated the drawing room, adorned with elegant chinoiserie lamps, Wedgwood porcelain and gleaming silver. A small, elegantly inlaid mezzaluna card table stood in pride of place at the centre of the bay window, just a few inches from my bicycle outside. Everything in that extraordinary room had been chosen with purpose, often with real care and some emotional investment.

I loved that room, immediately, just as I later came to love every inch of the house. Eventually, I was told all the stories of how and when Roger had acquired his favourite pieces. Roger had an infectious passion for his home, despite never having been able to see the finest features of his creation. Its beauty was in more than just what I could see: more than its elegance and careful curation. There was a restful, palpable calm to the place, a calm that seemed to be spread thickly throughout the house by the steady ticking and loud, regular chimes of Roger's gothic-arched clock at the back of the drawing room. For someone who had spent years living in temporary student rooms, largely stripped of the interior character their ancient facades implied, being in this environment was blissful.

Standing by a highly polished chest of drawers (Regency, of course), Roger pulled a square-bottomed decanter with a pleasing spherical stopper towards himself.

'Gin?'

'Gosh, absolutely! Thank you!' I almost pleaded. 'I got so horribly lost and thought I'd be far too late. I'm so sorry . . . Gin would be wonderful.'

My panting keenness was a little much in that wonderful room, but Roger just smiled and did what he'd do countless times more when I arrived at his home. Off came the stopper, opening up the decanter filled with gin (always Beefeater). Out came a can of tonic (always Schweppes). In came a tray of ice (always a bit mixed up with pastry flakes from the croissants Roger froze). Then came the cut-crystal glasses – ones into which I still occasionally pour my drinks, thinking about that moment.

I was invited to mix for myself. I was nervous. Here I was in the home of a man I didn't know, in an environment that was certainly not what I had expected, and unsure of what the evening would bring. Strong was essential: more gin, less tonic. Roger did the same, putting his finger into his glass as a measure.

We sat down – me on the deep, red sofa, facing the bay window, Roger on the matching chair opposite, the two of us framing Roger's open fireplace.

'So, then, shall we read something?'

Our first evening together began.

CHAPTER 2

A Journey from Angel

'One still had this feeling that there was something sort of underworldly about homosexuality and everything pertaining to it.'[1]

Roger sensed something different coming the moment he stepped out from Angel tube station onto Upper Street, one early evening in November 1958. He began walking towards Islington Green and, as he turned left into Liverpool Road, away from the traffic and the glare of the brightly lit shops, the atmosphere changed. It was suddenly darker, quieter and he felt a slight wintry haze – not quite a fog – in the air, blurring the street lamps and making it even harder for Roger's eyes to focus on the house numbers. As he made his way down the street in the mist he felt almost like an agent on a secret mission.

```
I passed a short row of dingy little shops, one
or two still open - a café and a newsagent -
throwing a soft light across the pavement.
The road widened to reveal a long terrace of
once handsome later-Georgian houses now in a
melancholy state of neglect - front gardens
```

overgrown or cluttered with debris, chinks of
light showing between ill-drawn curtains.

   Next, on the corner ahead where the road
narrowed again so that it seemed to be jutting
out across the pavement, a solid Victorian pub,
dim lights glowing through its frosted and
engraved plate glass windows, but no sounds of
life let alone revelry coming from within as
I passed. A few yards further on and I came
to another row of shabby little shops, all in
darkness.

   A few doors along I came to the one that had
been described, double fronted with its windows
whitewashed over. There was a faint light
from deep inside. I glanced up to check the
number, then rang the bell. I felt just a shade
uneasy having no idea what to expect. In my
imagination there was a conspiratorial air to
the whole scene - the dark November night, the
seedy locality, the mystery of what lay behind
these blanked out windows.

Two short hours in Leicester Square had changed everything
Roger thought he knew about himself. Now he was answering a
summons to Liverpool Road, to a covert meeting of gay activists
whose very gathering put each of them at risk of arrest.

Roger's Wildeblood-inspired revelation was more than a realisation about his own identity. It was a realisation that his identity

was criminal and that men like him went to prison simply for being who they were.

A few months after he had read *Against the Law*, on 4th September 1957, the final report from the Wolfenden Committee was published. Roger wanted to get his hands on it as soon as possible and he rushed to Her Majesty's Stationery Office to obtain a copy. His anticipation was well-placed: the committee's membership had backed, 12–1, parliamentary action for a complete overturning of the laws prohibiting homosexual activity.

The following is a summary of our Recommendations:–
Homosexual Offences

We recommend: –

(i) That homosexual behaviour between consenting adults in private be no longer a criminal offence (paragraph 62).

(ii) That questions relating to "consent" and "in private" be decided by the same criteria as apply in the case of heterosexual acts between adults (paragraphs 63, 64).

(iii) That the age of "adulthood" for the purposes of the proposed change in the law be fixed at twenty-one (paragraph 71).

(iv) That no proceedings be taken in respect of any homosexual act (other than an indecent assault) committed in private by a person under twenty-one, except by the Director of Public Prosecutions or with the sanction of the Attorney General (paragraph 72).[2]

This was a stunning proposal from an establishment body and it offered an opportunity that was quickly recognised by people who wanted the law changed. It wasn't long before the report created enough of a stir to leave breadcrumbs that guided Roger into the veiled, secret world he was so eager to discover.

Soon after the Wolfenden Report was published, notices about the existence of a new pressure group began to appear in major publications: the Homosexual Law Reform Society (HLRS) had been established specifically to achieve the recommendations of the report. It swiftly became the leading voice of the campaign for the decriminalisation of homosexual acts between men, and in 1958, Secretaries of the HLRS began to write diligently to the press. Announcing their arrival in letters first to the *Manchester Guardian* and *The Times*, they moved to a broader range of political magazines, including the *Spectator*:

SIR, – May I have the courtesy of your columns to announce the formation of a new society? It is called the Homosexual Law Reform Society, and is concerned to work for the implementation of the major recommendation of the Wolfenden Report upon private homosexual acts between consenting adults.
- Yours faithfully,
A.E. DYSON
Hon. Secretary
[6th June 1958]

The HLRS began to place regular notices in the classified sections of those magazines – discreet but direct appeals for people to get in touch to support their work. Roger, a reader of the *New Statesman*, spotted the call almost immediately:

THE Homosexual Law Reform Society now exists, to work for the implementation of the major Wolfenden proposal. Details from the Hon. Sec. 219 Liverpool Road, London, N1.
   [28th June 1958]

There it was – Roger's first real chance to find a community of people like him. He jumped at it, writing the first letter that would bring him into the gay rights movement. He was one of the earliest respondents to the HLRS appeals.

```
Once I had worked up the courage to take the
step of replying to such an advert, dropping
the letter into the box at the Strand post
office on the way to work felt like a fateful
step into the unknown. When the printed
material arrived a few days later there was a
written note saying extra voluntary help would
be welcome to keep the Society running. By now
I knew I must go for it - in for a penny, in
for a pound - so I rang the name given, Len
Smith, and was told an address and a time.
```

It would soon become clear that Len was coordinating the HLRS's volunteer operation out of his own home. Doing so was an exceptional act of bravery, especially because Len was living in the house with another man and had put up only cursory barriers against public and police harassment when he published their address in the national press. Officers had shown up at Peter Wildeblood's home without a warrant, searching through his letters, photographs and visiting cards before arresting him. There was no reason for Len to believe that he and his visitors wouldn't at least be surveilled.

When Roger knocked on the door of 219 Liverpool Road, he was as excited as he was anxious. He waited, convinced that a whole new area of experience was waiting for him behind the anonymous windows. The door opened and a wiry man in early middle age, sharp featured and with iron grey hair, introduced himself briskly but affably as Len. Roger stepped in to the front part of the house, which had obviously once been a shop. Now stripped of its fittings, the room was being used as an artist's studio, with an easel, a work table and rows of paintings leaning against the walls.

The studio, Roger could tell, was tacked onto the front of a pretty Regency cottage. He was ushered through and up some steps into the house itself, and to a little sitting room at the back. Len introduced Reiss Howard, a bearded Canadian in his mid-thirties and the painter for whom the studio had been created. The couple, Roger later learned, owned the house and ran an antiques business together.

```
There were two small connecting rooms,
immensely cluttered but cosy with the gas fire
softly hissing. The atmosphere was friendly
and easy so that such small qualms as I had
```

were soon dispelled. Shortly, two more men
arrived who were obviously already known,
both were middle aged and unremarkable in
appearance. After some perfunctory chat we all
settled at any available writing surface and
began the business of dealing with the mail
that was flooding in daily from the various
advertisements such as I had noticed.

Part of this tiny group who made up the HLRS's earliest recruits, Roger took on a sense of purpose, which quickly evolved into a new feeling of belonging and confidence. For several hours that evening, he was working in a small gathering of men, stuffing envelopes with the printed literature of the HLRS and writing short accompanying notes for individual recipients. He was addressing potential supporters as if he had been doing so for years.

Mugs of coffee appeared and the evening's work yielded to drinking from them. To Roger, it felt like he was among old friends, but with one small and crucial difference: these were homosexual friends and in Len and Reiss's house, they were all openly so. The group talked about the work of the HLRS and about political, homosexual issues. They also spoke freely about their lovers and the romantic entanglements of their friends, and gossiped about their sex lives. And for the first time, Roger saw two male lovers be affectionate with one another. Len and Reiss kissed, and Roger felt a 'physical jolt'.

Roger offered very little into the conversation. It seemed to him as if he didn't have much to contribute – unless he could somehow find a way to mention losing his virginity to an off-duty policeman, and he was too nervous to manage that. Instead, he just listened, taking it all in and marvelling that here he was in company with people who were talking about being gay and about living the lives of gay men: 'four queers chatting queer talk'.

These four queers chatted their queer talk as if it was the most natural and everyday occurrence, but for Roger it was an absolute first. After reading *Against the Law*, he had realised what he was, immediately accepting the fact and seeking to find out more about it. Now, Roger had placed himself in a room of homosexual men, where, from the outset, he identified himself as a homosexual, albeit one with very little experience.

When Roger walked out of the studio and back onto the dark street outside, he felt the magnitude of this moment. He had found himself at the heart of the emerging campaign for law reform:

But I couldn't possibly have imagined its long-term consequences, how profoundly it would change my life. For the time being, I could see that it had been a good instinct, a good choice that had led me to seize the opportunity to become part of something into which I fitted so naturally. Walking back to the tube station, the neighbourhood no longer felt like alien territory. Now it looked just like any other run-down area, even quite friendly.

To bolster their position, leaders of the HLRS did their best to make a show of the famous and respectable names who supported their cause. The advocacy of such people, they were sure, would be important for gaining both publicity and public support, and from the earliest announcement of their formation in the *Manchester Guardian* they name-dropped aggressively:

A Homosexual Law Reform Society has been formed . . . Among the committee members are Dr J. Bronowski, Sir Basil Henriques, Miss Ethel Mannin, Lord Russell, Professor A.J. Ayer, Sir Robert Boothby, Mr R.H.S. Crossman and Mr Marcus Lipton. The Society believes that 'our present law is unjust and no longer acceptable to medical opinion, the leading spokesmen of the Christian Churches, or to humane good sense in general.'

[30th May 1958]

But it was ordinary people like Roger who would do the hard work that sustained the society for the next nine years as it battled with successive governments to implement the recommendations of the Wolfenden Committee.

Just as it was on Roger's first night in the movement, much of the work involved writing and responding to letters. In post-war Britain, the letters pages of newspapers and political magazines were crucial forums for the airing of talking points on the legalisation of homosexuality, from speculation about 'causes' and ideas of 'cures' to perspectives about the right of the law to dictate individual morals. The Homosexual Law Reform Society's Secretaries and supporters in particular made use of those pages, pleading with readers to consider the pain inflicted on homosexuals by prosecution, and prison's lack of efficacy in making men less homosexual. They usually succeeded in drawing out their opponents and the debate could go on, back and forth for weeks, as new voices chimed in, the originators of the argument tried to rebut them and the letter-writers ended up bickering – even with their allies.

The more liberal publications rarely printed the diatribes of disgust that could be found in tabloid newspapers. They also gave space for leaders of the reform movement to complain that they had won their argument with right-thinking people and yet still nothing was changing in practice:

> Sir, – . . . It will be a much graver evil if we continue to allow adult homosexuals to suffer long terms of imprisonment simply because the forces of modern knowledge, expert opinion, and humane good sense, which are now almost wholly opposed to such persecution, lack the dignity and guts to fight for justice.
>
> A.E. Dyson,
> Hon. Secretary, Homosexual Law Reform Society
> 32 Shaftesbury Avenue, W.1.
> [*Observer*, 14th September 1958]

Even progressive publications, though, did not always refrain from printing letters of moral outrage, linked with conspiracy theories and spurious claims of medical truth.

> SIR,– . . . The man suffering from disease accepts treatment, and wishes to get well. The homosexual, on the other hand, very often claims that his disease is preferable to the

normal state; that he is a forerunner of a third sex which Nature is about to evolve; that *Uranian* love is superior to the love of a woman. With the help of these dubious arguments and through his hold in certain semi-artistic quarters, he recruits his ranks from silly young men, with hankerings for the arts and no very clear sense of values . . .

I can suggest no remedy for this state of affairs. The law of libel effectually protects groups of people whose influence is pernicious, but can only be diminished by a common persecution, in which they have generally the sympathy of the liberal-minded man. A series of objective articles on the homosexual's psychology . . . might help to remove the glamour with which these pathetic, sometimes talented and often dangerous men have succeeded in surrounding themselves.

My argument, of course, holds equally true of the Lesbian, who is usually to be found in the same company as her abnormal brothers.

Yours faithfully,

J.M. COHEN

London, N.W.11

[*Spectator*, 13th November 1953]

Sir,—Even if it is true, as the vice-chairman of the Homosexual Law Reform Society states in his letter of November 14th, that 'in a small minority of men homosexual impulses are both deep-seated and ineradicable,' that is no reason why a licence should be granted for their gratification. Impulses are not the whole of a man's nature.

Man has been endowed with conscience to understand when his impulses are evil and ought to be suppressed, and will-power to suppress them when evil. What a world this would be if we all felt free to give free rein to our impulses!

So infectious is this vice that, given the protection of law by the ancient Canaanitish nations, it became 'an abominable custom' amongst them, and . . . not only the practice but the sense and notion of morality was corrupted amongst them . . .

Arthur Carrington,
4 Bantam Grove, Morley, Leeds
[*Manchester Guardian*, 19th November 1958]

Roger had grown up barely ever hearing about homosexuality, but he could now read plenty of people discussing it in detail and know these people were talking about him. Supporters of the HLRS and its cause at the end of the 1950s urged compassion, but their missives were hardly more cheering for a homosexual than expressions of revulsion or claims of impossible cures. They wrote repeatedly, describing the persistent tragedies the present laws were causing homosexual men up and down the country.

SIR, – I am reluctant to write another letter on the subject of homosexuality . . . However, during this week, there have been reports in the press about a case of a type which is, unhappily, very much more common than those who are complacent about the present state of the law would have us believe.

60

Two men, aged sixty-six and forty-one, gassed themselves at Bilston, Staffs, because they had been questioned by the police in connection with allegations of indecent actions between men. There is no indication that anyone other than consenting adults was concerned in these incidents.

It is hard to see how the Government can feel justified in continuing to allow this type of intrusion into the private lives of responsible adults. Only by the most twisted reasoning could it be argued that the result in this case was in the public interest. –

Yours faithfully,

A. HALLIDIE SMITH,

Secretary

The Homosexual Law Reform Society,

32 Shaftesbury Avenue, W1

[*Spectator*, 26th December 1958]

Meanwhile, populist newspapers were the loudest voices in opposition to law reform, making use of any scandal involving homosexuals to stoke fear and outrage in the general public. Well-known figures were the best fodder for this kind of reporting and in October 1953 there was a particularly salacious case when the actor John Gielgud was arrested in a public lavatory in Chelsea 'for persistently importuning' (i.e. cottaging). The editor of the *Sunday Express*, John Gordon, made frequent, virulent attacks on homosexuals and took Gielgud as evidence that any caution in condemning homosexuality encouraged the spread of a dangerous disease.

It has penetrated every phase of life. It infects politics, literature, the stage, the Church ... It is time the community decided to sanitise itself. For if we do not root out this moral rot it will bring us down as inevitably as it has brought down every nation in history that became affected by it. There must be sharp and severe punishment. But more than that we must get the social conscience of the nation so raised that such people are made into social lepers.

[*Sunday Express*, 1st November 1953]

It wasn't just the popular press that described homosexuality in this way. Academic studies, couched in the language of scientific thinking and balanced investigation, were often equally brutal. *They Stand Apart*, a self-described 'critical study' of homosexuality by J. Tudor Rees and Harley Usill, published in 1955, was one especially unpleasant example. It promised to offer expert views on the issues surrounding homosexuality from legal, social, religious and medical perspectives, 'quite objectively' and bearing in mind 'that there are two parties to be considered – society and the individual, each having inherent rights which have to be safeguarded.'[3]

All that said, in that same set of introductory remarks, Rees and Usill made it perfectly clear how they felt – disgusted:

Although each contributor has been left entirely free to express his own views, editorially we are entitled to ask whether this thing is a 'cancer of the soul', a 'twist in the mind', a 'bodily affliction', or a commixture of them all, perhaps acting and reacting on one another. Whatever it may be, there can be no question about the potential evil, in varying degrees, resulting from the practices associated with homosexuality.[4]

They went on to compare homosexuality to tuberculosis in the 1890s: something that should drive society towards finding a cure. In their thinking, if an individual could not or would not be medically treated, his homosexuality should not be given freedom of expression and should be punished when it occurred.

The printed page was an intellectual battleground for people eager to keep discussing the topic and propose action. In Parliament, however, there was limited support for any change to the status quo. In November 1958, members of the House of Commons argued over the content of the Wolfenden Report for the first time, the only debate in Parliament prior to this having been in the House of Lords. Roger was watching from the viewing gallery of the Commons, having made sure to obtain a ticket well in advance. He arrived just as Home Secretary R.A. ('Rab') Butler was making his opening speech, in which he was deeply unsympathetic to enacting the recommendations of the report. Roger felt a pang of betrayal from his namesake, who was known for being intellectually liberal but whose position seemed to be one of political expediency.

As the debate warmed up, Roger spied Peter Wildeblood also sitting in the viewing gallery. Glancing down to his left, Roger saw another one of his heroes. Winston Churchill, then aged 83, tottered in through the Churchill Arch, dressed in a familiar bow tie, black jacket and pinstripe trousers. He took his

THE LIGHT OF DAY

customary front bench seat and, with hands on knees, remained as motionless as a waxwork for the next two hours. To Roger's frustration, these cameo appearances were about the most interesting feature of the debate. He left before the end, by which time the outcome was already obvious: there wasn't enough support for decriminalisation to take a vote on it.

```
Only one catchy phrase stuck in my memory, when
Leslie Hale, a rumbustious Labour MP with a
rich, fruity voice, loudly declared, 'What we
are discussing today is not so much a question
of buggery as of humbuggery!'
```

A decade would pass between the publication of the Wolfenden Report and the realisation of its recommendations on homosexuality in law in the Sexual Offences Act of 1967.

Len's house on Liverpool Road remained the base of HLRS operations for some time, even when the society's first full-time professional Secretary, Andrew Hallidie Smith, was appointed towards the end of 1958 and began to set up a new headquarters on Shaftesbury Avenue. Len was suspicious of Hallidie Smith and of the changes this heterosexual clergyman was making. He kept the volunteers close to him, initially refusing to hand over records for fear that names would not be secure in the new premises.

Roger liked Hallidie Smith and the two became lifelong friends, keeping in touch even after Hallidie Smith left the HLRS and moved with his family to a parish in Canada. Roger agreed with him that the HLRS needed to grow up and professionalise in order to succeed, but he also stayed loyal to Len, sustaining friendships with both men throughout the period of wrangling. Len had been Roger's first contact with the gay world and took on an almost parental status in that environment. And it was through quietly and persistently turning up to volunteer at Len's house that Roger had finally found his way into the hidden gay society that had eluded him for so long.

Oxford, 2003

My first journey to Regent Street began a weekly pilgrimage that would continue for the next five years. We moved the appointed time to 6pm so I could cycle back for dinner, but I almost always stayed later and missed the meal in 'Hall'. Tuesday nights became Roger nights – 'blind man' nights, I called them with my college friends, to explain where I was going without elaborating much more.

Our routine stayed largely unchanged until I left Oxford. I would fight the rosemary (which was not, it turned out, neglected – simply loved as it was), lock my bicycle, ring twice, see the house light up, watch Roger's thin, beige figure approach slowly through the frosted glass and hear him unchain the door. Then I would step inside. An initial, uncertain hello evolved into a friendly greeting, a wide smile, soon a 'hello, love' from Roger. Gin remained our staple – at least two each visit. Normally more. Sometimes Roger would move to red wine – the sole purpose of the hatch between the kitchen and drawing room being to hold his latest 'work in progress' bottle of the Wine

Society's claret, always sealed by the same old rubber stopper. I'd be offered crisps or nuts, which Roger would pour into a small bowl and place on the low wooden cabinet next to the red sofa (a cabinet built to conceal a radiator, which would never have matched Roger's chosen aesthetic).

Roger suggested that we wait before deciding together what our first big project might be. For several weeks, this mostly meant me reading aloud from recent issues of the *London Review of Books* so Roger could decide if any items stood out as ones he would like to return to. Sometimes it meant reading a story or review he'd noticed with another reader or in a prior week with me. The material was unremarkable – thought pieces on new biographies or historical memoir, comments on emerging new authors – but this was intentional: Roger was deliberately treading water until he could work out what might be of mutual interest.

Almost always, with every new edition of the *LRB*, we would finish by looking over the personal columns. Roger believed this would provide great amusement (people tried hard to be clever and funny in what I suppose was a place to meet literary-minded soulmates). I never quite shared his enthusiasm but was too polite in those early days to say so.

Over strong, weekly drinks, as we continued to read, we also began to get to know one another. The two went hand in hand: we would stop midway through some article or other and talk, about the content but just as often about ourselves. Roger was interested in Christ Church as a college and in how much student life had (or hadn't, it turned out) changed since he had been an undergraduate at Balliol. He was especially curious about my subject area. He had always rejected any form of religion, so my choice of theology was both intriguing and perplexing to him. I talked about my upbringing in a clergy family – everything from swinging incense and ringing bells during services from a young age, to the unique experiences suffered by children of vicarages, always being in some way public property, living life somewhat on show. Roger's bemusement only intensified.

He could, however, understand my interest in church history, which by 2003 had become my Master's subject. Roger, it turned out, had developed a strong interest in the Oxford Movement as a younger man, attracted in particular by the aesthetics of this Victorian Anglo-Catholic revival in the Church of England. Although that particular piece of church history began some 1,500 years after the Roman imperial church that I was studying, it offered some common ground, allowing us to bypass Roger's conviction that, ultimately, believing in God was like believing in the tooth fairy.

Roger asked most of the questions but he spoke just as much as he listened. We were beginning to learn who the other was and as our first term together passed, I found myself looking forward to my visits more and more. Arriving at Regent Street and stepping into Roger's home signalled the beginning of a few hours of quiet, measured conversation between two men, cocooned in an elegant room behind thick, embroidered curtains and accompanied by Roger's beloved clock. Those few hours each week, each Tuesday, were a world apart from the Oxford I otherwise knew, which was rushed, busy, frenetic.

Not that the life I was living the other end of my weekly cycle ride wasn't everything I had hoped. I was doing well academically – something that had mattered deeply to me ever since secondary school. There, success had given me an identity in an environment where I was a strange creature, not particularly interested in rugby or football or girls. It had also offered the possibility of an escape to places where I would find people like me – places like Oxford – and I carried this need to achieve with me there. Unlike most of my friends, I actually went to lectures, really not the 'done thing' at Oxford (I sometimes lied and said I hadn't), and I took on extra languages, though I still scoffed at science students who spent long days in their labs. But I was coming to see that success wasn't just a question of academic achievement – having a crammed social calendar meant just as much.

A pattern formed at the beginning of my undergraduate days that was largely unchanged in 2003. Monday nights were for a 'cheesy music' disco at the Old Fire Station (the club's designated gay night). Wednesday afternoons meant 'pink teas' in college (a collection of gays would sit in someone's room with pink wafers, party ring biscuits and mugs of tea). On Thursday night, it was university-wide 'LGB Soc drinks': plastic cups of cheap alcohol served in whatever college function room the organisers could book. These could end messily. I remember being pushed (or perhaps I was pushing someone – the memory is hazy) in a shopping trolley out of Mansfield College after one of them, en route to whatever the late-night venue might have been that week.

For several years, we were spoiled by having a lesbian and gay community centre, located in an old Methodist chapel called the Northgate Hall, which also hosted a drop-in centre for people who were homeless. It reopened after a fire and started hosting a gay afterparty on Thursdays that would close with 'New York, New York' and a can-can line. On other days we might go to the Ultimate Picture Palace – an independent cinema halfway to Roger's house – which was the likeliest place to watch queer films (anything from classics like *The Rocky Horror Picture Show* to movies like *Shortbus* that seemed especially avant-garde). From time to time, when the opportunity presented itself, LGB Soc would arrange special outings – somewhere I still have the hat that accompanied my Austrian costume for a group trip to 'Sing-a-Long-a *Sound of Music*'.

When, at the end of my first year, I stood for election to become Christ Church LGB rep, I did so on a joint ticket. Amy and I ran unopposed, and our prize was no more than a title and about £50 of college money to spend on parties, but our victory was no less sweet: in 2001, Christ Church claimed proudly to be the 'pinkest' college in Oxford. We were so sure of ourselves that we decided to mimic the college rowing societies and their regular 'crew dates'. We would, we determined, invite the LGB reps of another college to bring their community to Christ Church for the evening and lay on some wine and cheese, a staple of Oxford socials in those days. Magdalen turned us down but Toni, the LGB rep at University College ('Univ'), jumped at the chance.

When the night came, twenty-five people gathered from Christ Church to welcome our guests. Amy and I leaned out of large sash windows, looking across Peckwater Quad from rooms named the 'drag suite' (because of their length, not their use), hoping to catch sight of the Univ masses arriving up the cobbled street and through Canterbury Gate. We spotted just three people. Toni had managed to round up Louise and only one more student.

Toni and Louise keenly entered our bigger pink bubble, and Louise never left. Like me, she had taken Oxford as a chance to live a gay, grown-up life for the first time. At the freshers' fair, with offerings from clubs oriented around everything from Methodism to judo to the Labour party, she had prioritised finding one sign-up sheet over all the others: the LGB Society. Just as there was a New Christopher, there was a New Louise. And as we had hoped, we had access to a gay enclave, not cut off from mainstream university life as much as floating alongside it, allowing us to go back and forth.

I had never been especially interested in activism, but Louise had a campaigning side to her and in 2003 there was still plenty about which to be political. After the equalisation of the age of consent, the new battle was to overturn Section 28, part of a law passed under Margaret Thatcher that banned local governments and schools from doing anything to 'promote homosexuality'. There was also the struggle for civil partnerships and same-sex marriage. Louise somehow ended up being a fake bride in a staged mock wedding in front of the Bodleian Library. She knew it didn't make a lot of sense even at the time, but we drank champagne anyway.

With all this going on, it might seem odd that Roger and I didn't much speak about my social life. He asked a lot of questions in that first term (just as he carried on doing) but he – we – skirted around anything too exposing. We stuck to family, to my studies, career ambitions (I had none to speak of) and the day-to-day. In later years, there was more at stake – or, more specifically, more to lose from Roger knowing what I was doing, who I was with and why. But in the early stages, I think it was just reticence: two slightly shy people avoiding subjects that the other might consider impolite. Perhaps there was some residual reluctance on my part to talk openly to new people, to older people outside of that world, about sex and my own sexuality. It would be untrue to claim I've lost that reluctance completely, even today.

I know now that there is some considerable irony in this. Roger, at about the same age I was in 2003, had revelled in his gay social life. Realising how lost he had been before this, Roger pitied men who hadn't been able to find what he had. Once he had discovered it, Roger had rushed into a gay community, just as I had.

CHAPTER 3

An Underground Party

*'I very quickly got in with people who knew
where one went'*[1]

Barely a month after his initial, apprehensive venture to Islington,
Roger was sitting on the top of a number 12 bus with some of
his new HLRS friends, bearing bottles. They were heading
south across the Thames, on a Saturday night, to Roger's first
gay party.

> Word had gone around that Edward, whom everyone
> else seemed vaguely to know, was giving a party
> in his basement flat on Peckham Rye, opposite
> the common. I had only been to one party
> before and little cared for it, being pressured
> to talk to girls and feeling decidedly out of
> place. I safely assumed this party would be
> of a very different order. As we approached
> Edward's flat, I wasn't sure whether it was
> curiosity or expectation that was uppermost in
> my mind, but I felt for the first time properly
> at ease in the company I was keeping.

THE LIGHT OF DAY

The party was as different as Roger had hoped, though not necessarily in all the ways he had assumed. The lighting was low and so was the music: Frank Sinatra, Ella Fitzgerald, more jazz and blues, coming from LPs on a record player. It might have passed for a straight gathering, he thought, given the number of women who were there, until several couples began to dance together, giving the game away: while some of the men and women paired off, so, too, did some of the men, and some of the women. Everything still seemed relatively decorous until Roger noticed young men slipping away to the bedroom together from time to time.

Roger himself spent most of the evening clutching a glass and talking with people he already knew, all the time watching this compelling scene unfold in front of him through the spectacles he would have preferred not to have to wear. Around two o'clock in the morning, the party was running out of steam.

```
Like a fire that has burned itself out, only a
glow and a few embers remained. For some time,
people had been drifting away, back to their
bed/sits and shared flats, accompanied if they
were lucky by a new partner for the night.
The last buses had long since gone so those
of us who were car-less and unable to cadge a
lift had to settle to make a night of it where
we were. Our host now retired to bed with
a friend, accompanied by at least one other
pair; the rest of us who had failed to make
any attachment sat around drinking whatever
```

76

was left and idly talking. One couple glided
languidly around the room to the accompaniment
of soft, romantic music; another couple lay
obliviously entwined on the sofa.

By some lucky chance I found myself sharing
some cushions with a passable, slim young man
I hadn't even spoken to previously. The lights
were switched out and we occupied ourselves for
some time, fumbling, but it was clear we hadn't
been designed for each other.

Eventually, pale daylight began to filter in,
people stirred, drifted to the kitchen, made
tea and toast, discovered eggs to scramble.
Edward and his friends remained oblivious while
the remnant of the party, tired and unkempt,
emerged into the grey morning of a Peckham
Sunday and made their various ways home.

By turning up each week at Liverpool Road, Roger had
quickly fallen in with the other men on the volunteer rota. To
his delight, they started inviting him to meet them outside of
Len Smith's living room and Roger finally had his ticket to a
semi-underworld of gay pubs and clubs. Many of these establishments were technically neither illegal nor completely secret,
but they were places in which men could talk about, and even
take part in, illegal activity. By necessity, this meant they could
be found only by people who already knew the way to them.
Now Roger was in the know and he had a clique of friends to
take him with them.

For me, this was a rapid and amazing
transformation in my way of life. I found
myself, overnight it seemed, becoming gregarious
to a degree I could never previously have
imagined. I felt I was leading a double life,
which added a frisson to it all. It all seemed
quite daring, and liberating, too, being
in company where all the usual crippling
inhibitions were irrelevant because you knew
everyone was on the same wavelength.

Roger's progress into this queer world was moving at an
exhilarating pace. He was still in his twenties and suddenly he
had a vibrant social life, which seemed to offer the potential for
romantic relationships, too. For about three years, Roger was
part of a large circle, brought together by a common cause and
a common sexuality, and he thrived in it.

The first time Roger was taken to a small gay club in Soho,
he really felt he had arrived. Before long, he was a regular at the
Fifty Club, or 'Old Fifty', run by a married couple called Johnny
and Patsy.

The so-called club was nothing more than a
bar - not the famous 'Colony' where I wouldn't
have fitted - it was just a large first floor
room above a restaurant in Frith Street, not so
much sleazy as tarty with its pink wall lights,
striped Regency paper and a white grand piano
at which sat a good-looking, rather too smiling

young man called Gary, who ceaselessly tinkled out tunes from the current popular musicals. His favourite at the time seemed to be an unmemorable show called *Flower Drum Song*, then running at the Palace Theatre just around the corner. But this was also the period when *My Fair Lady* had just opened at Drury Lane . . .

This discreet little hideaway was a handy place to drop in to at any time. At weekends, it was a regular meeting place for a small group of us who formed a kind of nucleus to which a wide range of acquaintances temporarily attached according to what was being proposed.

Here arrangements were made for other meetings or excursions - sometimes to the theatre or a concert - sometimes simply to move on to the other recognised haunts. I became familiar with all these in no time, some of which I had been walking past for years without realising their true nature - the various pubs and clubs dotted around central London, all well known to the informed but not then widely advertised.

There was even a lesbian club, 'The Gateways', a drab and dingy dive in the King's Road and opposite to this an exclusively gay coffee bar which was open into the early hours and packed to bursting point, especially after the pubs closed.

That coffee bar, Gigolo, was in the basement of the Casserole Restaurant at 328 King's Road. It later became renowned enough as a gay venue to make it into *The London Spy* – the notorious self-described discreet guide to the city's pleasures – as a social spot for men wanting to find sex with other men:

> Aptly named, hot, incredibly packed coffee bar. A frotteur's delight. Lots of Spanish waiters and terrified Americans. A surprising variety, however. The Rolls-Royce outside *could* be the one to whisk you away from it all.[2]

Roger's preference for these less salubrious places over somewhere like The Colony Room Club was understandable for a young man taking his first steps into gay society. A members' club at 41 Dean Street since 1948, The Colony's lesbian founder, Muriel Belcher, went to some lengths to attract wealthy and famous patrons, regularly paying people like Francis Bacon to visit. However intriguing that might have been to Roger, it felt well beyond his reach.

Roger only went to the Gateways a few times, as somebody's guest, but he was unusually negative in his down-at-the-heels description of this much-loved venue. *The London Spy* dedicates six pages to Gateways, which had been in existence since the 1930s, painting a thrilling picture of it in the early 1970s as an exclusive but eclectic setting.

Still, there were many other options available to him, across many spots in town, both public and private. At this time in Roger's life, a typical week could easily include trips to the Queen's Head in Chelsea, to the Salisbury in St Martin's Lane, the Rockingham in Shaftesbury Avenue, and several gay establishments in Earl's Court and Battersea. Some of these were far from respectable, which made it all the better. Roger, at the time, simultaneously played it up and tried to assume an air of casual sophistication:

A jaunt which I enjoy on occasional
Sundays . . . is to go down to 'The Boltons'
and the 'Coleherne' in Earl's Court. These are
always overflowing at this time, and here, as
arranged, I meet a few of the 'boys' - last
week there were six of us. Within the space
of an hour, we tend to imbibe an alarming
amount of liquor and, at closing time, sally
forth riotously in the direction of a 74
bus which takes us to Putney. Here, in the
slightly shabby, but still sedate, Victorian
road, we cram into a minute room (with kitchen
attached) belonging to one of our number,
and for about the next hour helpfully hinder
the preparation of vast quantities of curry
and rice, or spaghetti. This, surprisingly, is
very good and is enhanced by flagons of beer
which, miraculously, always seem to survive the
journey from Earl's Court. All very primitive,
but great fun. After this, everyone lapses into
inactivity - sleep or reading any odd bit of
the Sunday paper that can be found: sometimes
aloud, though no one ever takes any notice.

THE LIGHT OF DAY

At opening time there is a general revival
and a mass departure for the West End
once more. Of course, if any of us ever
found ourselves in court all this innocent
conviviality would certainly be presented as the
most orgiastic debauch since the Borgias.

Roger loved the camaraderie established by the common denominator, this shared criminalised attribute. It was elating for him to be in places where he at last felt that he could be himself, and rub shoulders with people from all classes – from the rich and famous to younger, working men – especially in one of the two 'queer pubs' on Dean Street:

One of the places I liked to drop into
occasionally was a seedy, rather sinister Soho
pub called 'The Golden Lion', where much of
the clientele had the appearance of being
(and probably was) rough trade picturesquely
supplemented as a rule by two or three
sailors obviously also plying their wares. The
atmosphere had something in it of feasting with
panthers.* Someone who was often in there and
was easily recognisable from television with
his bright blond hair was the journalist Daniel

---

* In his letter, *De Profundis*, Oscar Wilde used this phrase to describe his relationships, especially with younger, working men.

Farson.* He was usually chatting up the sailors and sometimes he was with a friend, a stocky, almost uncouth-looking man of perhaps 60.

. . .

It felt as if I had at last discovered where I belonged. Whenever you met anyone for the first time there was no need for pretence or evasion: you began from a quite different starting point. It was as if a large obstacle had been removed beforehand.

This freedom brought together men who might otherwise never have met as equals. It was a notable feature of queer life in the pre-legalisation era – one that heightened police hostility to gay venues but, to Roger at least, made everything feel extraordinarily inclusive:

I believe, and I think most others would agree, that this is the sort of friendship which is far and away the greatest advantage of being 'in' gay society: the opportunity of simply having the company of a few others all united by just one, common bond, with whom one can just relax and feel perfectly at ease, without having to guard constantly against looking too long

---

* Daniel Farson (1927–1997) was a writer, broadcaster and photographer, associated closely with Soho in this period. His book *Soho in the Fifties* is a celebration of London's West End culture.

in one direction, or letting slip a give-away
remark, or in any way pretending to be anything
that one isn't. And furthermore, this 'common
bond' is a tremendous breaker down of social and
racial barriers: people who, in normal society,
would remain rigidly within their artificial,
bourgeois social pale, here mix freely with all
and sundry, and find that they enjoy it, even
though, in nine cases out of ten, there is never
the slightest physical attraction involved. For
example, out of the six of us who spent last
Sunday together, the other five were Irish, South
African, Jewish, American, and one from Trinidad.

Roger's entry into London's queer world was his first real taste
of a life which he could shape for himself. There was something
magical about its secret language, the need for contacts to help
uncover it and the prohibited aspects of what transpired there.
He loved it so much in some ways that, later in life, Roger
found himself looking back fondly on the 'enchantment of the
forbidden' in the pre-legalisation era, which came with 'a kind
of erotic excitement'. He recalled this especially when he read
Joe Orton's diaries from the 1960s, describing the aphrodisiac
kick of illegal sex, even if Roger had been afraid to take things
particularly far himself.

The 'sweet edge of terror' enjoyed by a drug
and alcohol-fuelled young poet was not the world
of the majority. This was not a choice about

right and wrong - I claim no moral rectitude -
but one about risk. There could be no such
lifestyle choice for the ordinary man with an
ordinary job. The dismal truth is that I was
far too timid for such high-risk pranks. Insofar
as I needed to be deterred, this came quite as
much from fear that I might find myself in a
situation I couldn't handle - being beaten up -
as from being picked up by the police. I had
too strong a sense of self-preservation.

Despite his fears, Roger experienced two sexual encounters
that might be called cottaging:

. . . a couple of occasions when I succumbed
to temptations which were, so to speak, thrust
upon me. I hadn't sought them but I was swept
along by the impulse of the moment.

And in those moments he felt for himself 'the intense excitement of the circumstances – the spontaneity, the anonymity, the
risk, the whole terrible pull of it.'

The first of these was in the toilets of the Woolwich pub Roger
had begun visiting because of the new landlord: the attractive
Maurice who previously worked where Roger met the policeman
with whom he had his first sexual experience in London.

It happened that the only other occupant was
a tiny soldier, aged about 18. We glanced at

each other and the glance said everything.
Everything was proceeding very nicely without a
word being spoken until, of course, a tiresome
intruder came in. We left together and went
to the bar where I bought him a drink and
we chatted aimlessly for a while, until he
suggested we might 'go for a walk'. We wandered
around the backstreets for some time, eventually
finding a dark corner behind Woolwich Arsenal
station, where at last we could get down to
business. But once again, no sooner were we
thoroughly absorbed in each other than there
was the sound of footsteps coming down the
street. At this point we gave up. He had to
return to barracks and I had to catch the last
train home. We arranged to meet again at the
weekend but, of course, he never showed up.

Roger and Maurice, incidentally, did themselves spend one
night together. The outcome was, as Roger put it, 'not altogether
successful', but the two stayed friendly, and following Maurice as
he moved from pub to pub seemed to work out well for Roger.
About a year after the Woolwich encounter, he was at Maurice's
latest establishment, in Peckham Rye, where he had his second
experience of public sex with a handsome man of about 25, in
the toilets.

Here, in the old fashioned way, the gents was
outside at the back, open to the sky and at

night completely dark except for faint reflected
light. When I made a call here one night, it
happened that once again there was only a
single patron in place. As always, we looked at
each other with the usual questioning curiosity.
And as I looked down, I could just discern his
hand moving rapidly. Without hesitation he moved
next to me and I turned to him, taking his
considerable size in my hand. Just then, right
on cue, there was the sound of approaching
footsteps. Instantly my partner pulled away and
fled into the night.

Neither of these incidents gave me an
addiction to the activity.

Later, Roger characterised his sense of self-preservation as
fortunate. Very few men could survive the fallout of being
arrested for cottaging. John Gielgud was able to harness public
affection to his advantage and continue a career in showbusi-
ness, despite the negative press, but this was a rare, unusual
privilege, which Roger very clearly did not share.* The reality
for most men, and certainly for men like Roger, was that the
publication of the Wolfenden Report and the early work of the

---

* Roger reflected later that Gielgud's continued public success was a sign of
changing social attitudes: 'it did Gielgud little harm in the long run to have been
caught in this way. In many ways, the persecution increased his popularity, and
this demonstrated the broad tolerance – or indifference – of the public even at
that time, in sharp contrast to the approach of the authorities.'

HLRS had done almost nothing to change the practical implications of being known to be a homosexual, or even of being
thought to be one. The anti-homosexual police campaigns
continued unabated.

Giving evidence to the Wolfenden Committee in 1955, one of
three homosexual witnesses, named in proceedings only as 'the
Doctor',* set out the repercussions for gay men:

> I happened to be visiting a country parson the other day
> who was very willing to come here in person – I do not
> think I need mention his name – who cited five people
> he knew personally who had committed suicide for fear
> of police proceedings going on in the neighbourhood or
> inquiries actually being made and prosecutions being made.
> Three, as I remember it, were discovered on the round robin
> business, the police overheard some conversation, grilled
> him, frightened him, and he then declares the names of
> the people he has had homosexual relations with and these
> people are all put in the dock . . .³

Almost nothing had changed by the end of the decade.
Homosexuality – confirmed, suspected, merely inferred – often
quickly became a police matter, just as much as it brought shame
and the prospect of dismissal from employment. And with
these came isolation and despair for the man implicated. The

---

* 'The Doctor' was Patrick Trevor-Roper (1916–2004) – a wealthy opthalmic
surgeon who was involved in a number of homosexual campaigning charities and
who would later become a good friend to Roger.

threatening reality for ordinary homosexual men was described powerfully in a 1958 letter to the *Spectator*:

> SIR, – Even though the Government, for reasons which they are not prepared to give, are to throw over the recommendations of the Wolfenden Committee, one would still have expected the police authorities to pay *some* attention to them . . . The pogroms, however, continue, one in this neighbourhood having started with long and weary police-court proceedings on the eve of Christmas . . . The pattern is much the same in all these cases. The police go round from house to house, bringing ruin in their train, always attacking the youngest men first, extracting information with lengthy questioning and specious promises of light sentences as they proceed from clue to clue, i.e. from home to home, often up to twenty. This time the age range is seventeen to forty, which is about the average. Last time, a man of thirty-seven dropped dead in the dock at Assize. Just because this happens in country places and at country assizes, it all goes largely unreported . . . we still have moralists in high positions who imagine that they do good by this cruelty and in whose hands rests the destiny and happiness of so many of us, heterosexual and homosexual alike.
> R.D. Reid, 8 Chamberlain Street, Wells
> [3rd January 1958]

These incidents were easily recognised, and criticised, by other readers of the *Spectator*, which by this time was championing the law reform cause.

SIR, – If more people had the courage of Dr R.D. Reid in speaking out against these multiple vice prosecutions and the unhappiness and personal tragedy they entail, then our savage and vicious homosexuality laws might well be eased in a comparatively short time. As it is, these cases involving sometimes as many as fifteen people continue to come before the courts all over the country.

The dubious methods employed to track down the offenders reflect no credit on the police force. Nor do they reflect any credit on a law which, by its harshness and by its interference in personal matters, necessitates the employment of such methods in order to be effectively enforced.

MICHAEL NICHOLASS

16 Lampton Park Road, Hounslow, Middlesex

[10th January 1958]

Homosexual men were among those moved to write against what Reid called the pogroms – although none dared to imply that this was a matter of personal concern.

SIR, – Dr. Reid's disquieting account of the police prosecutions at Wells should receive all possible publicity. Evidently the scientific conclusions and humane recommendations of the Wolfenden Report cut no ice in that city. Nor is Wells unique. I have it on good authority that in another provincial city the police had under their control a homosexual whom they employ as bait. He encourages homosexual advances and then reports them. No doubt most police officers would refuse to adopt this disgusting technique.

They are a decent body of men. But if they wish to adopt it they are legally entitled to do so.

For divergences in police procedure, see the Wolfenden Report, paragraph 129. That Report is not dead because the present Government has chosen to ignore it. It is a living document which will be constantly discussed and will gradually influence public opinion.

Yours faithfully,
E.M. FORSTER
Reform Club, SW1
[17th January 1958]

Forster's novel about homosexual love, *Maurice*, was published only posthumously, in 1971. His letter to the *Spectator* shows vividly the problem for the law reform movement which Roger was coming to recognise: famous homosexuals were unwilling to state publicly and in their own words that this matter affected them personally.

Roger felt pressure to be careful as much as any other man of his generation, if not more. He was also capable of almost crippling reluctance to act on his feelings of sexual attraction, even in the safety of his own home. Never was this more obvious than when he joined the high-end estate agency, Keith Cardale, Groves & Co., and found himself smitten with a junior member of staff.

Harry was 'a little on the chubby side with crinkly gingery hair, but he had the most sunny disposition – open, cheerful, good natured, easy-going, always smiling'. He was also, it seemed, 'unmistakably quite straight', but the two men got on well and fell on the idea of sharing a flat. Roger had been lodging in Lewisham, and the possibility of subletting a room and sharing bills meant he could afford to lease somewhere of his own. He moved to Tonbridge for a short while during the search, but quickly found a flat just off the Old Brompton Road for an annual rent of £350.

All this time, Roger was worrying about more than just his rent. He was afraid of how Harry would react when he found out Roger was gay. He poured this out in letters to a friend.

He is younger than me, delightful company, full of fun, gusto, enthusiasm, noisy and boisterous, but, with it all, basically steady and - I am sure - once committed to anything completely honest and reliable; sees everything in clear black and whites; is utterly, utterly, charming . . . Yet, of course, there is one big complication so far as I am concerned (why are other people's lives always so much simpler than one's own?!) in the fundamental difference that there is between us - a difference which only I am aware of . . .

Not long after they moved in together, Roger told Harry everything.

Harry now knows it all. It's a TREMENDOUS relief now it's over but it was a terrible ordeal at the time . . . I was worked up in - for me - an

unusually high state of tension . . . I was just
not sure what Harry's reaction would be and our
living together complicated it all so much more.

In fact, Roger discovered his anxieties had been misdirected –
by some significant distance:

There can be no denying that I was rather
captivated by him, but he was so obviously
straight that I had no problem accepting that
our relationship must always be platonic. Then,
on one of those rare golden summer evenings
when the air is heavy with warmth, about three
weeks after we had moved in, we walked all
the way home after work diagonally across Hyde
Park and Kensington Gardens to Gloucester Road,
arriving at the flat hot and sticky. I went
to run cold water in the bath so that I could
freshen up and when I turned around I was
startled to find Harry standing right behind
me, naked and with a full erection.

The two settled into what Roger described as 'an easy-going
sexual friendship', but this lasted only a few months, when
Harry decided to leave his job and move back to his family home
in the countryside.

As the 1960s were beginning, Roger was finally part of the
community he had been looking for in London.

```
It was a world I had vaguely heard about but
never expected to be part of. Now that it's all
so open and advertised it's hard to appreciate
what a private world it then was. It seemed so
daring to have this secret life.
```

Secrecy was a double-edged sword. On the one hand, becoming part of a hidden world had made Roger feel special. It brought him into contact with people far outside of his previous experience, while sustaining a veil of excitement, even erotic mystique. But the continuing need for gay men to remain in the shadows also brought with it misery and isolation, and terror of the ever-present dangers of violence and exposure. It destroyed the lives of men up and down Britain.

The more confident Roger became in his own gay life, the more he urgently felt that the law compelling men to live secretly needed to change. Leaders of the HLRS had already felt Roger's energy for activism and were encouraging it. Several forces were pushing him to take personal, direct action.

Oxford, 2003

I understand now that Roger intentionally steered our reading relationship into a formational experience for me – the kind of formation that can characterise relationships between people so different in age. There was often a common thread to the material, but the wide-ranging subjects, forms and styles brought me to people and worlds I would never have otherwise known.

From the early days, this included 'dipping in' to small collections of letters and poems that held a particular, personal interest for Roger. He enjoyed being able to go back into specific volumes from time to time and remind himself of passages, chapters or references, but Roger's regular schedule of planned reading and admin with other visitors didn't leave much room for this more piecemeal activity. Audio 'talking' books, even when cassettes were phased out for the newer CD format, didn't allow him to scan for dates, names or places, so I was pleased to do it for him – especially so when I began to notice that this habit of Roger's was as much a way for me to learn more about his own past as the subjects of the material.

In some cases, this dual education was especially direct and emerged from places that took me by surprise. One of the first volumes we picked up, *A Bookseller's War*, was an edited correspondence illustrating wartime, high society living in London. These were letters between a husband and wife – Heywood and Anne Hill – who lived in the strange sort of world where it was perfectly natural just casually to employ Nancy Mitford as a shop assistant. When a postcard, used as a bookmark, fell from the pages, signed 'with love from Anne' in large, curly handwriting, this was Roger's chance to mention that he had been close friends with the couple since the 1960s. (A year later, we found a namecheck for Roger in the published volume of Heywood and Nancy's letters.)

Another time, we opened the diaries of Frances Partridge – the last survivor of the Bloomsbury Set. Roger had wanted to remind himself of an occasion in the 1970s when Partridge spent time at the Aldeburgh Festival and made a derisory remark about Benjamin Britten's *Albert Herring*. Roger's name just happened to appear in the entry and her assessment of the opera just happened to quote Roger's own lukewarm words. It was becoming clear to me that Roger's life had once been very different and through these moments I was starting to discover more about it – now distant things Roger valued, and which he thought I, too, should get to know.

Given the intentionality of this, the degree to which the two of us avoided discussing anything about his (or our) sexuality as we settled into our early routine at Regent Street seems quite remarkable. Roger told me years later that he'd telephoned Nick (who had introduced us), asking whether he was absolutely, definitely sure that I was 'one of us'. From New York, Nick managed to assure him of that. Neither of us was ashamed nor embarrassed, but that shy politeness between us meant the ice needed to be broken somehow.

Body language, a raised eyebrow or a quick glance at the right moment, might eventually have done it with someone sighted, but we needed a more direct approach, and those *London Review of Books* personals, tedious as I found them, allowed it to happen. As we began our way through one of them describing – in some witty way or other – a man looking to meet another man, and apparently bolstered by his conversation with Nick, Roger quickly threw in the question, 'Do you have anyone . . . a boyfriend?'

There was no great reveal to be made. At the time, I was going through an uneventful period on that front, but the question allowed me to talk about having had the same boyfriend for most of my undergraduate years and about some of the short-lived relationships I'd tried out since. The deed was done, the unspoken finally spoken.

After this, a wall had come down and there was a sense that we could be more open with one another – perhaps more relaxed in the knowledge that our common experience was no longer off limits. Roger, certainly, became more enthusiastic as he suggested what we might read together. I had slotted into the gap Nick had left and we could now carry on as Roger had hoped when I was sent his way.

Roger started to suggest we read books he had been saving for someone who shared his interests, someone like me. It was always a discussion. He had been building a list of titles he thought he might enjoy, but he wanted us to consider them together and pick ones that appealed to me, too.

Reading aloud was an unfamiliar experience for me when we started. Roger said I read well and that he liked my 'boyish' voice, but it took some time for me to get used to a way of reading that was both led by me in one sense, but also steered by Roger – a way of reading together, collaboratively. Progress is slow when you say the words aloud (or it was the way we did it). Skimming isn't an option, skipping ahead takes some negotiation and if the reader doesn't pronounce a word correctly, or sounds uncertain about its meaning, it usually prompts a conversation with (in this case, at least) a more knowledgeable, more articulate listener. And so – slowly – we began to work our way through our choices: some Hollinghurst novels, an enormous biography of Christopher Isherwood, Edmund White memoirs, that sort of thing.

At the end of our first term together, on the last Tuesday before I went home for Christmas, we talked about my plans for the vacation. Roger, he said, loved Christmas but he would spend the day alone. He had a special ritual for Christmas Day: he would light the open fire, cook himself sausages (his absolute favourite), listen to his talking books and to the radio (always BBC Radio 3), and speak with some old friends on the telephone. This, he said, was how he had done it for more years than he could remember, perhaps changed this year only in one way, should I feel inclined to call. He would love to speak to me.

The idea of spending Christmas alone sounded to me – then, at least – alien: something reserved for . . . well, I'd struggle to

Oxford, 2003

know who. As a family, we often collected up others who might be on their own and this year could well have been the one (it was certainly around this time) that I celebrated Christmas with a convicted arsonist just released from prison and invited by a prison visitor friend of my mother. He probably didn't expect to find himself sitting next to my probation officer sister at the vicarage table, as I pulled faces with my mother in the kitchen, giggling naughtily about who would risk lighting the Christmas pudding in front of him.

How could Roger, whose home spoke of a person who ought to be surrounded by interesting and loving people, spend Christmas by himself? I later understood that Christmases alone were more by choice than by necessity. People had been inviting Roger to join their families for many years, but he preferred the peace and familiarity of his own home and the traditions he had made for himself.

As I was saying goodbye on our final Tuesday in 2003, I regretted leaving that lovely man to his lonely Christmas in the cold. I kissed him as I left. 'Oh!' he almost laughed, and then smiled widely. 'I wasn't expecting that!'

A kiss on the cheek was a perfectly standard way of greeting or parting for an Oxford student at the start of the millennium. It was, though, the first time we had touched in any meaningful way and it seemed to Roger a bold and unexpected move. Unanticipated by me, this gesture turned me from a visiting reader to something closer – a friend, or perhaps something more than the friends he seemed otherwise to keep.

Had I known the power of that kiss, I'd probably have hesitated. I'm glad I didn't.

CHAPTER 4

A Research Subject

'It was brushed under the carpet and thought not a
suitable topic for general conversation'[1]

The freedom, the fun and the fascination that Roger found in London's underground homosexual scene in the late 1950s did not distract him from the activism that had led him there. It was the opposite. The more Roger experienced what he called the 'great age of queerdom', the more sharply he felt that the law governing it had to change and the more determined he was to do what he could to make that happen.

After only a few months in the movement, Roger was being trusted with more responsibilities. As Andrew Hallidie Smith was pressing ahead with establishing the HLRS office at 32 Shaftesbury Avenue, he relied on Roger to the extent that he asked him to look after the office when Andrew took a holiday in the summer of 1959.

Roger was willing to take on whatever was asked of him: 'anything that would contribute to greater enlightenment and the softening of homophobic prejudice'. This is how he found himself, in the autumn of 1959, recruited by Hallidie Smith to take part in a new study commissioned by the Home Office. Roger was to be a research subject for a sociologist called Richard Hauser. Hauser was beginning a study of homosexuality in which he would be listening to the views of both homosexuals and people with a personal or professional interest in same-sex attraction.

For months, Roger traipsed one evening a week to Hauser's flat on Clapham North Side, which happened to be next door to Hallidie Smith's own home. There, Hauser fired questions at his guests, and made notes from the discussion that ensued. From the outset, Roger was sceptical of the project. Hauser claimed to have organised the Italian probation service and to have worked miracles in the development of Australian mental health services, but Roger suspected that he was little more than a failed Viennese schoolteacher, riding on being married to the pianist and human rights campaigner Hephzibah Menuhin.

He was, Roger found on meeting him, 'a lumbering, unkempt man around the middle forties, who appeared vaguely genial but was provocatively irritating in conversation and very self-opinionated; also extremely dogmatic.' And Roger's misgivings only deepened as time went on.

```
Between noisy bites at an apple, Hauser
talked a lot about himself, expounded his own
opinions, and occasionally mentioned why he
was interested in homosexuality and what he
intended to do about it. The general impression
was that he was feeling the ground and had
no clear idea how to start. Periodically, he
would throw in a provocative comment which
```

would immediately excite argument and much note
taking by Hauser. I have always felt that these
aggravating remarks were deliberate on Hauser's
part in order to stimulate argument, and so I
never really took them seriously; but everyone
else took them as simple rudeness.

Halfway through the evening, Hephzibah appeared
and took orders for tea or coffee. Occasionally
the 'phone would ring and fascinating one-
sided conversations would take place: the
instrument itself rested on a very low shelf
and appeared to have an uncommonly short lead
which meant that Hauser, in order to conduct his
conversation, had to kneel on the floor. I grew
to look forward to these interruptions.

Hauser said he planned to use these sessions to compile two
questionnaires: one on homosexuality generally, to be answered
in discussion by groups like this one, which could be formed
all over the country, and the other an individual, personal one
to be completed anonymously and posted back to Hauser. The
latter, Hauser hoped, could be distributed through some kind
of snowball process, whereby homosexuals would pass it on to
others they knew.

Roger couldn't imagine that happening, especially after
Hauser abruptly cut contact with the group, apparently now
having more important things to do. They didn't hear anything
for several months. Then, faced with an impending deadline
in March 1960 to turn in the report, Hauser summoned them

hastily for one last lunchtime meeting. But he didn't ever follow
through on his promise to show the participants his work or
to include any comment they wanted to make in an appendix.
Roger was left doubtful it was ever finished, explaining his irritation in a letter later that year.

> Everyone that I know who has met him seems
> convinced of only two things - that he is a
> complete charlatan and one of the rudest people
> alive . . . and the result? NOTHING . . . how on
> earth Hauser came to be entrusted with such a
> commission Lord alone knows!

The chief impact of this experience on Roger was to confirm
in his mind that the government wasn't serious about imple-
menting Wolfenden's recommendations – that studies were
being conducted so that the Home Secretary could say, whenever required, 'We have researches in hand,' and then file them
away the moment they arrived and do nothing more.

What Roger seems never to have learned is that Hauser did
actually publish his findings. A lengthy report on homosexuality
in Britain appeared in 1962 under the title, *The Homosexual
Society*. At the start of the book, Hauser described the process
of his research, suggesting that it had been more extensive than
just what Roger had seen:

> It may be said at once that although our approach is socio-
> logical, we are nowhere concerned with measurement. We
> have listened to the comment and views of about four

hundred people of whom most had experience of living homosexually while others had either a personal or professional interest. If such words as 'many' or 'often' jar on the ear of the statistician, it may be borne in mind that we have been more concerned with people's opinion about themselves, their aims, their difficulties and their potentialities . . .

Although some opinions have been gathered from personal interviews, we have worked mainly in groups, some of which did not survive more than a few sessions while others lasted for months. Out of deference to expert opinion, we made use of questionnaires but have no hesitation in saying that sole reliance on this means would have proved to be disastrous. The interviews quoted are often excerpts from discussions and debates. Care has been taken that no person could possibly identify himself from the text.[2]

It may have been for the best that Roger didn't see what Hauser claimed to have learned from him and the others who gave him their time. The main thesis of *The Homosexual Society* was that, while large numbers of men would class themselves as homosexual, only a tiny number are actually homosexual by nature. Hauser called the latter group 'biological freaks (and this is said with full sympathy for them; few of them are happy and nature has played them a dirty trick).[3] The rest, Hauser believed, had become stuck on an idea about themselves through corrupted social conditioning and a lack of proper guidance.

It was a conclusion grotesquely different from anything Roger could have imagined, and certainly not what the HLRS had thought would happen. Hauser called homosexuality a 'social infection' and argued everything should be done to prevent impressionable straight people from being influenced to become homosexuals. And so it followed:

> If it is true that homosexuality can be environmentally produced, there is a great need to understand the issues, primarily in order to *contain* the evil, secondarily to handle it properly when it occurs, and, last but not least, to deal with the cultural damage done to society . . .[4]

> The best defence, as always with people, is in their own minds, in understanding the problem clearly. Beyond this there should be certain safeguards to prevent homosexuality spreading and becoming a threat to society and to prevent people becoming fixated in it and then consumed by misery and regret.[5]

The majority of Hauser's book is caught up in a strange determination to describe 'types' of homosexuals. Homosexual men, he claimed, can be identified according to a range of groups. Among these Hauser included 'The Psychopath', 'The Paedophiliac', 'The Cottage Type', 'The Ship's Queer', 'The Bodybuilder', 'The Self-masturbator', 'The Homosexual Voyeur', 'The Woman Hater' and 'The Homosexual "Virgin Chaser"'.

Unsurprisingly, the most positive reviews of the book came from other people determined to stop the spread of homosexuality:

Richard Hauser is a sociologist whose enthusiasm galvan-
ises a pessimistic and complacent majority into taking
action . . . The value of the book lies in its revealing conversations with the 40 types of homosexuals . . . The
book has three sections: the prevention in society of the
breeding places of homosexuality; a better handling of
the matter when it occurs; and the consideration of the
normal cultural relationship between men and women to
see whether all is well there, which Hauser rightly thinks
is not.[6]

[*Mental Health*, April 1963]

Perhaps fortunately for Roger, the HLRS and Hauser's other
research subjects, reviews in more scholarly journals were dismissive:

This is an odd book. It can be said at once that it has no
scientific value to anyone with any knowledge of the subject.
Though the Home Office financed a 'survey,' which is said
to be reported in the text, to a tune of £525, it cannot be
said that anything new has been discovered. There is no
index. There is not a single reference. Mr Hauser appears
to have begun and completed his study entirely unaware
that anyone else had ever studied or written on the subject.
Apart from the 'data,' mainly recorded snippets of conversation, the book consists of obiter dicta, unsupported ideas
and conclusions.[7]

[*The British Journal of Criminology*, October 1962]

*

Smarting from his interactions with Hauser, Roger, in the spring
of 1960, was both more impatient and more determined to find
a different way to change the law. He could sense an opportunity with the arrival of a new decade and was determined not to
waste it:

```
Although I wasn't a particularly perceptive
observer of the changing political and social
scene, no one could be unaware that traditional
stuffy attitudes were fast being undermined in
a whole host of ways and life was being opened
up. Social difference and officious interference
in how people chose to live their lives was on
the way out.
```

Roger's experience of Hauser's research taught him that proceeding only within the established boundaries of discourse
would not be enough to change the position of homosexuals
in British society. Anonymous, hidden discussion groups led
by dubious researchers would not help. Public campaigns for
change led by well-meaning straight people who were believed
to be more palatable to the general population than homosexuals themselves would not be enough either. He concluded that
change would demand more personal action from the people
who lived their lives under the oppression of the law.

There were, of course, plenty of homosexuals among the campaigning voices of this era. But how could the law ever change,
Roger worried, unless the people most affected by it were willing
to say out loud that they did not see themselves as shameful or

unworthy? The problem was, there were so many reasons to be afraid that even the early leaders of the homosexual law reform movement who were themselves gay felt bound to secrecy. They were convinced that they could only work effectively if they continued to hide their own homosexuality or their names – they certainly could only continue to enjoy their jobs, homes and liberty that way. It was a vicious circle.

When Anthony (Tony) Dyson worked to found the HLRS in 1958, he gathered the support of numerous heterosexual patrons, whose names he cited in letters to the press about the need for changes to the law. Dyson himself was a public figure – an English literature academic at the University College of North Wales in Bangor – and a homosexual. But in his campaigning work he did not make his arguments personal – the homosexuals he described when the society put out its call for support were 'them' – as in somebody else.

Sir, –The present situation is seldom appreciated at its true worth. The main assumption behind the present law, which alone can justify it, is that homosexuality is a deliberately chosen perversion. This is now known to be untrue ... Now that this is known to be, to continue to treat them as outlaws and subject them to the constant fear of blackmail, imprisonment and social ruin is indefensible.
A.E. Dyson,
Hon. Secretary, Homosexual Law Reform Society
32 Shaftesbury Avenue, W.1.
[*New Statesman*, 15th November 1958]

Allan Horsfall, an early member of the Homosexual Law Reform Society who went on to found and lead the Campaign for Homosexual Equality, looked back on this time as one in which anonymity felt essential.

Had it been conceivable to produce a gay man's survival guide at that time it would have urged him never to reveal his name or address, never to discuss how he earned his living or where he worked, never to take anybody to his home or give anybody his telephone number and never to write letters, whether affectionate or not, to anybody with whom he was sexually involved or even to anybody he knew to be gay.[8]

And when a gay man called Anthony Wright took up the secretaryship of the HLRS in 1962, he used a name he had adopted for himself to shield his identity – Antony Grey. (Wright had also participated in Hauser's sessions; his account echoed Roger's bemusement.)

The lack of openness in this period led even members of the HLRS to be confused about who among them was or wasn't gay, and to believe that law reform relied on their deception. The acceptable face of its campaigners was a heterosexual one – as John Mathewson, a recruit to the HLRS in the 1960s, later reflected:

My first experience was in the mid 1960s with the Homosexual Law Reform Society who had offices in Shaftesbury Avenue. I think it was run by *Guardian*-reading type straight people (anyone who was gay couldn't openly admit it before the 1967 act anyway).[9]

Mathewson's characterisation of gay rights campaigners in this period is understandable, but not completely accurate. Before 1960, there was one campaigner for decriminalisation who had been willing to acknowledge his homosexuality publicly and explicitly in writing without adopting a pseudonym: Peter Wildeblood, who wrote *Against the Law* after his trial and conviction left him with little opportunity to deny being a homosexual and nothing to lose by speaking up.

For other men, who had not undergone that experience, there were devastating costs to identifying themselves. In Wildeblood's subsequent book, *A Way of Life*, he elevated some of their stories. 'Gordon Poole' is a cautionary tale about a man who confided in Wildeblood that he, too, was a homosexual. He had formed a friendship with a younger shop assistant at the hardware store where he was a manager. It took just a hint of suspicion to lead to gossip by an interfering colleague, Gladys, for Gordon to be dismissed along with the shop assistant, Patrick Stone.

> They could think of nothing more to say. Gordon ordered a plate of fish-and-chips, and sat staring at it miserably. After a while Patrick said: 'Why can't they leave us alone? I don't want much. I just want to be left alone.'[10]

Patrick spoke for a multitude.

*

On 12th May 1960, more than a thousand people gathered for the first public meeting of the Homosexual Law Reform Society. They packed Caxton Hall in Westminster: an ornate building that did double-duty as a registry office for high society civil marriages and as a public gathering space. It had a storied history of hosting pressure groups, not least the annual 'Women's Parliament' of British suffragettes in the years before the vote was won. (Its less vaunted occasions included playing host to the founding of the National Front in 1967.)

As people crammed into the largest chamber, Andrew Hallidie Smith hastily secured another room to serve as an overflow. Roger and many of the attendees still had to stand, filling the main hall right up to the balconies where the Women's Social and Political Union had draped their banners fifty years earlier. Many of the WSPU slogans would have been perfect for the new moment – 'Who Would Be Free Themselves Must Strike the Blow' – but that wasn't quite the tenor of this event.

Proceedings began at 7.30pm with a speech from the Bishop of Exeter, who declared the criminalisation of homosexuality a 'monstrously unjust law', but not before telling the gathering that he was certain the view of the Church would never change:

> . . . homosexual practices between men or between women are gravely sinful, . . . unnatural in a sense and in a degree in which heterosexual misbehaviour is not . . . as cancer kills the body, so homosexual tendencies, if not controlled or eradicated, are destructive of human personality and of human society.[11]

The next two speakers were supporters of the kind the HLRS had typically relied on for its campaigning work so far – concerned straight people (though today they would hardly be considered allies). Anne Allen, a Justice of the Peace, spoke of how as a mother of two sons, she would be horrified if they were criminalised as a result of having to face this 'problem' in their lifetimes. Then came Dr W. Lindesay Neustatter, a psychiatrist and member of the HLRS executive committee, who bemoaned:

> Ordinary members of the public only know what they call the 'Nancy boy' – the very obvious homosexual. I am perfectly certain that many homosexuals are never recognised as such, and it is as absurd to judge all homosexuals by the unstable 'Nancy boy', as to judge all women by prostitutes.[12]

Roger was becoming increasingly frustrated by these speeches. Then came the final one from Kingsley Martin, editor of the *New Statesman*. Martin told the attendees that in the past he had published letters from homosexuals under pseudonyms, and he would continue to enable their voices to be heard in that way. It was a practical approach, based in the reality of a legal and social environment in which known homosexuals experienced oppression and shame. But it infuriated Roger.

Roger was energised by the visible support for the decriminalisation of homosexuality, which was cemented with a vote taken at the end of the meeting. (A collection hat also appears to have been passed between speeches, garnering £110.) It was the nature of this support that angered him. Surely, Roger thought, these arguments made by heterosexuals – keen to change the law but hardly positive about homosexuals as people – could not be the best hope for men like him. And, surely, nothing would change if the only visible champions of the cause were calling for pity on behalf of nameless and pathetic shadows. It was about time that homosexuals took charge of their own destinies.

> After this highly successful meeting a dozen of us adjourned to a nearby pub. Here, inspiration fired by indignation, overcame me: 'Why the hell,' I said, 'should we write letters under pseudonyms? What have we got to be ashamed about?'

The beauty of the letters pages in newspapers and periodicals, where swathes of Britain debated the issues of the day in the 1950s and 1960s, was that they presented the opportunity for anyone to take part. This included a 25-year-old junior estate agent with few connections and too shy to have had anything approaching a meaningful romantic or sexual relationship.

Roger lamented that the likes of E.M. Forster and Tony Dyson used those pages only to support changing the law from an abstract point of view. He only had his own name to give – and what weight was carried by an unknown name? On the other hand, since nobody else had ever done it, perhaps his name might actually carry some weight?

> The proponents of legal reform always wrote in a detached manner, as if they were personally disinterested, merely expressing a rational

114

```
and commonsense view. After a while this
pusillanimity, as I saw it, began to irritate
me. I felt it was time for the cause to move
on, for someone to come out of the closet, as
it came to be described, and defiantly say, like
Luther, 'Here I stand.'
```

Roger had come to believe that decriminalisation would rely on the leadership of homosexuals themselves – on acts of personal bravery by as many homosexuals as could make them. Three weeks after the Caxton Hall gathering, Roger would go ahead and take his stand.

Oxford, 2004

On the rare occasion Roger talked about his feelings, normally brought on by an excess of gin and wine, he described just how empty of meaningful companionship and affection his life had become. He had no family to speak of, no partner, and the friends with whom he had felt entirely at ease were now mostly gone.

He had a retinue of visitors who attended religiously (the only religious aspect of Roger's life) to read and to help in other ways. But his world was still bounded almost entirely by the walls of his house and he often spent entire days alone. Later, he told me that the kiss I had given him before Christmas was his first for many years. When I returned after the winter vacation, Roger moved from his usual seat opposite me to spend our evenings on the sofa beside me, and a kiss and an embrace – a cuddle – became expected on my arrival and departure.

It was hard to know how much Roger had chosen to isolate himself and how much of the isolation had been imposed upon him. What was clearer was that he was comfortable when at home, having gone to great efforts to turn that house from battlefield into haven, ordering it with exact precision. Objects and papers had to be put neatly away, books kept on their right shelves, in their right order, and lights were not to be touched by anyone else without express instruction. His ability to fill his small freezer with what seemed to me like mountains of food was astonishing, and his ability to extract from it immediately any item he wanted was masterly. He told me that, long ago, he had developed a Braille labelling system for food, but in the end it proved easier just to learn ways of remembering what and where everything was by touch.

This strict order gave Roger a level of freedom he couldn't have elsewhere. Only by knowing everything was in its proper place could he move about without fear of tripping and be sure that he could find what he needed in the moment he needed it. But living almost exclusively within 41 Regent Street had obviously drained much of the joy from his days. Roger's world felt small, shallow, even, and not just for its lack of human relationships – physically, too.

He had been without a guide dog for twenty years at this point, mostly because of the time and energy involved in having one. He had also largely given up on the method of tapping a short cane as he walked almost as soon as he'd learned the technique in the early 1970s. It was clumsy and exposing, he felt, and Roger feared using it more than he wanted whatever it might offer him.

Roger told me he had loved to travel, and still longed to explore as many new things as he could, whether short trips around the corner to new local restaurants, visiting unknown parts of the country, or even abroad. He talked often to me about his many holidays as a younger man, both before and after he lost his sight, when a wide circle of friends took him with them to Suffolk, Cyprus, Tunisia, Morocco. But most of that seemed to have dropped away long before I arrived on the scene. Old friends still visited, but came only rarely. Perhaps Roger could have made more efforts to visit these old friends himself, but he felt unable to travel independently.

When I first met him, I wondered why Roger hadn't bothered to take on some of the newer technology that could give him more freedom. The answer became obvious fairly quickly: after more than three decades of having to cope on his own, Roger was exhausted. Braille, talking books, a typewriter and a few basic gadgets – his 'talking clock' and, more latterly, his talking mobile telephone (clunky, difficult thing that it was) – allowed him to do some of the things that he wanted to at home, and he had settled into accepting that this was enough. Taking bigger steps came with a price he was no longer willing to pay.

But now, there was me.

When I took my Master's exams in the summer of 2004 I had already been accepted onto a doctoral programme (more early Church history) and, unless things went very wrong, I was assured at least three more years in Oxford. A cause for celebration, we toasted to three more years of Tuesday evenings with Roger. By then, though, it had already become more than just Tuesdays.

I had started visiting Roger more often initially for practical reasons, for odd jobs around the house that required both sight and some dexterity. But by being in Regent Street more, becoming more familiar with how he lived from day to day, seeing more of who and what he was, I began to realise I could help Roger with more important things than finding lost objects in the cellar or reordering his bookshelves. Even just from time to time, even only for short distances, I could help to break him out of his red-bricked walls.

When I started leaving the house with Roger, the practical difficulties unfolded, one after the other, in great numbers. Steering us around Oxford involved negotiating a minefield of cobbled streets and ancient, uneven steps where any distraction on my part might cause Roger to tread wrongly and fall. Keeping Roger safe – keeping us going – required continuous concentration, sharp eyes and quick reactions. When we were walking, normally arm in arm or hand in hand, Roger's old, white cane would make a reappearance. A small, collapsible stick, it provided just enough warning for fast-walking pedestrians to give us a wide berth and avoid otherwise inevitable collisions.

Roger was a good teacher, talking me through it all as we went and only rarely commenting if I got something wrong (instead, he warned me about the physical perils of travelling with him through vivid and memorable stories of other people's failures). Having been sighted for so many years, Roger understood what someone in my position needed to know. By doing things – by actually following life as Roger lived it – I began to understand how best I could help and become someone on whom he could confidently rely.

For a while, taking Roger outside his home had a largely practical focus. Most useful for him were Saturday visits into the city centre, stopping for lunch on the way there – Italian was always Roger's preference – and at Marks & Spencer to stock up on the way home. He loved visiting Oxford's old covered market to pick up the niche foods his local Tesco (and his local helpers who shopped for him there) would never provide: speciality coffee from Cardews (250g Kenya AA, 250g continental: mixed, medium ground), puff-pastry mince pies (all year), rare breed sausages, traditional pork pies. After that, we'd head to Boswells, Oxford's traditional department store, to pick up other small luxuries (highly fragrant Yardley soaps were an essential) and to one of a handful of chocolate shops.

What Roger really wanted was to get out for longer spells away from home, so by the summer, with golden stone walls gleaming around us, we started to take extended walks at weekends. These were sometimes punctuated by meals in Oxford's pretty surrounding villages – old pubs with riverside gardens – or something more upmarket in town if we'd taken one of Roger's favourite routes back into the centre through the university parks and past Keble College.

Keen to try something different, and always happy to 'splash out' when I was with him, Roger would leave me to book places I thought he'd enjoy. The success of my choices became, as much as anything in those days, an insight into how differently Roger and I experienced environments outside the controlled familiarity of Regent Street. Once, I booked us into Gee's – an atmospheric restaurant in a glass house, which I was sure he would like (everyone did!). It was a terrible choice. Glass walls, stone floors and crowds of people made it impossibly loud for Roger – overwhelming for someone who relied so much on sound to navigate somewhere new. He couldn't even hear me read the menu from across our table.

The Old Parsonage, a beautiful seventeenth-century hotel, was my next attempt. We would sit in the courtyard, I decided, so noise couldn't possibly be a problem. Again: a disaster, despite the surroundings and the ease of hearing. Above us a tree was dropping pollen all through lunch – pollen which I could easily bat off my plate but which Roger found himself spooning into his mouth several times when I failed to spot it landing on his food.

Gradually, just like the cobbles and the steps, I learned to anticipate at least some of Roger's experience of places like these – and we honed our dining choices down to a few of the more overpriced options on Oxford's High Street.

All this time walking and eating was time not spent reading, of course, but it did give us the opportunity to talk a great deal about almost anything Roger wished. I took my lead from him, normally. Roger would speak about the books he had been reading as much as anything, but he also kept up with the news in ways I didn't back then and was interested especially in the patterns of history he saw unfolding and examples of them repeating. In the later years of the Blair government, after the invasion of Iraq, he talked a lot about his fears for a world descending into violence. Roger had been a supporter of nuclear disarmament in the 1960s, attending several of Bertrand Russell's rallies – the ultimate failure of that movement being something he regretted. And, with a smile and a gentle tease, he would explain to me exactly why religion was to blame for so much of history's warfare.

Oxford, 2004

In those conversations, it was always more him than me, which suited me well. I absorbed a great deal, or at least I tried to, from a man whose knowledge and memory were impressive. Roger would have refused the idea that blindness had sharpened his mind. He was keen always to reject careless or simplistic narratives about the loss of sight leading to the improvement of the other senses. 'Certainly not!' he scoffed with absolute conviction when I first asked him about it. But there was, I learned, some truth to the idea – losing his sight had caused Roger, by necessity, to develop ways better to remember things, people and facts.

By sheer force of effort, Roger had learned to be as self-sufficient as any person I have known. His prize for accomplishing self-sufficiency, though, had become loneliness. Three more years of Oxford: time enough, I thought, for us to change that.

CHAPTER 5

The Letter

'Why not stand up and be counted?'[1]

It was the last week of May 1960 and Roger was sitting anxiously in a café on one of the narrow, muddled streets behind the Charing Cross Road. He was looking out through the heavy lenses of his glasses, hoping anxiously that his friends would hold their nerve, that they wouldn't let him down. When they appeared, Roger opened a neat leather folio, setting out on the small table in front of him several identically typed sheets of paper and envelopes addressed to the editors of England's major periodicals.

Raymond Gregson and Robert Moorcroft pulled their chairs in close. The three men had a solemn purpose, something which, they knew, would shock most of the people sitting around them, unsuspecting folk accompanying this historic moment with the rattling of metal teaspoons against white china mugs. But there was nothing to cause anyone to stop and look over. In fact, the three men didn't even have much to talk about. They had resolved the difficult discussions before even agreeing to meet.

Frustrated by the Caxton Hall meeting, Roger had managed

to persuade two Homosexual Law Reform Society volunteers to join him in a radical plan to send to several national publications an unprecedented letter, in which they would identify themselves to the entire country as homosexuals as a way of making their own case for law reform.

Roger drafted what he considered to be a suitable text, which stated plainly both their opposition to the criminalisation of homosexuality and their personal stake in the matter. Raymond and Robert approved Roger's composition and, a few days later, they were meeting to sign the copies he had prepared and unleash a new political tactic in the struggle for gay liberation.

The co-signatories weren't close friends of Roger's and both are now even more lost to history than him. 'Raymond was from Lancashire, a nice, gentle, if somewhat willowy-watery young man,' is all that Roger recalled. 'Robert, in his late twenties, was from Yorkshire with characteristic grittiness and weather-beaten good looks who had, I think, been married but was so no longer.'* They were the only activists who had agreed to go along with Roger's idea – and he had asked many.

Gathered around the café table – 'rather in the manner of an international treaty' – they passed around four identical versions of the missive, signing, then signing again, and again, and again. Roger sealed the envelopes and packed them back into his folio, walking hurriedly to the nearest postbox to send

---

* Roger doesn't mention Raymond or Robert again in his writings, except to note that they were also present for the *Sunday Pictorial* debate soon after this, described in the following chapter. We would be delighted to learn more about their lives from anyone who knew them or knows about them.

the letters immediately to the *New Statesman*, the *Spectator*, the *Daily Telegraph* and the *Guardian*.

The daily papers would not publish the letter. The *Guardian* sent a polite refusal and the *Telegraph* didn't even do that. But the country's two leading political journals printed it. The *Spectator* was the only publication which agreed to feature Roger's letter in its complete form. Even then, Roger received a telegram from an editor, Bernard Levin, who wanted to make absolutely sure that the letter was genuine and that the signatories wished it to be published.* An abridged version appeared in the *New Statesman*, whose editor, Kingsley Martin, was unaware that his remarks at Caxton Hall had goaded Roger into writing his letter in the first place.

> SIR, –We are homosexuals and we are writing because we feel strongly that insufficient is being done to enlighten public opinion on a topic which has for too long been shunned. Furthermore, because we deplore a situation which requires that most homosexuals who write letters for publication are obliged to do so under a pseudonym, we have determined deliberately to sign our real names, even though, by so doing, we realise that we are making only a token gesture which may well be foolhardy.
>
> Over the past few years an enormous amount has been

---

* Levin had been political correspondent for the *Spectator* since 1956. He became well known for his willingness to champion progressive thinking, having voiced his support for the publication of the banned novel *Lady Chatterley's Lover* during the 1960 obscenity trial.

spoken and written about the homosexual situation. Most of it has been realistic and sensible, some has been vicious and singularly ill-informed. But whatever its form we welcome it, because we must welcome anything which brings this topic, for so long taboo, into open discussion. Only in this way can prejudice, which is fear born of ignorance, be overcome.

It was one of the recommendations of the Wolfenden Report that research be instituted into the aetiology of homosexuality. If anything is being done about this it has received little or no publicity and, therefore, is unlikely to be effective. We who sign this letter are anxious to do everything in our power to bring about better general understanding of our situation; it is often called a problem, but is only a problem because of the prevailing attitude towards it and because of the ludicrous law which encourages such an attitude and hinders every attempt to overcome it. The reform of this law, which has often brought more discredit to the police than to homosexuals, is, of course, inevitable, and we can only hope that the Government will soon have the courage to realise and accept this.

Even so, reform, though essential, is only a first step; there will remain the much larger and longer task of dissolving the centuries of accumulated and deeply ingrained misconception. We are under no illusions that this can be effected overnight, but we believe fervently that much can, and must, be done now by homosexuals like ourselves towards breaking through the barrier of public prejudice. Already, since the publication of the Wolfenden Report, breaches have been made in the general attitude towards issues at one time thought 'not nice.'

We will leave the last word to Dr. Sherwin Bailey, who, in a book published under the auspices of the Church of England Moral Welfare Council, wrote: 'Education alone can remove the irrational prejudice which persists in some quarters against those handicapped by inversion . . . despite the imputations of the ignorant or malicious, there is nothing sinful or disgraceful in being homosexual.'

Yours faithfully,
ROGER BUTLER
RAYMOND GREGSON
ROBERT G. MOORCROFT
[*Spectator*, 3rd June 1960]

The letter's revelatory and unambiguous announcement, to the widest possible audience, crossed a red line. Using their real names, Roger, Raymond and Robert were announcing their homosexuality entirely voluntarily – not because it had already been made known and they had nothing left to lose, but because they believed that freely identifying themselves could further their cause. The fact that such an act was dangerous was, so far as Roger was concerned, exactly the reason for doing it.

Roger was well aware of the high stakes involved in signing a public letter coming out as gay in 1960. It admitted criminal activity of a kind that opened the possibility of real trouble for him and his co-signatories. That, he suspected, was why an open declaration of this kind had never been made before.

I didn't quite know what I might be letting
myself in for, or all of us into, and didn't
know what repercussions there might be or what
publicity it might or might not stir up.[2]

Roger did not flinch. Perhaps it was 'an act of youthful bravado fired by a combination of indignation and the impetus of the reform movement which was just beginning to roll', as he himself described it. Still, he had a clear idea of what he hoped to achieve: to make the British public aware of the real men whose lives were on the line in the debate over decriminalisation, and to say that those men saw nothing about themselves that was wrong or needed to be denied.

I was unaware of anyone who had come out
unequivocally at that time. In the case of public
figures at that time - actors, politicians,
writers - there was a power of difference
between being widely known to be homosexual and
openly making a declaration of it. We felt it
was high time that the likes of us should be
prepared to stand up and be counted.

In politely and measuredly showing that he was willing to be identified as a homosexual, Roger immediately punctured some of the most vicious assertions about sinister deviants. Homosexuals couldn't be so bad, he was telling straight people and gay people alike, if he was so comfortably announcing he was one of them.

The Letter

Gay men working for homosexual emancipation in Britain throughout the 1950s included people generally assumed – known, even – to be homosexuals themselves. But acknowledging and declaring their homosexuality as part of that work was something categorically different. The declaration, 'Sir, we are homosexuals', was a revolutionary act: the first coming out in the struggle to change the law.

The act and the process of coming out as we now understand it entered common usage in queer culture in the early 1970s, but the term was already established among gay people by then. Gay groups in the early twentieth century held 'drag balls' in cities across the United States: large, collective events modelled on the debutante and masquerade balls of the heterosexual mainstream in which young women 'came out' into high society. Moves to shut the drag events down increased sharply after the 1920s, but the balls continued into the 1950s, and from them emerged the idea and the language of gay people coming out into gay society.

> The coming out of new debutantes into homosexual society was the outstanding feature of Baltimore's eighth annual frolic of the pansies when the Art Club was host to the neuter gender at the Elks' Hall, Friday night.[3]

This version of coming out was an entry into a sub-culture inhabited by homosexuals and gender-nonconforming people who were aware enough of their identity to seek out queer society and brave enough to take a step into it. Coming out was an announcement to others, a decision to enter the spaces and the lives of other queer people. But it was an announcement made to, and within, queer communities. As much as drag balls drew attention, participants were not intentionally speaking of their individual identities to the wider world.

In 1970, the Gay Liberation Front also began talking about 'coming out' – this time as a public act, openly identifying as gay, including to straight people, in order to change perceptions about queer people. The GLF has been widely credited with adopting this idea first. They were, however, asserting the same language and the same foundational principle as Roger had set out a decade earlier: change for gay people required them to come out, and coming out couldn't mean simply acknowledging homosexuality in private.

The British GLF had formed in October 1970, with a meeting of eighteen men and one woman in a basement room at the London School of Economics. Two students had travelled to the US to see what was being done there for gay rights and decided to bring the campaigning zeal they saw back to Britain. At one of the very first meetings, new members were pressed, more than anything else, to come out, as a young gay attendee named Stuart Feather recalled:

We were encouraged to buy the GLF badge (badges were the cool fashion accessory of the time) and urged to 'Come Out' and show pride in being gay by wearing one. Someone said that despite the fact that there must be one gay person in every family, heterosexuals feared lesbians and gays because our invisibility had led them to believe that they didn't know any. By coming out, by being visible in the family and community, a lot of that fear and prejudice would be allayed. The heterosexual would see we were as human as everybody else, and that we counted and had to be reckoned with.[4]

The GLF both petitioned gay people to come out and fought to create safe spaces in which gay people *could* come out, understanding that the two reinforced each other. From the start they declared that coming out meant more than just being open in mutually supportive queer communities – it required declaring individual sexual identity openly, specifically to the dominant heterosexual majority. This, campaigners argued, would free individuals from the oppressive and restrictive life of secrecy and change the fate of a maligned minority. Ultimately, coming out would force society to do more than just tolerate gay people – heterosexuals would have to welcome, include and celebrate them instead. This was a significant expansion of ambitions and became a cornerstone of gay rights activism, but it all rested on the same idea that Roger had pioneered.

It is only by coming out, and coming out proud, that we can ever be truly liberated. Not only does it confront straight people with our existence, but it also liberates ourselves from the tensions, guilt and hypocrisy of pretence.[5]
[*Come Together*, May 1971]

Gay Liberation fixed coming out at the heart of queer rights discourse and made it a prominent feature of queer rights activity. For the GLF, coming out (a Good Thing) would become contrasted with being closeted (a Bad Thing): a paradigm and a language central to its campaigning. For individual homosexuals, of course, reaching the stage of being willing and able to come out to the general population required a personal journey to have taken place already – one which began with breaking down the self-loathing in their own minds.

> You must kill the old society within your own self and your own life, or it will take you with it in its endless grey cage. You are a free agent . . . You and only you, perpetuate our past and make our present.[6]
>
> [*Come Together*, February 1971]

Jeffrey Weeks, another early member of the GLF, described coming out as having three stages, each of which was essential before someone could be said fully to have come out:

> . . . first of all it involved coming out to yourself, recognising your own homosexual personality and needs; secondly, it involved coming out to other homosexuals, expressing those needs in the gay community and in relationships; but thirdly, and most crucially, it meant coming out to other people, declaring, even asserting, your sexual identity to all comers.[7]

This idea still holds for what it means to be really, fully 'out'. As for Roger, he first came out to himself privately on a London bench when he acknowledged, 'I am a homosexual'. His arrival at the HLRS volunteering headquarters was the second step: sitting, mug in hand, listening to 'queers chatting queer talk' for the first time. The letter of June 1960 was Roger's third and final stage of coming out – telling the nation that he, Roger Butler, was a homosexual.

Looking back after three decades had passed, Roger characterised his letter in just the same way as the GLF explained their mantra: 'It was what's now called coming out into the open . . . out of the closet, they now say. Another expression which wasn't dreamed of at that time.'[8] In fact, two of Roger's letters from 1960 demonstrate that he was, even then, describing what he had done as 'coming out'. More than that, he was taking opportunities to come out to heterosexual friends and calling on others to do the same – in petitions that might just as plausibly have come from the 1970s literature of the GLF.

Roger was the innovator here.

```
I feel it is very important that as many people
as possible come out into the open, and the
more eminent the people the better.
```
[9th October 1960]

```
I agree it would be ideal if everybody did come
out into the open. I do it whenever I can.
```
[18th October 1960]

At the start of the 1960s, no man had ever come out in the way that Roger, Raymond and Robert chose to. To the extent that homosexual men campaigning in the preceding decade declared their personal interest in changing anti-homosexual laws, the accepted practice was to use pseudonyms or no names at all. Anthony Wright did this when he wrote a powerful campaigning letter to the *Sunday Times* in 1954, emphasising his own sexuality, but signing it, 'Yours faithfully, HOMOSEXUAL'.[9]

Outside of Britain the situation was hardly very different for gay rights campaigners. In the United States, for example, the 1951 book *The Homosexual in America* played an important role in articulating the experiences of the homosexual author and his homosexual friends and partners. It helped to nurture American gay rights organisations, but it was published using the pseudonym Donald Webster Cory. Edward Sagarin, as a result, continued his double life as a respected sociologist in New York, and the truth of his dual identity was only revealed in 1974, by someone else. In 1954, the national secretary of the secretive Mattachine Society, Dale Olson, became the first man to appear on television in the United States and self-identify as homosexual in order to further the gay rights movement, but he did so with his face literally obscured and under the name Curtis White.

Roger's sexuality had been entirely unknown outside of the hidden gay community of London, and that would have likely remained the case for ever, had he stayed quiet. In 1960 he voluntarily exposed himself to the prospect of persecution for no personal gain, for no reason other than that he believed it needed to be said in order to help change the law. Finally, the public was seeing a homosexual who had not been dragged into their view, but who stepped up, freely, calmly and confidently, to claim the name. This was unimaginable to most people in 1960.

It would also have seemed extraordinary to the leading figures of queer emancipation in earlier criminalised generations. Those heroes of the past, even men understood now to be homosexual, rarely spoke openly or directly about their sexualities. In Oscar Wilde's case of libel against Lord Queensbury and his trials for indecent activity, to take one famous example, he denied his homosexuality. In court, Wilde explained away his relationship with Queensbury's son – and what 'Bosie' Douglas had called the love 'that dare not speak its name' – as a spiritual affection between the intellect of an older man and the hope of the younger.

Some of Wilde's homosexual contemporaries did grapple more explicitly with same-sex attraction in their writing, using evolving language and concepts including 'urnings,' 'uranians' and an 'intermediate sex.' But arguments for social acceptance and legal reform were still deployed with academic detachment by men who sent conflicting messages about their own lives. John Addington Symonds suppressed same-sex attraction for much of his life, was married to a woman and left his memoir acknowledging erotic feelings for men to be published only after his death. Edward Carpenter, a man who has been described as a Victorian gay rights activist, lived with a same-sex partner but wrote about giving homosexuals 'their' fitting place. Late in life, in his 'autobiographical notes' he described his 'temperament' using opaque language, so carefully constructed that a reader can be left wondering what he actually means. Further afield, amid the beginnings of what has been characterised as the first homo-sexual emancipation movement in Germany, Magnus Hirschfeld published his studies of gender and human sexuality as a scien-tist, not as the homosexual that he also was.

When Roger looked around himself he could not see any

men who had revealed their homosexuality to campaign against anti-gay laws – only people who made public statements after their sexuality was already a matter of official record. In Britain, Peter Wildeblood had been arrested and identified as a homosexual before he wrote *Against the Law*. In the United States, the poet Robert Duncan wrote a 1944 essay for the periodical *Politics* intimating he was a homosexual, but only after he had told the U.S. Army he was gay in order to secure his discharge from military service. Karl Heinrich Ulrichs had alluded to his homosexuality in pamphlets written to challenge the spread of anti-gay laws as Germany unified,* but he began his campaigning work after being forced from the civil service in 1854 by scrutiny of his scandalous – though not then illegal – relationships with men.

In 1960s Britain, it was no secret that gay men were living gay lives – and sometimes even writing about homosexuality for wide audiences. It was because of this that Roger could go out and buy James Baldwin's *Giovanni's Room* and hope that some famous homosexual like E.M. Forster would write a letter to declare publicly who they were. But the reality was that someone like Forster wasn't willing to do that. And nobody involved in the law reform movement would do it either. Nobody whose homosexuality wasn't already a matter of record appeared to be willing to state in plain terms 'I am a homosexual', and to say it to the world as themselves. Nobody other than Roger, Raymond and Robert.

---

* Ulrichs' 1868 pamphlet 'Gladius Furens' describes his thwarted attempt to speak out against anti-gay laws at a forum of the Association of German Jurists the previous year. By his own account, he did not identify his sexuality in that speech, but in the pamphlet he says that laws criminalising 'urnings' are injecting poison into 'men of my nature'.

Oxford, 2004

I tried my best not to disrupt Roger's ordered existence as we spent more time together, but I didn't always get it right. I remember vividly a strong ticking-off one Tuesday evening after leaving the lights on when I'd brought Roger home from dinner the previous week. I'd casually pushed the hallway light switch on when we returned to Regent Street, forgetting to turn it off when I left. A simple mistake and hardly a problem anywhere else, but in Roger's house, most of the lights were controlled by that one dimmer switch, so they remained on all weekend. Roger only found out his house had been lit up like a beacon when another visitor asked if he'd intended to have so many lights on at lunchtime on a Monday.

As I learned more about how Roger lived, I tried to develop the same habits I saw him exercise to sustain the order: do what Roger does, I told myself, and nothing much should go wrong. And even with the occasional mistake, he had come to trust me. This meant more than just allowing me to guide him around. Outside of his house, doing very basic things made him exceptionally vulnerable.

Shopping, for example, meant him handing over his credit card. If Roger needed to write a cheque, it would be up to someone else to fill it all in – set out the amounts and the payee, and then guide him, pen in hand, to the dotted line, pointing to where his signature should start at the bottom. Some experiences Roger faced when leaving the house were deeply personal – intimate, even. Accompanying him to a restaurant didn't just involve the business of reading a menu, clearing the table of obstacles and guiding his hands to his glass. More often than not, it involved taking him into a bathroom, manoeuvring him to a toilet, waiting next to him, helping him to a sink to wash.

I had been seeing the many physical and practical obstacles the world presented to Roger for some time already, but I hadn't always understood how distressing these could be for him. The extent of that hit me most fully when Roger asked me to accompany him to the memorial service for Stuart Hampshire, the former Warden of Wadham College.

When I arrived to collect Roger at Regent Street, I was relieved to see he had changed out of his standard home attire and into something more formal (he was still in beige, mind you). I knew how snobbish Oxford could be about appropriate dress. As we set off, he opened up his folding stick and we walked up to Wadham, taking one of Roger's favourite routes through the city centre, through the high-walled Queen's Lane and under Hertford College's 'Bridge of Sighs'.

Stuart had been a famous philosopher, and he and Roger had been friends since the 1970s. As we walked, Roger gave me a brief summary about Stuart's first wife, Renée, who had been married to another philosopher, A.J. Ayer, when her relationship with Stuart began. As we approached the entrance to Wadham, Roger casually dropped in that Stuart was, for a period, rumoured to be the fifth man in the famous Cambridge ring of secret Soviet agents, along with Kim Philby and Anthony Blunt. The idea was generally dismissed, he said, but he still had a tantalising flicker of doubt – 'Perhaps he was the smartest of the lot, the one who actually got away with it?'

At the memorial service, there was a bizarre performance by a pianist who, some way through his piece, started playing with just one hand, lifted a mouth organ from a pocket with the other and continued for quite some time, accompanying himself. I tried to tell Roger through a giggle but couldn't get it out until after we'd left.

Then came the reception, in a crowded, stone-walled, stone-floored hall, with the clinking of wine glasses, the clattering of trays and people shouting to be heard over one another. Roger was defeated. He couldn't spot people he knew – and of course I knew nobody and nobody knew me – so we relied on others approaching Roger to introduce themselves. Amid the large crowd, we were bumped about until we found a table to hold on to near a quieter spot. Even then, when people came over to talk, Roger struggled to sustain conversation. Unable to watch lips to make out one voice over the others, not seeing any body language, not knowing who else was looking or listening . . . it was just impossible.

As we walked home, from the elegant sandstone facades of the city centre to the disorder of the East Oxford residential streets, Roger was visibly relieved and exhausted. This, he explained, was typical. At best, at that kind of event, he would find one amiable person and be able to talk with them throughout. At worst, he found nobody and was stuck alone and helpless, unable to spot a friend. More likely, he would end up pinned into a corner by someone he longed to escape. Having me there helped – I could whisper into his ear or he could pull on my arm to seek an exit (we developed a code later on) – but these were minor improvements.

After our Wadham experience, I recalled with new understanding a time I'd been waiting on Roger's sofa one Tuesday evening. As I sat – was sitting – nursing my gin and tonic, Roger's telephone rang. An unfortunate undergraduate, obviously working a vacation job for the college's fundraising office, had called Roger to invite him to a reunion event at Balliol. The student received an extraordinary scolding from Roger, who said he had left money to the college in his will on the condition he never be bothered by them. At the time, this struck me as out of character, but now Roger's rapid irritation made more sense to me. He was determined not to revisit college and subject himself to the sort of suffering I had witnessed that day. What might be a pleasant chance for an overdue catch-up with old friends to someone else brought for Roger, instead, the prospect of trauma.

Roger's blindness made these gatherings unbearable, but it took a little longer for me to learn that he was unhappy about more than just a few hours lost at a party he couldn't enjoy. Roger had a keen sense that in those rooms filled with intellectuals and high achievers, he would never measure up. Roger delighted in his closeness with Stuart and Renée and admired many of the impressive friends he had made over the years, but he believed that he shone only by association – and not for any other reason. With no career to speak of, nor wealth, status or honours to his name, why, Roger wondered, would anyone be interested in what he had to say?

I accompanied Roger to various kinds of gatherings over the years and over time met several of his surviving friends. Never once did I get the impression that the people he spoke to felt this way about him – and this wasn't just politeness. Roger was knowledgeable, extremely well read, with a clear and insightful intellect. He was an excellent conversation partner. And it's likely his friends grasped just how much effort and energy it took for him simply to be in a room filled with people. That alone might be considered an accomplishment. No – this concern of Roger's was entirely his own.

It is a shame, though, that so many of his friends seemed not to know that Roger had also done something of historical significance, which would have stood up among the achievements of anyone else in any room he occupied. In 1960, the young Roger Butler had quietly gone and started a revolution.

CHAPTER 6

The Quiet Revolutionary

'If you really believe in the rightness and justice of a particular cause, why not be completely open about it?'[1]

THE MEN IN THE WOLFENDEN REPORT

+ One man in every twenty-five in Britain today is a homosexual. A shocking figure? It is the estimate of the Wolfenden Committee on Vice.

+ These men live in towns and villages all over the country. The problem of homosexuality is not confined to the big cities.

+ This week Parliament debates a proposal by the Wolfenden Committee to change the law as it affects homosexuals.

+ The Committee's proposals to drive prostitutes off the streets have already become law. MPs will now debate the Committee's other controversial recommendation –

+ THAT HOMOSEXUAL BEHAVIOUR BETWEEN CONSENTING ADULTS IN PRIVATE SHOULD NOT BE A CRIME.

+ If this proposal became law it would change the lives of a million men who are attracted to other men. Many

145

of them have sexual relationships with each other which are at present criminal offences.

◆ What are homosexuals like? Can they be cured? Would a change in the law free them to increase in number? Are they a basic danger to society?

Four self-confessed homosexuals met at a consulting room in Harley Street, London, last week to discuss the questions above. With them were two leading figures in the battle to change the law – Mr Kenneth Walker, famous sociologist and surgeon, and the Rev. A. Hallidie Smith, secretary of the Homosexual Law Reform Society. Also there were Mrs Anne Allen, Britain's youngest woman magistrate, who has two sons and two step-sons, and Mr William Shepherd, Tory MP.[2]

So began Roger Butler's next appearance in print. Within weeks of the publication of his letter, he was a subject of a double-page spread in the *Sunday Pictorial*, a major tabloid newspaper that would become the *Sunday Mirror* in 1963. The paper was offering its readers the findings of a 'special inquiry' into homosexuality and, more unusually and significantly, directly interviewing what it referred to as 'the men in the Wolfenden Report.' Roger was one of the four 'self-confessed homosexuals' in the piece that appeared on 26th June 1960.

The *Sunday Pictorial* was a hugely popular paper and had flourished for years under the editorship of Hugh Cudlipp. It had also been running a persistent hate campaign against homosexuals for most of the preceding decade, launched in May

1952 with a three-part series under the heading 'Evil Men'. The homosexual problem was presented as a conspiracy of corruption, and the campaign for tolerance as a war on British values:

> TODAY the 'Pictorial' begins an Investigation into a grave and growing social problem.
> IS IT TRUE that male degenerates infest the West End of London and the social centres of many provincial cities?
> IS IT TRUE that their influence is exerted in important spheres of national life?
> [*Sunday Pictorial*, 25th May 1952]

By the summer of 1960, with MPs again preparing to consider the Wolfenden Committee's recommendations, the *Sunday Pictorial* had contacted Andrew Hallidie Smith to help it put together a more balanced feature on the hot topic of the moment. They asked him to nominate members of the HLRS who could participate in a recorded discussion, apparently aiming to bring together people with differing views and present both sides of the argument. Roger's letter had made him an obvious choice.

Participating in the project was risky, in different ways than writing the letter had been. There was no certainty about how the men would be presented. There was, in fact, every reason to believe it could be a set-up, especially given the newspaper's history. Still, Roger and the HLRS decided they had to try to get their points across on the pages of such a widely read publication. They gambled that they could do this best by offering the *Pictorial* real, live homosexuals – ones who happened to be crushingly ordinary.

The impact of Roger's letter in redirecting the campaign for homosexual emancipation was clearest in the composition of the group that gathered in Kenneth Walker's consulting rooms. The heterosexual supporters for legal change sitting there had all also been on the stage at Caxton Hall as the public faces of the movement, leading the work of the HLRS. Now, for the first time, openly homosexual men had secured an invitation to join their ranks.

Two of the other self-confessed homosexuals featured by the *Sunday Pictorial* were Roger's co-signatories, Raymond Gregson and Robert Moorcroft. The trio that had risked their own safety and security to personalise law reform had now become leaders in that movement. With his letter Roger had seized, from sympathetic heterosexuals, ownership of the narrative about homosexual people.

Just as they were beginning their discussion, on what Roger recalled as a balmy summer evening, a man in his forties arrived and joined the group. He struck Roger as very charming, but also a little shy, with a slight stammer. This fourth homosexual participant had an intriguing aura of anonymity, and indeed was introduced to Roger by Andrew simply as 'an eminent surgeon' – the descriptor which appeared also in the *Pictorial*'s article.

It was the newspaper, rather than the participants, that decided not to identify the homosexuals present at what it described as 'a meeting of brutal frankness, often charged with bitter emotion'. Roger, Raymond and Robert had already shown themselves willing to take a visible stand in the national media, but that was more than the *Pictorial* would contemplate for its own pages. Instead, the men were assigned false names, ages and professions, and the printed photograph of the meeting concealed the faces of the homosexual participants (Roger appears to have his back to the camera, but has still removed the glasses he disliked wearing – something his parents had encouraged him to do for photographs since he was a child).

The explosiveness of what they were doing by appearing at all is made clear by an inset fact box in the article, with pictures and a short biographical description of three famous – and very much dead – homosexuals.

Oscar Wilde, the Victorian playwright whose life has recently been filmed, was sent to prison for homosexual associations. He was married and had two sons.

James I was notorious for the homosexuals in his court. One was said to have escaped punishment for murder when he threatened to make public his relationship with the king.

Tchaikovsky, the composer who wrote 'Swan Lake', had strong homosexual tendencies and at one period of his life was in love with a girl and her brother at the same time.[3]

These were apparently the only homosexuals whom readers might have previously encountered. Now, they were about to hear from some who were alive, in the present, and ready to defend themselves.

William Shepherd MP more than justified his role as the group's hostile voice, generating blockbuster quotes such as: 'There is every reason to believe that homosexuality would spread like a prairie fire if the law was changed.' The others

THE LIGHT OF DAY

present gave him no reason not to be cordial, though, and he ultimately conceded, 'I would not say that homosexuals are necessarily disreputable members of society.' He ended somewhat weakly: 'we mustn't get away from the fact that these relationships between men are unnatural.'

At times, the real debate appeared to be occurring between the supporters of law reform. Kenneth Walker, referred to in the piece as 'THE SOCIOLOGIST', was in reality the first chairman of the HLRS, but not identified as such in the piece, and his comments lay bare what Roger and his friends were up against. Walker and Hallidie Smith – 'THE PRIEST' in the abridged version of the discussion that appeared – offered bloodless and at times downright negative comments about the homosexuals on whose behalf they were meant to be campaigning.

'No increase in homosexuality has been reported from countries such as Holland and Sweden where the laws have been amended,' Hallidie Smith promised. 'Most experts agree that a man who is exclusively homosexual can't be turned normal. Borderline cases may be helped to make the change. With expert advice on how to adjust their lives they could become happy and useful citizens.'

Walker made the point again before opening up on his theories of the causes of homosexuality. 'Homosexuals I've met over the past thirty years don't expect to be cured . . . I can only advise them on the best way to accept a disability which is making their life very difficult and lonely,' he told the reporter. 'The likelihood of a man getting dragged into homosexuality is very slight. Sometimes it's hereditary, but normally it's acquired . . . because a boy is brought up "girlishly" by his mother, perhaps. There are so many emotional factors in childhood. Fear of normal relationships is also a cause. Much more research is needed before a definite answer can be given to this question.'

The agenda set by the published questions of the *Pictorial*'s reporter was unavoidable. The four homosexuals were drawn into discussion about the prospect of a cure and a link between homosexuality and paedophilia. But they offered succinct and compelling defences, even as they fought on terrain they could not control and under identities they were forced to assume.

'The normal homosexual is revolted by men who run after little boys, just as a normal man, presumably, is revolted by men who chase little girls,' said 'STEVEN G. 27, a technical clerk and homosexual' (and whose description comes closest to Roger). 'They don't represent homosexuals. They are a sick minority.'

Each man also managed to land at least one blow in support of gay men. When 'THE MP' told the group that some of his friends were homosexuals who didn't act on their desires and he admired them all the more for it, he was scolded by 'LESLIE S., 41, a clerk and homosexual'. '*Admire* them! You should *pity* them for having to restrain their natural – natural to them – sexual instincts. Your friends must live terribly unhappy lives. Would YOU like to have to restrain your natural desires for women?' 'DAVID K., 22, a junior diplomat who is a homosexual' argued similarly: 'I can see nothing morally wrong in acting according to my instincts.' The 'EMINENT SURGEON [not Mr. Walker], aged forty-two, who is a homosexual', threw the most decisive punch. 'There are 1,000,000 of us, remember.'

Homosexual voices were finally being heard.

'These, then, are the questions to which MPs on Wednesday will have to find their own answers,' the piece concluded. 'The basic problem they face is: Are so many men to be treated as social outcasts indefinitely?'

At the same time that readers of the *Pictorial* were being asked to sympathise with anonymised homosexuals for the first time, readers of the *New Statesman* and the *Spectator* were grappling with the realisation that some of those homosexuals were actually willing to identify themselves. If Roger's family or colleagues saw the letter, they didn't mention it to him, and no policeman came knocking on the door. Instead Roger could sit in his flat and read the flurry of reactions that he had provoked. Responses were printed for an entire month in the *Spectator*, while the *New Statesman* featured responses and counter-responses for a further month after that. Many of the correspondents wrote in more than once about the subject, showing the passion with which they held their views and their insistence on airing them as frequently as possible.

The submissions selected by the editors show some of the same dominating preoccupations around homosexuality as the *Pictorial*'s: causes, consequences and the effects of its criminalisation. It would take time for the letter-writing classes to adjust to homosexual men speaking as themselves, for themselves, but some of the responses did quickly engage with the main point of Roger's letter: that living, breathing homosexuals were proof that there wasn't anything particularly wrong with homosexuality.

SIR, – Your homosexual correspondents should not suppose that all who fail to rally to their cause are constrained by 'irrational prejudice'. There are practical considerations. The demand for the implementation of the Wolfenden recommendations is not pursued solely for the benefit of those men who wish to establish conjugal fidelity. Homosexual practices are, and will continue to be, largely promiscuous ... Once the desired legislation has been achieved, clubs in which men solicit men will be accepted as legitimate, even respectable. Only those clubs which encourage or facilitate heterosexual promiscuity will continue to be denounced as 'dens of vice'.

R.L. ARCHDALE
Darenth House, Leigh-on-Sea, Essex
[*Spectator*, 10th June 1960]*

SIR, – ... On the question of homosexual law reform, it is surely obvious that homosexuals are being driven by the law to act like any other persecuted minority. It must be remembered that homosexuals are not homosexuals *by choice*. If the law regarding acts between consenting adults were changed, we should soon hear no more of the whole business than we do of, say, Lesbianism. Does Lesbianism spread and increase because there are no laws to restrain it? Certainly not ... Most homosexuals, under great strain, are good and useful

---

* On 24th June, Archdale underlined his point: 'In short we may well arrive at a situation in which lonely men with bisexual tendencies will find it easier to obtain homo- than hetero-sexual satisfaction.'

members of society. Many more could be so, if given the chance. The neuroses induced by fear and ostracism lie at the root of the whole trouble. – Yours faithfully,

G.F.

London, SW1

[*Spectator*, 24th June 1960]

SIR, – The three signatories to the letter in your issue of 4 June complain that insufficient is being done to enlighten public opinion on this subject. They also rightly state that an enormous amount has been spoken and written about the homosexual situation.

Over the past few years we have had conclusions from Peter Wildeblood, the Wolfenden Report, intellectuals, social workers, priests, and psychiatrists including Dr West, whose Penguin is on sale at every bookstall throughout the country[4] . . . The result of all this has been to make the normal man, who likes women and enjoys regular sexual frolics with his girl friend or wife, feel the odd man out and to have some doubts as to what now constitutes normal sexual behaviour.

What the normal man (if he really exists) finds acutely embarrassing and unpleasant are such overt manifestations as homosexuals engaged in mutual masturbation in a public convenience, and the synthetically blonde males with made up faces and exaggerated feminine mannerisms. No amount of persuasion and education will make him like these things and the most that homosexuals can expect from the more enlightened sections of the community is tolerance.

So we have got to live with it. And now please, is it too much to ask that we may have a respite from a subject which has become excruciatingly boring?

WALTER DESTEFANO

17 Hogarth Road, SW5

[*New Statesman*, 11th June 1960]

SIR, – Perhaps Mr Walter Destefano would not be quite so 'excruciatingly' bored if he were faced with the possibility of two years imprisonment when he 'enjoys regular sexual frolics with his girl friend or wife' which he states the 'normal man' likes.

It is no more amusing to see heterosexual couples copulating in Hyde Park than it is to see homosexuals engaged in what he calls 'mutual masturbation' in public conveniences. It has to be faced that these people are perhaps driven by environment and circumstances to have their 'frolics' in public places; the difference lies in the penalty if they are caught.

Next time Mr Destefano is having his 'frolic', or is overcome with his terrible boredom, perhaps he will remember that fact.

SYBIL MORRISON

6 Apollo Place, SW10

[*New Statesman*, 18th June 1960]*

---

* Sybil Morrison (1893–1984) was a veteran suffrage and peace activist, known most widely for her pacifist stance. Her relationships with women were not hidden and, although not illegal, caused her some notoriety.

SIR, – I write in admiration of the courage of your correspondents (4 June) Roger Butler, Raymond Gregson and Robert G. Moorcroft.

I still, in these days of so-called enlightenment, come across incredible ignorance and therefore intolerance of inversion, and this becomes ironical if not tragic in the cases known to me of parents whose grown children are homosexual, these parents claiming that they have never met an invert, as though all homosexuals go about branded with some sort of identifying stigmata.

As long ago as the turn of the century Krafft-Ebing,* when he was over 60, possessed the mental resilience and moral integrity to state publicly that his belief over many years that inversion was disease or degeneration had been proved false by his research and that it was in fact a biological anomaly; while Kinsey, 50 years later, concluded that 'it is difficult to maintain the view that psychosexual reactions between individuals of the same sex are rare and therefore abnormal or unnatural, or that they constitute within themselves evidence of neuroses or even psychoses . . . Homosexuality is an expression of capacities that are basic in the human animal.'

MICHAEL R.C. LAURIE-BECKETT
Broadway, Worcs
[New Statesman, 18th June 1960]

---

* Richard von Krafft-Ebing (1840–1902) practised in psychiatric asylums, after which he made a career in psychiatry, forensics and hypnosis. His work was influential in the scientific study of homosexuals and for medicalising homosexuality as a congenital condition.

156

SIR, – I am sure that no experienced psychiatrist will accept Mr Laurie-Beckett's contention that homosexuality is not a neurosis . . .

In 1937 I published a book on psychosexual diseases, based on considerable experience, in which I stated that homosexuality is a neurosis; and since then I have had further opportunities of seeing many cases. Nothing in that experience has caused me to alter my views. The very fact that homosexuality, in a certain number of cases, is curable, demonstrates that it is a neurosis. Successful cures have been published by London, Naftaly, Lilienstein, Laforgue, Stekel, Gordon, Serog, Frey, Bircher, Sumbaer, Hadfield, Ellis and others.

Homosexuality is caused by the conditions in which a boy is brought up. All boys mould their personality on their mothers during this first few years of life – up to about the age of six. A normal boy should then mould himself on his father (and so acquire male reactions – 'Learn to be a man'). However, if the father dies, or is an unsuitable person, a drunkard, too busy, etc. then the boy will go on moulding himself on his mother and so acquire an excess of feminine reactions . . . visible in all the classical homosexuals, for example Oscar Wilde and Lord Alfred Douglas. In the case of women, excessive moulding on the father produces the female homosexual. This is clear in the autobiographical novel *The Well of Loneliness* by Radclyffe Hall.

Naturally prison will not cure homosexual neurosis any more than any other neurosis and the unbiological isolation from the opposite sex tends to aggravate it. Those who

suffer from homosexuality need psychiatric treatment . . .
Greater facilities for treatment and wider publicity that
it can sometimes be cured would be of more help than
to make it permissible in young people. Older, incurable
cases, unless they interfere with other people, should not
be prosecuted, but allowed to live as happily as they can.
CLIFFORD ALLEN*
148 Harley Street, W1.
[*New Statesman*, 25th June 1960]

SIR, – . . . It is untrue that 'there is no doubt that homosexuality is curable by psychotherapy'; there is considerable
doubt. If a homosexual becomes heterosexual after treatment this does not prove that it was because of it. One
would want additional evidence . . . In modern medicine,
clinical impressions have repeatedly been shown to be
fallacious when tested by modern research techniques.
Psychiatry falls behind other branches of medicine if
psychiatrists forget that it is a scientifically based discipline
as well as an art.
L.M. FRANKLIN
40 Midfield Way, St Paul's Cray, Kent
[*New Statesman*, 23rd July 1960]

---

* Allen was a London-based psychiatrist, who had published *Modern Discoveries in Medical Psychology* in 1937. He wrote specifically about homosexuality (with Charles Berg) in *The Problem of Homosexuality* in 1958 and in a number of further works relating to homosexuality and sexual 'disorders'.

The Quiet Revolutionary

SIR, – The whole subject of homosexuality seems bedevilled by two considerations: the question of what is natural and unnatural, and whether it is a disease . . .

The only way in which the term unnatural can be used of sexual relations between the same sex is from a purely biological standpoint, in that bodies of the same sex are obviously not formed for sexual fulfilment in the same way as bodies of the opposite sexes. That, however, is to restrict the term natural to a purely biological sense . . .

Nor can I see any evidence which would lead one to think of homosexuality as a disease or even a neurosis in the sense which the latter word is usually used . . . is it not rather a matter of what is or is not socially acceptable? I am very dubious . . . whether homosexuality can ever be 'cured' . . . All that can be said of homosexuality is that it is probably a retarding of sexual development, which yet has little or no effect on the rest of the personality.

If we are to stop thinking of homosexuality as either unnatural or a disease, we should understand how best to help the homosexual, which is surely to encourage him to develop his personality to the full in the highest rather than the lowest way: to help him find someone whom he can love . . . and not to place any legal or social barriers in the way of his finding that love . . . As a Christian priest I would say that the fulfilment of love is never wrong, the mere satisfaction of animal lust is always wrong.

D.A. RHYMES, Vicar
All Saints, New Eltham, SE9
[*New Statesman*, 30th July 1960]

159

These are just a selection of the responses and counter-responses to Roger's letter. Many more were published. His words had sparked debate and discussion among medical professionals, social campaigners, clergymen and academics, and inspired strong feelings of support and resistance from members of the general public, including people with no particular role in the debates about decriminalisation or personal investment in the issue. As Roger had hoped, there was now a very real current running through the ensuing printed correspondence that addressed Roger, Raymond and Robert specifically when they were talking about homosexuals.

And those homosexuals had found their way into living rooms around the country, on the pages of both the tabloid and the high-brow press.

As letters and debates continued, leaders in the homosexual law reform movement started to use Roger's line of thinking, to adopt his logic about how to achieve change and to ask him to help other people make his argument too. In the early summer of 1962, John Newall, the then-Secretary of the HLRS, sent Roger a manuscript of *Queer People* by Douglas Plummer, a book which made the case for legalising homosexuality in very similar terms to Roger's letter. In the published book, Plummer portrayed homosexuality as just another way of being – a natural characteristic, like being left-handed – and laws banning homosexuality as the criminalisation of something innate.

I believe this love should now be accepted and should be freely discussed in schools and family circles and everywhere

where social problems are debated. There is nothing un-usual about it. It is part of the natural pattern of life.[5]

Just as Roger had, Plummer argued that society would benefit from understanding that gay people are everywhere and con-tributing to it. There was, he agreed, an urgent need for the identities of homosexuals to be known in order to achieve broader acceptance, and he repeatedly made the point that change would happen when people came to understand homosexuals as ordinary people, part of ordinary life, doing ordinary things.

Plummer's work shows how the arguments made by Roger were gaining traction, and not just in the political media. In fact, they were becoming central for the detailed, intellectual writing underpinning the law reform movement.

Perhaps it is part of our national character to stick our heads into the sand and ignore what is really happening in the outside world. But now more people are beginning to realise that the condition of homosexuality is right next door and often in the same house. With at least a million of us in Britain, *you* probably know at least one homosexual. It could be your own son or brother or uncle . . . So a primitive law remains, which can easily send *your* son or nephew or brother to prison for the so-called 'crime' of having been born a little different from most people. And different only in *one* respect.[6]

In his novel *Love Among the Ruins*, Evelyn Waugh looked into the future and satirically saw a time in which homosexuals could be easily recognised because they all wore green. I wish that it could happen here, now. The public would be astonished to discover, one bright Monday morning, that an unexpectedly large number of people was wearing green – the bank manager, the butcher, the bus conductor, several passengers on the morning train, business acquaintances, perhaps an employer, the barber who has cheerfully cut your hair for ten years, and the man who sells you your evening newspapers. After all, we are everywhere.[7]

Queer People extends what Roger wished to do and the point he wished to make – even though Roger thought it was very badly written. But in one significant, fundamental way, Plummer's argument falls down: he himself was unwilling to live out the practical implications of his own argument. He would not actually come out. 'I am a homosexual, a so-called "queer" or "pansy",' Plummer began his book. 'I admit it without shame, although I must hide behind a false name because of fear of the law, vindictiveness, and ignorance.'[8] 'Douglas Plummer', it turns out, was not Douglas Plummer at all. He was John Montgomery, author of many other books (of a very different kind) under his own name. It was a decade later before he revealed – to the fortnightly newspaper *Gay News* – who he truly was: 'I was then a partner with a leading literary agent, and hesitated to risk offending clients,' he explained.[9]

To understand how central Roger Butler was for the homosexual law reform movement in 1960, we should look again at that

Harley Street gathering in June and in particular to the older homosexual participant who arrived late. The so-called 'Eminent Surgeon' was treated somewhat reverently by those gathered, including Roger, though he had no idea of the man's name.

```
[He] left the meeting rather hurriedly at
the end, shaking hands all round but without
being properly introduced. He spoke softly in
a low tone, almost slurring his quick, jerky
sentences. He created an excellent impression:
after he left everyone remarked what a nice
person he seemed.
```

Roger learned a few days later from Andrew Hallidie Smith that this was Patrick Trevor-Roper, an ophthalmic surgeon, brother of the well-known historian Hugh, and one of the few homosexual witnesses who had given evidence directly to the Wolfenden Committee.

Pat had used his social connections to push his way into the room of the Wolfenden Committee, with the purpose of ensuring that the body with the power to change the lives of gay men up and down the country actually heard from at least a few of those men. He arranged a dinner with John Wolfenden during the course of the committee's work, bringing with him the novelist Angus Wilson. Wilson, notable for writing some of the first books in the 1950s with characters whose homosexuality was only incidental to their portrayal, had also countersigned Tony Dyson's 1958 letter to *The Times* that gathered sufficient support for the establishment of the HLRS.

The two men lobbied Wolfenden that he needed to gather evidence from homosexuals who would not be regarded as outsiders and rebels, who could not be dismissed as unsavoury witnesses, criminals or prostitutes. The committee, they insisted, should listen to respectable, professional people.

Like Roger, Raymond and Robert a few years later, Pat was willing – without compulsion, and at personal and professional risk – to declare who and what he was, to straight people he believed needed to hear it directly. He had told Wolfenden that he was willing to participate without the protection of anonymity but Wolfenden advised against this, worrying about the threat it would pose to Pat. As a result, Pat maintained a kind of diffident public anonymity, while providing in private another one of the most important contributions to gay rights of the 1950s.

Pat's approach was on the one hand quiet and understated – deliberately, so as not to be seen as threatening to those whom he challenged – while also being determined and consistent. His commitment to living out his identity as fully as he could extended to the way Pat chose to conduct his personal affairs. In *Against the Law*, Peter Wildeblood lauded Pat for his courage, describing him – unnamed – as 'a surgeon, respected and discreet, who threw away his good name in order to remain, night and day, at the bedside of his friend who was dying in hospital.'[10]

Pat would find – create, even – all the opportunities he could to present the idea that homosexuals were just like any other men. Roger shared his desire to emphasise the normality of gay men but felt a much greater urgency to remove the cloak of anonymity. The next step in a measured, logical case for legal

164

change – the way by which society could be compelled to sit up and listen to it – had to be for those men to become known as real human beings: for them to come out into the open. And for that, they had to be known by name.

When Pat and Roger found themselves in the same room for the *Pictorial*'s gathering, they brought with them a revolutionary firepower that changed the course of the gay rights debate. Having asked Andrew Hallidie Smith to organise the meeting, the *Pictorial*'s reporter almost certainly had no idea that he would be sitting down with the four most significant 'self-confessed homosexuals' in the nation. Roger recalled that Andrew also brought along Len Smith and Reiss Howard, 'the Islington stalwarts', but it was Roger, Raymond, Robert and Pat – homosexuals who had freely identified themselves as such – who interested the reporter and made it to print. The attention they drew in 1960 makes it especially noticeable that these four men have been overlooked in sweeping historical narratives. But they were people who never made particular efforts to claim credit for their contributions. They simply carried on, focusing on their goals and persistently working to achieve them.[*]

These were the quiet, even shy, men who introduced ordinary homosexuals to millions of Britons – and with that introduction, the idea that gay men might have a voice in their own liberation.

---

[*] Pat continued in this manner throughout his life. At the beginning of the 1980s, he helped to establish the Terrence Higgins Trust, which spoke out for the gay community during the early throes of the AIDS pandemic. Its first meeting took place in Pat's London home.

Oxford, 2005

I began to sleep at Regent Street. Not by necessity and not frequently, but from time to time after dinner, by arrangement, for ease and because it made Roger happy to have another person in the house. We talked, we read and we drank. In fact, I often drank too much during those evenings, when there was no cycle ride home ahead of me. Roger encouraged it and it allowed him to feel free to do the same. Helped by gentle intoxication, we both became more confident during those evenings, open in ways which our generally restrained natures didn't otherwise allow.

Roger said how much he enjoyed this version of me: louder and more alive with movement. However many glasses down, though, Roger was always careful to be still and physically contained. He'd learned from experience that wide gestures and quick movements were a risky business for him in any environment, even at home. But the energy of those times was fresh and bright, and conversation flowed in a happy, unstrained sort of way for as long as we let it.

At Regent Street, mine was the back bedroom on the first floor, dominated by the Edwardian tallboy that stands opposite my bed in London today. A tiny Victorian fireplace was painted white, contrasting with the chalky green walls that surrounded it – a repeating feature of the house's careful décor. Silk curtains, a memento of a trip Roger had taken to India some years before, picked up both colours in their elaborate, floral patterns.

I struggled – struggle still, always – to talk over breakfast. After a night of drinking this was especially so, and Roger knew it. He would bring me orange juice in bed to start my waking process and then announce that he would put on some eggs. But by the time I was downstairs, semi-dressed, I was expected to be ready for conversation. As an early riser, Roger had always been up for hours and was eager to chat.

Breakfast was always the same. Out would come the blue and white china – Mason's 'Manchu' patterned plates, wide cups and saucers – with Mappin and Webb silver and bone-handled cutlery. Over to the kitchen table would come a small French coffee maker, often covered nearly as much on the outside as inside by grounds of the special Cardews coffee, clinging on to the damp glass. A fresh, white loaf would be cut using a special wooden slicer, and toast would follow, popping up blackened and ready to be heavily buttered. Then poached eggs would arrive – somehow cooked perfectly every time.

One morning, before coming down for breakfast, as I walked to the bathroom at the back of the house – down three stairs, up three stairs – I spotted a black and white, framed photograph on the wall of the narrow corridor. It was labelled: 'Balliol College

Victorian Society'. In it, a crowd of young people filled the deck of a vintage riverboat, the kind only ever used for tourists and private parties. On the top deck, propped up by some friends, was a smartly dressed, young-looking Roger, surrounded by bonnets and boaters, striped blazers, lace dresses and the sorts of adornment still typical of the sillier of Oxford undergraduate parties I experienced thirty years later.

Over breakfast, sitting at Roger's kitchen table opposite his pine Welsh dresser, I asked him about the photo. Our trip to Stuart's memorial service at Wadham had revealed to me the complexity of Roger's feelings about his student days – a knotty combination of his pride in being part of something special and feelings of inadequacy when he was with the people he had met there. But now Roger spoke at length about the Victorian Society (singing and frivolity seemed to be its only purpose, an annual summer boat party its peak) and about his affection for Balliol, and the people in the photograph.

It was also that morning that Roger first told me he had written some reminiscences about his years at college. Would I, he asked, be interested in reading them with him?

After I'd dressed, Roger showed me two hard, black binders which pulled together at the centre to hold loose sheets of his typed work. Both binders were about two inches thick, crammed with extremely thin paper, every page filled with black ink from what was obviously an old-style typewriter.

He would have been well aware from the feel of them what each of the binders contained – and I could tell immediately from the number of pages that they held more than just a few reminiscences. Roger told me how useful he would find us reading the typed sheets together: if we recorded as we went, he could listen back to his memoirs without needing me there and continue to polish them far more easily.

It was a given that I'd agree to this, that I'd want to do it. So, soon after, we began to read and from that moment those folders became a consistent presence in our shared life – and in my life ever since. We did carry on reading books, articles and even occasional *LRB* issues, but now, more often than not, when I arrived at Regent Street, a black binder or two would be waiting for me, along with a very old-looking cassette recorder, placed on a small, folding table in front of Roger's red sofa. After he poured our gins, we would sit together, side by side, and Roger would press the buttons to start the machine turning the cassette inside. As we went, Roger often asked me to number the pages – a repeating task every time the memoirs were tweaked after Roger had played back the recordings.

Those two binders he'd shown me were only a fraction of what he'd written – several more were eventually brought down from his study, and Roger explained the extent of his writing. Some pieces were connected, some stood alone. All of them were about his own life (though, Roger said, there were some historical pieces and family histories he'd written that were kept elsewhere). The first, he explained, was something he'd written back in the 1960s, edited, honed and augmented since, and by the time he showed me the work, it was an ordered library in two huge volumes: *Catching Up* and *Marking Time*.

After we'd worked through the black binders, new box files appeared, containing essays, usually focused on particular people

Roger had known: people he was now keeping alive by writing and re-writing about them. Renée and Stuart Hampshire, Lionel Fielden, Richard Cobb, Heywood Hill, Beth Britten (Benjamin's sister), Lennox and Freda Berkeley, Patrick Trevor-Roper, even the Gathorne-Hardy brothers, said to have inspired the characters of *Brideshead Revisited* (Eddie having made a big first impression on Roger by speculating with mock academic detachment on the need for pornography for blind people and how this might be produced).

But to me, the most important material was about Roger himself – his difficult childhood, blighted by anxiety that surrounded his poor vision, his desperate move to London to find a life he really would feel was worth living, the romance of his travels to Tuscany as a young man, and the terrible, painful procedures that left him entirely blind.

None of the pieces had a title or any kind of indicator, but most started with a close-typed section of text, before a double-spaced, main part. The front pieces were normally about two pages in length, mostly musings and reflections relating to what followed. Their opening sentences became the means by which we oriented ourselves through the mass of sheets and I came to learn those sentences by heart.

```
When the little turbo-prop plane from Milan
touched down at Pisa, the airport then, in
1962, was little more than a field . . .

Over the years there have been moments - though
not many, it must be said - when I've wondered
```

171

```
if marriage might ever have been possible for
me  . . .
```

```
"You'll like Balliol," said Chris Patten, "it's a
very friendly college".
```

Before we'd read the works in full, these lines were little moments of intrigue for me about what was to come, but some were more than that and read like a jolt. First among these was Roger's assertion, read several times together:

```
Naturally, it's depressing sometimes - and you
can't beat self-pity - to realise that I shall
go to my grave without ever having known the
joy of a completely fulfilling relationship.
```

Here began the process in which Roger started to hand me his legacy. As we read what became thousands of pages, Roger spent time explaining and embellishing what he'd written with extra details, happy memories, gossip or tragic endings. This protracted experience of diving completely into the life Roger had led, the thoughts he had thought, the relationships he had formed, and his musings about how all of these experiences had shaped him, was a far more deeply personal way of relating than I had ever experienced with another individual.

I see now more than I did at that time that Roger wanted to show me who he really was. And in knowing Roger Butler, I came to understand him, and also to love him.

CHAPTER 7

Italy Calling

'a very interesting, cultivated man, who I think
I learned quite a lot from really although
I hardly ever met him'[1]

When the little turboprop plane touched down at Pisa, the airport then, in the spring of 1962, was nothing more than a field with iron grating laid over the grass to form a runway. The passengers from Milan, where Roger had changed planes, stepped down and walked the few yards to a terminal building that was hardly more than a hut.

As he waited at the counter for his passport to be stamped, a voice at his elbow asked, a little tentatively, 'Roger?' Glancing up, Roger recognised Lionel Fielden, although they had never met before and his appearance was not quite as Roger had expected.

The only photograph that Roger had seen of Lionel was on the dust jacket of his autobiography, showing him in semi-profile leaning against a pillared loggia: a lean, handsome, older gentleman, aristocratic-looking with grey hair neatly swept back. The 65-year-old face Roger gazed at now took him by surprise – broader and fleshier than he had imagined, with a nose slightly bulbous and veined, and a white, nicotine-stained military moustache. Lionel's general expression as he smiled at the young man struck him as slightly bleary. Probably a fairly steady intake of gin or whisky, he imagined. The former, as it turned out.

Lionel ushered Roger to an ageing Mercedes and they set off, driving at speed along increasingly narrow roads that seemed to take them through every hamlet along the way to the villa Lionel had recently moved to just outside Lucca. Lionel buoyantly filled half an hour with what felt to Roger like a well-practised tour. In London that morning, as Roger walked up the Gloucester Road to begin his journey, it had been a fresh April day with brilliant sunshine. Here, a soft warm rain was falling, and Roger was amused as they passed a man on a bicycle holding an umbrella over himself as he pedalled.

The house, when they reached it, was not the tumbledown farm Lionel had described in his letters. Rather, it was a peach-washed, elegant lodge – centuries old – with dark green painted shutters and a large barn attached to one end, and a scattering of farm buildings close by. It was perched on a steep hillside, sixty acres of untended woodland rising behind the house. A broad grass terrace ran the length of the front and a pair of cypresses, one slightly larger than the other, stood at the centre of the stone parapets, below which the ground dropped down to the level of the tiny village of Massa Macinaia.

At 27, Roger Butler had made his first trip abroad, to the other side of Europe, alone, to stay in the home of a man he had never met.

*

Roger received a number of personal replies in the wake of his coming out letter, sent on to him by the post rooms of the *Spectator* and *New Statesman*. There were general notes of praise and encouragement, applauding Roger's act. There were letters from homosexuals hiding their own identities – either celebrating Roger's bravery in arguing for an acceleration to change in the law or expressing sadness that they themselves were unable to come out. Sometimes both.

But the most interesting letter came from Italy, written on elegant die-stamped paper with the address *Poggio Luce, Ripafratta, Pisa*. The letter was sent by Lionel Fielden – a man whose particular interest, as he described it, was that he was about to take the same step as Roger.

Poggio Luce
9.6.1960

Dear Mr Butler,

May I applaud both the matter of your letter and your courage in signing it. It is so surprising that I wondered for a moment whether it could be a joke. I am not sure even now if your action is wise in regard to yourselves. The prejudice is so strong that you may lay yourselves open to harsh treatment.

I agree with you that open discussion is needed and more particularly that it is not so much our idiotic laws as prejudice that must be overcome. But it is extremely difficult. Nobody – as far as I know – has written a first-rate best-selling novel or a highly successful play on the subject, and until something of that kind appears, I doubt if public opinion will be moved.

I have written a book called The Natural Bent, which will be published in September, in the original version of which I treated the subject at some length, though the reaction of readers of the manuscript (though not, I must say, the publisher, Deutsch) was so violently against it that I felt forced to cut it radically, though leaving it to be deduced that my life had been altered and imbittered by this curse.

I am inclined to think that prejudice in England is at least partly due to exceptionally high incidence, though why that should be so I can't imagine. Possibly anti-homosexual laws encourage homosexuality by giving it a fillip of danger. In Latin countries, as far as I know, it is regarded as a sort of light-hearted by-blow of love, but never as a serious or life-long proposition, therefore it is not regarded as a menace.

It seems essential to me that articles and books which are both persuasive and popular – very difficult – should be written, and I hope that they may be by one or all of you.

Yours sincerely,

Lionel Fielden

Roger didn't recognise Lionel's name but his interest was piqued, and in 1960s Britain, there was no better way of checking someone's credentials than consulting *Who's Who*. Roger's office had a copy. Sure enough, there he was:

Fielden, Lionel, C.I.E., born 1896. Educ Eton, Brasenose College, Oxford, served Artists Rifles 1914/18, Gallipoli campaign 1915.

Then followed an odd medley of impressive-sounding appointments including 'Head of BBC Talks Dept and first Controller of All India Radio, 1935/40'.

Lionel checked out and Roger couldn't pass up his opportunity to find out more. He replied soon after and an exchange began, in which Roger and Lionel speculated particularly about how anti-homosexual sentiment could be changed. They wrote just as Kenneth Robinson, a Labour MP, had secured a debate in the House of Commons for action on the Wolfenden Report's recommendations. Unlike the previous debate in the Commons that Roger had attended, this ended in a vote, but Robinson's proposal was heavily defeated.

Poggio Luce
1st July

Dear Mr Butler,

It was extremely kind of you to answer my letter at such length: indeed it was very kind of you to answer it at all. I hardly expected it. Your letter gave me great pleasure because it arrived at a moment when I was feeling abysmally depressed by the result of the House of Commons debate. I suppose that 99 votes are better than none, but what on earth were the 230 thinking about? I have argued this business with all and sundry for about forty years and have never yet found anyone who could logically defend our archaic laws: and yet they all shrug it off with 'Disgusting, unnatural'.

I simply cannot understand <u>why</u> the English have this intolerant attitude. Does it mean that in fact there is more homosexuality in Britain than anywhere else, and that therefore the laws are 'justified', or does it (the other way round) mean that our laws do in fact encourage the furtive and blackmailing parts of homosexuality? I don't know.

Really I sometimes feel that I would like to send out 230 very pretty boys to seduce those 230 MPs and then face them with the fact. It seems to require an earthquake to shake English prejudice. And nobody as yet has been able to tell me what harm homosexuals do to anyone else – or even to society. I can't think why the English don't have a law against masturbation!

I still feel that something much more forceful is needed before public opinion will move. That is why I admired your letter. It was bold.

The fact is that people, and especially 'respectable' homo-sexuals, i.e. Coward, Gielgud, E.M. Forster and so on, won't come into the arena. E.M. Forster, as perhaps you know, has written a novel on the subject but won't have it published until after his death: a pity. One actor whom I know was so terrified by what might be in my book that he threatened me with an injunction if I mentioned his name! That's the devil of it: people are so frightened, and well they might be: their careers are threatened. I myself, fortunately, am so old that I don't care what people think, and I have enough money to get by.

Anyway, thank you very much for your letter and good luck to you.

Yours sincerely,

Lionel Fielden

Two months later, the first reviews of *The Natural Bent* started appearing. Many of them were glowing, even when noting Lionel's propensity for self-congratulation.

These enthralling journals trace the career, not check-ered but gorgeously tessellated, of a dilettante of the first order ... Set down with breathless fluency, packed with incident, action, exotic scenery, notabilities, high-life, his-tory, opinion and confession ...
[*Spectator*, 23rd September 1960][2]

Mr. Fielden writes excellently; his gift of observation is acute, his experience has been manifold; he has been closely and deeply identified with many important affairs; and there are moments when he seems to be almost as clever as he himself believes.
[*Observer*, 2nd October 1960][3]

Roger had delighted in knowing that the book was coming before almost anyone else – and largely agreed with the reviewers. 'Naturally, I bought the book, read it, found it lively and entertaining.' He was disappointed, though, by Lionel's limited discussion of homosexuality: incidental references rather than lengthy description. The *Telegraph*'s reviewer made the same observation: 'He makes no bones about describing himself as a homosexual. I am not sure if this is entirely justified by his narration.'[4]

Still, Roger was impressed, better aware than anyone that 'to go public in this manner was a bold step at the time'. And he was thrilled that an actual *Who's Who*-listed public figure had been honest about his homosexuality. Roger wrote again to Lionel.

                                                    9th Oct. 1960

Dear Mr Fielden,

   I wonder if I may offer my own insignificant, but nonetheless very sincere, congratulations on the generally friendly reception which your book has received.

   . . .

   I feel it is very important that as many people as possible come out into the open, and the more eminent the people the better. This is one of the most effective ways of bringing home the fact that homosexuality is nothing to be ashamed of. But, even more, it is the majority of homosexuals themselves who need convincing of that. So long as they continue to accept it as a stigma - for, in my experience most do - the general public will go on treating it as such. Therefore, when someone like yourself comes along and blandly acknowledges the situation as one of the facts of life in a book which is widely praised, I feel it is a very important step forward.

   Very sincerely yours,

   Roger Butler

These letters were the beginnings of a regular and frequent correspondence that continued until Lionel's death, fourteen years later. Early on they mixed polite discussion about the legal and social struggle at hand and their places in it with questions and answers allowing each of them to satisfy their curiosity about who this other man really was, how he spent his time, and how he understood the world he inhabited.

For Roger, here was a man, a world apart from his own middle-class experience, with the social connections (and the inclination to drop names) to make him a wildly intriguing correspondent. Over and again, Lionel's letters offered Roger a window into the lives of his friends who just happened to be artists, authors and painters Roger had only dreamed of meeting.

Of course I have had a few sympathetic friends, and what a very odd collection they make – Robert Harris, Godfrey Winn, Noel Coward, J.R. Ackerley, Eric Portman, and to a lesser extent now, John Gielgud.

. . . Cecil Beaton isn't as bad as you think he is. He is a nice, kind bloke, you would like him, and, at his best, he can write very well. I don't think it's altogether his fault that he has had to climb through snobbism, and he can be quite funny about himself. The trouble probably is that he is getting a bit old and garrulous. He is like me – nothing much left to do.

. . . Yes, Priestley is good – better even, I'd say, than you think him. I know him quite well and like him immensely. He was not only guts and gusto, but a stormy fury against the littlenesses of life.

Some of these men also happened to be the same 'eminent' homosexuals whose fame Roger believed could be used to promote the cause for law reform, if only they would come out publicly and unequivocally. Lionel shared Roger's disappointment. In too many cases his friends' sexual proclivities were well known, but they were unwilling to risk taking the next step:

It is maddening – E.M. Forster, Somerset Maugham, Harold Nicolson, J.R. Ackerley, Raymond Mortimer, and so on and so forth – but none of them will play.

Lionel, for his part, had at least one obvious and self-declared motivation for sustaining the conversation with Roger: he was bored. At the end of the Second World War, he had inherited a large fortune and promptly given up any idea of continuing to pursue a career (not that he'd ever really had a career). Instead, he pulled strings with the Secretary of State for War to have himself recalled from Italy, where he had been leading aspects of the Allied Forces' public relations efforts, and returned to organise his affairs in London. After calling on the *New Statesman*'s Kingsley Martin to give him journalist credentials so he could re-enter Italy (no easy task in 1945), Lionel promptly flew back, bought a Rolls Royce and went about looking for a home.

He eventually decided on Le Tavernule: a fifteenth-century villa in the hills near Florence, adorned with cloistered quadrangle, hanging gardens, private chapel and views over its grounds stretching down in all directions through the unspoilt Chianti countryside. Lionel appointed servants and spent his time restoring his new home and its gardens, entertaining a constant stream of guests and driving about in his Rolls, social-ising with the large ex-pat community resident in Tuscany.

By the time he wrote to Roger, though, this life had dimin-ished. Lionel, who made a personality trait of not understanding money, always spent more than he had. Within a few years, he had been forced to sell Le Tavernule and move to the smaller, less grand villa of Poggio Luce near the village of Ripafratta. His household was reduced and the Rolls Royce was exchanged for an old Mercedes, and by 1962, when Lionel and Roger met in person, Lionel's spending habits had continued their pattern and Poggio Luce had been exchanged for the old hunting lodge and its farm close to the ancient town of Lucca.

Further from the high society of Florence, isolated also by having driven many of his friends off, Lionel often only had his household staff for company. With the autobiography project over, there was little more to fill the hours not spent tending his garden than to write letters. Most of his correspondents were people Lionel had collected in the years before moving to Italy, including the BBC's Lord Reith. They were his age or older – largely, like him, living in decline – and steadily decreasing in number. But now, here was someone new – a generation younger, gay and at the centre of gay society in London, offering descriptions of nightlife that Lionel declared 'is to me sheer Arabian Nights. I have never known anything of that kind.'

From his hillside in Italy, Lionel became hooked on Roger's letters.

Among all the drove of letters which have come to me this week, yours has delighted me far the most. I have stuck it

into my scrapbook for future pleasure. A lonely old idiot
like me gets a tremendous kick out of this sort of pen-
flirtation with someone young and gifted, and I do hope
that you will go on writing. Your letters will shine like stars.
I have been all alone these days and not very pleased about
it. I terribly need someone to talk things over with (what
frightful grammar).

Before long, Lionel's interest in Roger's life and boredom with
his own turned gentle flirtation into explicit lust.

Now look – let me say just this, however silly it may sound.
NOTHING, NOTHING at all has pleased me so much
about this half-baked book as the letters from Roger Butler.
Ancient randiness, do you think? Not quite, but sort of
something I can't quite define, which makes me look for
your letters and air your criticisms. I am entranced by
them . . . You come along and you have everything – style,
taste, courage. I can't really express myself. It is too complicated. I look for a Lewisham postmark, just as I – fifty
years ago – looked at a love-letter, but it is now a mental
thing. A kind of mental masturbation perhaps.

Roger, in his replies, was always more reserved. He never
responded particularly to Lionel's provocations, which appeared
to increase with the amount of gin he consumed before writing.
But this did not put Lionel off – in fact, it encouraged him:

Dear Roger, I have a great affection for you, did you know?
Yes really I have . . . I should like to throw you on a bed
and turn you upside down and screw you and put your toes
in your mouth and throw you around, and I'm certain I'd
find a wonderful person, whom you cover up all the time
with your so careful writing, oh so careful you are. I wish
I could hop over to London, just to annoy you.

Theirs had quickly developed into what Roger called 'an odd
kind of friendship at a distance with me enjoying, as I've always
done, the reminiscences and accumulated experience of an older
generation, while Lionel was stimulated (in more ways than
one) by the attentions of a younger acolyte.' It wasn't long before
Lionel proposed that Roger take a holiday from work and spend
some time in Italy, at his home.

Until now, Roger had enjoyed spending his holiday time
with his parents, however snobbish Lionel might be about him
'sludging about at Banbury'. But the idea of a foreign trip was
very appealing indeed and he told Lionel as much. Lionel, in
turn, suggested that Roger first meet an old friend of his, the
novelist Lettice Cooper. Lettice had been visiting Lionel since
he first moved to Italy, and she was devoted to him, although
Lionel was often unkind about her.

She is a very plain old spinster whom I first met at the
Ministry of Food, where she was the only person with a
sense of fun. She cottoned onto me and has been to stay
with me every year since I have been in Italy. She isn't rich
or aristocratic or anything of that sort, & she writes rather

bad novels which have a library success. But she is pure gold through and through.

The meeting was presented by Lionel as a chance for Roger to find out more about Italy, but Roger understood it was an interview, serving as Lionel's own screening mechanism. He played along, attracted not only by the idea of learning more about Lionel and proving his own worth for a visit to Italy, but also by the prospect of becoming more closely associated with Lionel's circle of literary friends. He rang Lettice, who invited Roger to tea at the flat she shared with her sister.

A short walk from Finchley Road tube station, 95 Canfield Gardens was a large, tired-looking Victorian house, standing in an unkempt garden. Climbing up the stairs, Roger found that the top floor had been converted into a spacious flat, more pleasant than the exterior suggested. Lettice invited Roger to take a lopsided wing chair beside a lively coal fire, and Roger focused on sitting upright, eating his sandwiches correctly and providing engaging conversation to make sure he passed his test.

Shortly after their meeting, Lettice travelled to Italy for her own, annual visit with Lionel, and in May 1961, Lionel reported to Roger that Lettice had given him her stamp of approval: 'She gave me a very nice description of you and said among other things that you had exceptionally beautiful hands. She thinks you are very equable and not easily rattled – how different from me.' With the matter decided, Lionel went about both fixing a date for Roger's visit and making sure his descriptions of what the young man would find there were compelling.

Italy Calling

I wish I could have you here today: after two months of wretched weather, we have now had a week of sparkling sunshine and blue sky: the mountains circling the horizon are crystalline and clear: daffodils and iris stylosa already in flower, and the witch-hazel buds are opening: this winter, with the promise of spring, in Italy, is magical.

And so it was that Roger found himself, that April of 1962, climbing out of Lionel's car and surveying views over Massa Macinaia that he found breathtaking. With Lionel's live-in helper Guido away, Angela (whose main role was as Lionel's cook) led Roger inside to settle in.

At the centre of the house a double staircase
led to a pergola in front of the entrance
doors on the first-floor level. The floor was
all polished grey marble, the walls plain white
with a charming vista straight ahead through
an archway to a vestibule and beyond this,
to a walled garden on the far side of which,
directly in line with the front door, was the
baroque facade of a small grotto set into the
hillside which rose behind the garden.
    I was showed my room, plain but charming,
a white wool carpet on a red tiled floor and
attractive old Italian furniture. Looking from
the window to the right, past the cypresses,
the campanile of the village church could be
seen above the olive grove on the hillside

```
bordering the drive. There was a luxurious
bathroom, all grey tiles and dusty pink
fittings. I felt this was going to be a very
pleasant couple of weeks.
```

Roger wrote about Lionel's house and his time in it repeatedly, recalling every last detail and colouring his descriptions as if he had, for one brief moment, inhabited a fairytale. The trip was not just an unlikely adventure – it was also an invitation for Roger to experience a way of living that he had long suspected existed, but which had been closed off to him.

No small part of this was the society into which Lionel now introduced Roger. Unlike his brief encounters with wealthy socialites while selling them houses, here he was being invited into their homes as a guest – as an equal. This began immediately. After being given a light lunch, Roger was whisked off by Lionel to see Poggio Luce, whose new owner – one Professor Tealdi – happened to be there inspecting renovation work and who greeted Lionel with great amiability. The trip was brief and, as they drove away, Lionel scoffed at the new owner's taste: 'The Tealdis have a lot of ornate empire furniture quite unsuitable for such a house.' But while Roger pretended to agree with Lionel, he was elated to have been welcomed as a friend by the husband of the Princess Livia Caracciolo.

Later in their trip, Lionel drove Roger over to the home of Vernon Bartlett, a former MP and political journalist, for a small lunch party to celebrate Bartlett's sixty-eighth birthday. Roger carefully noted down his recollections of a nice, kindly man, bespectacled and cherubic, somewhat reminiscent of Mr

Pickwick; of his Belgian wife, and their tall, square, plain house, exposed on a hill facing across an empty valley to a curious row of five little hills. Once again, Lionel was derisory about the house (despite having found it for the Bartletts) while Roger – although playing along – revelled in being there.

Roger could now count himself part of a privileged group, which included a string of far more impressive visitors Lionel had hosted in Italy (Roger loved to tell the story of how J.R. Ackerley had declared Lionel stingy because he'd limited the trips he would take him on across the rough Italian country roads to spare the damage to his tyres). Lionel took Roger to Florence, to Pisa, several times into Lucca, to the gardens of the Villa Collodi, to the unusual grounds of the private Villa Marlia and to Brancoli, a favourite place of his: a small village high in the hills up a steep, winding, precipitous road, with a tiny ancient church and vast panoramic views.

On the days they stayed home, Roger became enthralled by the splendid isolation of Lionel's life. Lionel's large, elegant house, his household, his daily rituals, all charmed Roger to the point of captivation, not least because so little activity was required.

```
This house ran - as all houses should - like
a finely tuned machine. It was supremely
comfortable with a regular, highly ordered
precision. I was never aware of any housework
being done but the place was immaculate with
never a thing out of order. Each day began
at 8am when Angela or Guido would appear in
```

my room bearing a large wicker bedtable laden
with silver teapot, milk jug etc. so that I
could luxuriate in bed with early morning tea
before bathing and going down to join Lionel in
the dining room for a full English breakfast.
Lionel would then disappear for his customary
long period of soaking and reading in the
bath, followed, I suppose, by dealing with the
day's business, such as it was, while I would
sunbathe. At half past eleven each morning,
with remarkable punctuality, Lionel would say,
"I think it must be about opening time," and
he would wander across to the house, returning
usually with a glass of apricot juice strongly
laced with gin, with which we would settle into
the basket chairs in the shade of the ilex
trees.

At one o'clock we both went in for a
leisurely lunch - soup, pasta, peaches with
plenty of the light, home-made red wine and a
pot of strong black Italian coffee. After this
I went to my room for the almost obligatory
siesta. Then, back to the garden for afternoon
tea, in the still, close warmth of the sinking
sun. The next opening time was about 6.30,
then back to the house for dinner at 8. It was
amazing how much we found to talk about. For
the last hour of the day we played records in
the drawing room.

Italy Calling

Roger's holiday unfolded as if from a novel: a young man suddenly immersed in the life of the leisured upper classes, comfortable, free from interruption and obligation, held together by a compelling routine, all decorated by fine art and expensive antiques, and set against a background of picturesque Renaissance towns and countryside views. This one short trip – one brief encounter with Lionel's world – would come to dictate many of Roger's choices for his future.

Roger's life-long love affair with Lionel's home and his way of living began as soon as he arrived in Italy, but any hint of a love affair between the two men themselves was extinguished the moment they met in Pisa airport. Lionel was attracted to Roger's writing – and his youth – but not his appearance. Nothing was said at the time. Even a man as blunt as Lionel conformed to the limits of propriety. But this did not stop him from writing directly on the matter, in a letter to Roger after his departure.

Is it possible that you lack some vitamin, or have some skin infection? No woman would put up with your skin, she would do something about it, and I am sure there are things to do. And it may be connected with your eyes – I am ignorant about these things, but I know that I should fight against them if I had them. Why allow handicaps?

Your eyes and your skin bothered me, and if you sometimes caught me frowning they were the cause. I wanted somehow to get AT you, take you to the professors in Pisa or something . . . I'd leave no stone unturned to get it better.

After several letters on the subject, Roger snapped. He had felt disfigured by his sight problems for as long as he could remember, and didn't need someone else to tell him he was unattractive.

```
What a fearful description of my plight.
Couldn't you have found an expression a shade
more tactful? I suppose ugliness as well as
beauty is in the eye of the beholder, so, you
see, there are advantages to being short-sighted
after all.
```

Lionel more or less dropped the subject, but his letters, while often affectionate, lost the provocative bent they'd possessed before Roger's trip to Lucca and his runaway fantasies were never repeated. And, in truth, whatever the impression he might have given Roger before the visit, Lionel's affections were already caught up in someone else.

In 1948, Lionel had engaged Guido Falconi, then 28 and beautiful, in a role that at the time he called a 'manservant'. By the time Roger visited Massa Macinaia, Guido's status in the household was very different: somewhere between butler and partner. This was perceived as so odd by some of Lionel's older friends that they stopped visiting.

Roger didn't think much about it at the time, but Guido's position must have been difficult for him, too. Guido was simultaneously one of Lionel's helpers in the house and also – and openly – his equal. Lionel made it clear the two slept separately but (as Roger overheard one night) they were also in a physical relationship. Lionel had signed over all his estate and finances to Guido: a gesture of commitment, but one that also led to complications, not least when Guido bought an expensive sports car and took to driving off with his younger friends on extended visits to various parts of Italy.

Roger more than once told Lionel exactly what he thought of the relationship:

```
What actually baffles me is why you should have
chosen someone so wildly unsuitable as Guido.
For one so fastidious and hypercritical I would
have expected you to choose someone who shared
at least some of your tastes and idiosyncrasies,
and might be expected to perpetuate something
uniquely of you after your demise.
```

Lionel, though, delighted in telling stories about Guido's jealousy and lack of refinement:

To give you an example, John Gielgud sent one of his young men to stay with me (while he was with another at Portofino) & this young man, though pleasant and handsome, was of no interest to me, but Guido was so maddened by our English conversation and laughter that he crept up behind my chair while we were at dinner and gave me a terrific clout over the head!

But Guido was polite and accommodating to Roger when he visited, and over time Lionel tried harder to explain the value he placed on their relationship.

Guido came to me 18 years ago and was from the first enormously helpful to me in running my house and staff and farm and garden, and still takes endless trouble. I regret his bad tempers for the sake of my friends, but in a sort of a way I rather like them, they ruffle my dull life a bit! I am not unaware of Guido's failings, how could I be, but I should feel very, very naked if I had to start a new life without him. And I must say – you need'nt [sic] send me up about this – I do feel quite desperate about the future. And who cares, apart, perhaps, from Guido?

Whatever their problems, and however strange the relationship might have seemed to Roger, here were two men, clearly devoted to one another, living together and having done so for well over a decade. Theirs was a functioning same-sex relationship, not hidden from the world, not lurking in the shadows: a rare and extraordinary achievement in the 1960s, even in a country where homosexuality was not criminalised. In their own way, Lionel and Guido showed Roger that homosexual relationships could, in practice, be all that Roger and the HLRS had argued they might be in theory.

Quietly, deep in the Italian countryside, Lionel and Guido were living a version of the dream for which Roger had been fighting since 1958.

Oxford, 2006

Roger loved his garden. Small, slightly unkempt courtyard that it was, for a good portion of the year it trapped the sun. Even out of season, it allowed him his 'golden hour', when he would stand, resting his arm on the kitchen window, his face to the light, breathing the air, listening to the bells and the birds.

From time to time, when the weather permitted, Roger invited me to spend long afternoons with him at Regent Street for a 'sort-of picnic' at his garden table, sitting on the bench he covered with an old, embroidered rug. Before lunch, I would normally go out with him to supplement the food he had at home with treats – cured meats, pâtés and fresh bread from the local Italian deli, sometimes French cheeses (the runnier the better) and, if the mood took us, baklava and other sweets from one of the local shops. Occasionally, Roger would decide to cook a soup, which he prepared with some secrecy, declining to tell me the ingredients until I guessed correctly. Beetroot and pea were his favourites, both served in white, double-handled soup bowls with a gold rim, with large dollops of cream (not optional) and pepper ground on top.

Whether or not Roger had cooked, once we moved outside with a glass of cold white wine to begin our afternoon together, I was 'in charge'. It was up to me to bring out the food in the correct order, arrange it in the best possible way, serve it, pour wine, pour water, clear away, bring desserts and make coffee. And when these occasions took place later in the summer, I would make sure always to do battle with the wasps, Roger having once told me about the horrid consequences of finding one in his glass far too late. The only thing he insisted on doing himself was the washing-up. He said he could feel on the plates afterwards that he was more thorough than anybody sighted.

Roger delighted in letting me look after him. After decades of living alone, he was used to doing everything himself. Now someone else could do the worrying and the work, even just for a few hours. But, preferring things always to be done a certain way, he instructed me as we went. Cheese should never be served straight from the fridge; milk should never be served from a carton (in fact, plastic should never be seen on the table); boiling water should never be poured onto fresh coffee.

As much an event as the lunch would be the post-lunch wine, these sort-of picnics being an excuse to remain sitting languidly in the sun, sipping and reading as we went. Roger would produce bottles from the Wine Society – white to begin with, but he would usually move to his favourite red (claret), encouraging me to finish what was normally most of a bottle of Burgundy.

Just as he had with the inside of the house, Roger packed his garden with things he loved, many of which had some kind of personal significance. Once we ate something that Roger's gardener friends had made from the gooseberries on the slightly spindly bush which grew in the flower bed behind our bench. Roger had planted it to remind him of a childhood home – I forget which – where his mother had grown her own gooseberries. And in the north bed was Roger's most prized plant: lavender, which had managed to become very leggy, with clumps at various points sticking out over the paved area next to our picnic.

Roger kept the bottom of the lavender as bushy as he could. He enjoyed the scent of its purple flowers in the summer, when his legs brushed past and caught the tips of its annual crop of spikes. Lavender, Roger told me, reminded him especially of Italy, of his old friend Lionel and the well-tended, formal gardens on the side of a Tuscan hill.

I knew about Lionel from Roger's essay, which we had read together one evening at Regent Street. In some small way, I had recognised then that Roger's fascination with Lionel and the relationship between those two men might be mirrored in my own relationship to Roger. Lionel had been a friend, but also a mentor of sorts, someone who profoundly influenced Roger's way of thinking. Having now known Roger for a few years, I could see him becoming something of the same for me.

It was in his garden, as he talked about Lionel's home in Italy, that Roger first suggested we start something he'd been waiting to do for over thirty years – something he could only do with someone he trusted fully and completely.

Fourteen years of letters between him and Lionel were resting upstairs in his house, all unread since the very first time they had been pulled from their envelopes. Could we, Roger asked, in the heat of the English summer, get them out and take a look?

He led me upstairs, to the top bedroom, which overlooked the garden. This was another pretty, little room where Roger often slept, behind the much larger study facing onto Regent Street. It had the same green, chalky walls and tiny, white-painted fireplace as the room below, where I slept, but it was lower, with a slightly pitched roof. A mock-Regency bookcase (the location, I later discovered, of Roger's emergency cash, hidden in unmarked envelopes inside certain book jackets) stood behind the bed, under a handsome print of a chaotic scene – 'Learning to drive a Dennett'. Opposite was a mahogany wardrobe, dominating the room and making it feel smaller than it was, next to a single dining chair and two metal boxes, one on top of the other.

Roger sat down, reached over to the boxes and raised the lid of the top one. It was stuffed full with neatly stacked, though irregularly sized, sheets of paper of various colours. Roger felt inside and picked up a couple of sheets. 'I'm fairly sure these ones are mine,' he said, 'so the other box must be Lionel's. Have a look.'

The top sheet was a large, cream piece of paper with neat, typed lettering set inside broad margins. I started to read:

```
129 High Street, Lewisham, SE13. 26th June 1960.
   Dear Mr Fielden, On behalf of my
colleagues . . .
```

'Ah yes, that's me. Well then, love, what do you think?' he asked as he closed the lid, slid the box onto the floor and opened

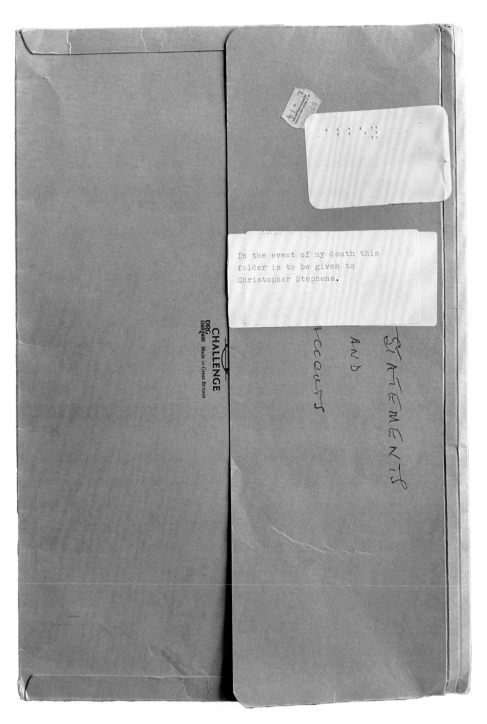

In the event of my death this
folder is to be given to
Christopher Stephens.

STATEMENTS
AND
ACCOUNTS

Roger's pink folder.

Roger as a young child.

With his mother. Oxford, 1944.

A rare childhood photograph of Roger wearing glasses,
accompanied by his grandmother and father. Malvern, 1947.

Some members of the *Sunday Pictorial* gathering.
Roger appears to be sitting with his back to the camera,
in the chair with a floral design. Harley Street, 1960.

One of the most successful photographs I ever took shows Lionel starkly outlined in profile looking immensely patrician, seated at a garden table with the tea tray on it.

Lionel's view over Massa Macinaia. Photographed by Roger, 1962.

Ipsden, Oxfordshire, 1974.

With Gay.
Blenheim Palace, 1975.

MA graduation.
Balliol College,
1977.

Goudhurst, Tunbridge Wells, 1977.

Renée Hampshire
with Cresco and
Gay. Wadham
College, 1978.

With Cresco.
Regent Street, 1980.

Visiting the Norfolk coast with Christopher, 2010.

the one it had been resting on, revealing another huge bundle of papers. 'Think you could face reading all this?'

'Of course,' I said without hesitation, 'I'd love to.' I didn't think much about it and, as we climbed down the stairs and walked back into the garden, I could hardly have imagined what Roger's question really meant for both of us.

Unlike Roger's various memoirs, all written and rewritten, thought about at great length and filled with retrospective consideration, those letters exposed Roger, on page after page, in unpolished, unrevised, uncensored form. They documented fourteen years of him as a young man, pouring out his thoughts and feelings, his hopes and ambitions, his loves and losses, describing his every action in private writing never intended for anyone other than Lionel. Asking me to read them was an invitation to know Roger more closely than he had allowed anyone to know him since those letters were written.

In that moment the significance of this didn't occur to me. That would come later. And yet, as we went back to the table and refilled ('refuelled', Roger always said) our glasses, a change had certainly taken place. 'Perhaps one day,' Roger mused, 'we might visit Italy together.'

CHAPTER 8

A Looming Shadow

*'I either was, or felt myself to be,
something of an outsider'*[1]

When Roger was about nine years old, towards the end of the Second World War, his mother took a crude black and white snapshot of him playing in the Oxfordshire countryside. She sent the picture to Roger's father, who was with the Royal Air Force in India, but it was lost sometime after Eric Butler brought it home with him. That photograph might have easily been forgotten, but it held so much meaning for Roger that he could recall the moment perfectly for the rest of his life.

We took a trip down river from Oxford, where we were then living, on one of Salter's steamers, disembarking at some point for a riverside picnic. As the wartime ration sandwiches and the thermos flasks were being unpacked, I occupied myself by balancing on a nearby stile. Noticing this, my mother stopped her preparations, took out of the basket the little Brownie Box camera in its canvas carrying case which she had been

given as a girl and made me repeat my balancing
act.

There I stand, perched boldly on the top
bar of the stile, feet apart, arms folded,
grinning broadly, eyes half closed against the
bright sunlight - a scruffy, tousled, rather
engaging little urchin, indistinguishable from a
million others. But, in its primitive way, this
photograph was every bit as stylised - just as
fraudulent - as any child portrait by Reynolds
or Raeburn or Watts. In its own way, too, it
was an idealisation. I remember it so clearly
because it presented the image of the small
boy I so much wanted to be. Perhaps even more
significantly, as I now realise, it depicted
the kind of robust, extrovert, games playing,
Just William kind of young son my parents would
rather have liked me to be.

The urchin on the stile was far from what the camera portrayed. This innocent little photograph was, as Roger described
it, 'a masterpiece of deception' – one born of Doris Butler's
discomfort and anxiety about her son's disability.

There's a very small clue to this enigma in
the photograph itself, but only a pretty astute
ophthalmologist might spot it. If you compare
the snapshot with two or three others from

```
around the same time, he might be struck by
the fact that in each case I am looking at the
camera through half closed, rather hooded eyes.
'What beautiful large dark eyes he has,' ladies
used to remark to my mother, little realising
what a curse this feature betokened.
```

When Lionel began nagging Roger about seeking out some medical assistance for his eyes after his trip to Massa Macinaia in 1962, he significantly underestimated how much time and energy had already been directed towards Roger's sight.

Doris Butler first noticed a problem with her son's vision when he was two years old. Roger always looked away from bright light, she said, and on sunny days he would turn his head towards the ground. She took him to London, where she received Roger's glaucoma diagnosis, along with a warning that this was an uncommon condition in children of his age and carried worrying implications for his future.

Within six months of his diagnosis, Roger was taken to the Western Ophthalmic Hospital, on the Marylebone Road in West London, to undergo an operation to relieve abnormally high internal pressure in his eyes. It was hardly a gentle or child-centred process. Roger was 'abandoned in the adult ward', waking after the procedure with his eyes firmly covered by bandages and his hands tied to the bed to prevent him from tearing them off.

The operation was considered a success, but did nothing to improve his vision. Roger emerged into consciousness with sight so limited as to be virtually useless without strong spectacles.

He could see the details and texture of objects only within a few inches of his eyes:

> More than a few feet distant everything simply dissolved into vague shapes, varying roughly in colour and mass but all merging one into another and not standing out clearly from their background. Even the largest forms were barely identifiable and then only with a kind of intelligent guesswork.

As their son grew up, Doris and Eric were frightened for Roger, but also slightly embarrassed. And so was he.

> No photographs from those early days show me wearing glasses because I was always made to take them off before the shutter clicked. No explanation was ever given for why this should be necessary but, somehow, I understood well enough. I certainly had no objection since I hated the ugly things anyway. They were unsightly and disfiguring, like a blemish, and perhaps deep down and unrealised my parents felt them to be almost a reproach which they preferred not to have permanently recorded. I hated them for more practical reasons. They made me feel self-conscious. They marked me out as being different.

A Looming Shadow

Having parents unwilling to grapple with the severity of his predicament meant that Roger sometimes deluded even himself, attempting to keep up with his schoolfriends as if there were no limitations on his abilities. There were, and even with glasses his left eye was significantly weaker than his right – and that was not strong.

```
The result was that there were so many things
that other people were able to manage much more
easily, and this made me feel inept . . . And
yet surely spectacles were supposed to make
everything all right?
```

Looking back at this time, Roger wondered if total blindness might actually have been easier for everyone to manage, including himself. The situation would have been more noticeable and his needs more easily defined. Instead, the young Roger faced day-to-day difficulties that were largely ignored but which added up to cause a lifelong psychological impact.

One of the effects was on Roger's ambitions. These were dulled by his parents' uncertainty about what he could or should do, as well as the wildly conflicting advice they were being given. There were trips to Harley Street that they could ill-afford, Roger remembered, in which he was pinched and pummelled by someone he decided in hindsight was a 'complete quack'. That doctor's (rapidly dismissed) recommendation was that Roger take up farming.

```
On the one hand, my parents wanted me to do
well enough at school, so to speak – though
```

well enough for what was never clear. On the
other hand, there was a constant nervousness
lest too much 'close work', as it was called,
might strain my eyes harmfully. Consequently,
at one moment there would be mild injunctions
to do better at school, the next moment
admonitions against doing too much reading
instead of being out and about indulging in
healthy outdoor activities.

Roger believed this was why he left school with just a few
mediocre O levels. Rather than nurturing any academic interests, he had spent the majority of his time developing skills in
making himself inconspicuous: 'It became my greatest wish to
attract as little attention as possible.' In terms of that particular
ambition, he achieved his goal. He did just enough work to avoid
being singled out for disgrace and nowhere near enough to be
scorned by other children.

But while academic indifference kept him in the realms of
the average in the classroom, Roger never managed to become
an accepted member of what he regarded as 'the tribe of boys'.
His sexually charged experiences with George and Jack were
one thing, but being in the group was something else entirely.
The limitations of Roger's sight made all the difference, he was
convinced: 'It was these, so it seemed, which shut me out of
everything that really mattered.' He was excluded from sports
teams, subject to awkward and embarrassing incidents on a
regular basis, ill at ease with other children. And so, while 'different' was the last thing he wanted to be at that time of life,

Roger couldn't help but give the appearance of being timid and standoffish: 'In a way I was,' he acknowledged, 'unintentionally and longing not to be.'

By the time Roger's classmates were discussing what they would do after school, he had already concluded there was little point in him planning a career. 'Of course, I don't suppose I shall have any sight left by the time I'm 30,' he casually remarked to a group of boys as they walked across the playing fields one afternoon. He recalled that this was the first time he had really understood this to be true.

```
No one had ever told me my sight was not likely
to last my lifetime, let alone fixed such an
arbitrary time limit, but it had hardly needed
much percipience to realise from an early age
that this most vital faculty upon which so much
depended was insecure. The constant injunction
not to take risks, not to strain my eyes, had
run like a chorus through my childhood.
```

Roger had little idea what he might do with his unimpressive education and didn't consider a trade, a career or a vocation, nor did he develop specific hopes for a future life. Instead, he resolved that it would be better to get on with the business of earning a living – any kind of living – and to make his escape to London.

```
I felt I must experience all this while the
going was good, while I still had the chance.
```

*

207

In the same momentous year of Roger's coming out letter, 1960, he also experienced the first major change to his vision, during a lunchtime walk.

Walking on a bright, if not sunny, afternoon in Harewood Place, all of a sudden, in an instant, I became aware of a deterioration of vision: in my right eye, the one I depended on almost entirely. There was no pain or physical sensation of that kind. I was glancing at the number plate of a car only a few feet away when quite suddenly the letters and numerals became blurred . . .

Everything – buildings around Hanover Square, the detail of the trees against the sky – had all become a little less distinct even than I was used to. It seemed also as if the very light itself had grown a shade dimmer.

He quickly took himself to Moorfields, the eye hospital in Finsbury where he went for routine monitoring. He left with only some drops, some ineffectual tablets (that had dismal side effects) and a sense that his doctors misunderstood the seriousness of his situation.

This new problem with Roger's sight started around the same time as he began writing to Lionel on a regular basis. In the winter of 1960, while the two men were beginning to get to know one another, Roger mentioned his growing difficulties.

The disadvantages of this to me, with the interests I have, are enormous and also it provides
me with my biggest complex which I just cannot
overcome. It prevents me entirely from reading
books or newspapers on trains and since so
much of my time is spent in travelling this is
really maddening. I enjoy reading very much and
would have liked an academic career, but this
has always been out of the question.

Reading wasn't the only passion of Roger's which his vision limited, and any further decline seemed to threaten his other loves, for photography, art and architecture. Lionel insisted that Roger take action – because there *had* to be action he could take. He made countless appeals during the next few years, his guidance and concern peppered with his signature name-dropping.

Surely you can do something about it, can't you? Aldous Huxley was a friend of mine for some time and he had the worst sight of anyone I have ever known: in fact, we all thought he would go blind at about the age of 30, when he could only read a book by holding it about one inch from his eyes. But then as you probably know, he took up with a man who gave him exercises and did wonders for himself and I must say when he taught me the exercises I was greatly impressed and I quite frequently do them myself if my eyes are tired . . . I'm going on like a Nannie. But at 25 you shouldn't have bad eyesight and surely you can do something about it.

For a while, Roger brushed off Lionel's pestering, but eventually concluded that the only way to shut him up was to tell him that he knew perfectly well what was wrong with his eyes, and to explain that while his operation in 1937 had preserved his sight for the subsequent twenty-five years, this couldn't last for ever.

```
It's what they call 'a congenital abnormality'
(sounds horrible). My eyes are unusually large
(as you noticed) and have a defective drainage
system. This means that a fluid which is
continually forming in the eye cannot drain
away properly and, consequently, a pressure
builds up which impairs the vision and, unless
it can be kept under control, causes pain . . .
Now, for several years past, I've been
given drops to put in daily but these have
a rather negative benefit in that, while they
may help to keep the drains unblocked, they
also contract the pupils so that vision is
diminished.
```

Lionel wasn't willing to admit defeat, offering a slew of additional suggestions that Roger ignored. Only one piqued his interest: had Roger considered going to see Patrick Trevor-Roper in Harley Street? 'People tell me he's a miracle man,' Lionel wrote in September of 1962, offering to pay the fee. 'Forgive me. I myself get such a lot of pleasure out of seeing things that I can't bear anyone else not to have it. I feel that you want some sort of PERSONAL interest, not just an institution like Moorfields.'

Recognising Trevor-Roper's name, Roger allowed himself to be taken up in Lionel's enthusiasm. 'It's absolutely amazing!' he explained, urgently writing back to Lionel that he had met Patrick twice already through the HLRS.

```
This strange concatenation of circumstances
seems almost to have been designed for a
particular purpose. I have a rather vague
belief in a kind of predestination: every
so often I find myself confronted with the
situation - seemingly without any sort of
engineering on my part - which I feel impelled
to act upon: impelled almost, as it were, by
some outside force. And in such cases the
result always seems to work out for my good.
All that sounds rather odd I know, it's
something difficult to explain coherently,
but I feel this is just such a situation and
'something' tells me I must act upon it.
```

Roger's belief that all this was somehow meant to be was further validated when he called Trevor-Roper's surgery and learned he was on holiday in Italy – only to read from Lionel in his next letter that Pat had just turned up on his driveway in Massa Macinaia, the visitor of a neighbouring homosexual couple, art historians Hugh Honour and John Fleming. Lionel had been charmed by Pat, who offered to see Roger without any fee and blew a kiss from his sports car as he left.

But having a well-placed and personal connection was not enough to overcome the facts of Roger's condition, as he found when he met with Pat shortly after his return from Italy.

22 Gledhow Gardens, SW5

Tuesday, 2nd October 1962

My dear Lionel,

Well, my dear, kind friend, there isn't a lot to tell you. I saw Trevor-Roper this morning - felt very easy and comfortable with him - and after the usual examination which I'm so familiar with his verdict boiled down to: 'Your condition won't get any better, but neither should it get any worse; the drops and tablets you are using are quite harmless and should continue to keep the situation under control; at present your situation is as satisfactory as you can expect it to be'. So there! Nothing startling: no prospects of magic cures, but at least very reassuring - and comforting, too, to know that apparently Moorfields are doing all they can be reasonably expected of them. (T-R, I learned, runs a clinic at the Holborn branch of Moorfields.)

. . .

I feel much more contented in my mind after T-R's reassurance because before things seemed

```
to be going downhill. How amazing, what an
influence you can exert from your remote eyrie!
Thank you a million times.
    Fondest regards,
    Roger
```

At this, Lionel backed down, but he did so unhappily: 'Everybody seems to think that T-R is the best oculist in London, so I suppose you can't do better . . . how I hate all medicine-men. I think they know damn little.'

Assured at least that his vision would get no worse, Roger decided he would go back to living his life. He wanted to learn Italian. He also wanted to meet more men with whom he could have a meaningful connection. With Mario, he appeared to be able to do both.

Roger began by taking Italian classes with a Mrs Momigliano, who lived in a dreary flat in Earl's Court, crammed with shelves of books covered with plastic dust sheets and sparsely lit by just two 40-watt bulbs. Lessons proved hard. Studying in the evenings, after long days of work, with his eyes struggling to read the words in front of him, Roger made very slow progress. So, in the spring of 1963, he fixed on a new idea, better suited to his situation: he would host an Italian in need of accommodation in London, in exchange for some conversational coaching.

He wrote to Ian Greenlees, director of the British Institute of Florence, to ask for introductions to suitable candidates. Greenlees initially proposed a 35-year-old university lecturer, but Roger hastily replied, expressing concerns about whether Dr

Corti would fit in with his lifestyle. Whether Roger knew it or not, Greenlees was also homosexual and seemed to understand the implications of what Roger was really asking. In May, he sent three further recommendations, with the advice that Mario – a Florentine student – 'might be the one that you would prefer'.

Roger contrived to deploy the trick Lionel had used before settling a date for his own trip to Italy. Mario was to be invited for lunch at Massa Macinaia, ostensibly for a conversation about Roger and London, and to discuss the technicalities of arriving into England. In reality, this would be his interview, and Roger's opportunity to get Lionel's opinion of Mario. The minute the young Italian left, Lionel wrote his review – making sure to include the details he knew would be of most interest.

> On the whole both I and Lettice thought he would do you pretty well and fit easily into your life. He is affable and not at all shy. He seemed rather surprised that you did the cooking; I think he visualised a servant.
>
> He is about your height, reddish blonde with light-lashed very blue eyes and a ruddy complexion; he does not look (to me anyway) like Love's Young Dream, but he is quite passable and well brushed and turned out and all that . . . Not 'gay' at all, I think: he said he wanted to find an English girl to marry. You might possibly find him a handful – I mean, he might want to bring in girls and whatnot.

Roger decided to take his chances and in September 1963, his new lodger arrived, rather more heavily laden than Roger had expected. Mario (whose non-Italian looks, it turned out, were accountable to his being half Austrian) turned up with several large suitcases: 'four suits, an overcoat, divers jackets, trousers, shirts, pairs of shoes, a typewriter, books, and even his own soap, towels and soap powder for washing his shirts!' 'I like him,' Roger reported back to Lionel. 'I met him at Victoria on Thursday evening, we've been together ever since, and we've got on famously.' Mario was polite, with a good sense of humour, and was willing to muck in with the housework, even if he did regularly mention that he was the younger son of the younger son of a marchese.

Roger took a week of leave from work to show Mario around London and settle him in, after which he wrote enthusiastically: 'Mario is sweet: we couldn't possibly get on better. I think Ian Greenlees must have known what he was at when he recommended him.' This was as much as Roger would admit to Lionel on the subject, but in truth it wasn't long before, with 'a hint of sex in the air' one evening, Mario simply arrived at Roger's bedside naked and jumped in.

The two began a physical relationship which lasted for several months. During that time, Roger spoke affectionately about Mario in his letters to Lionel, telling him about the parties they attended together (including one of Lettice's, where Mario spent the evening charming the author Hester Chapman), their trip to The Colony and how Mario had helped Roger host a New Year's Eve party. Roger just couldn't bring himself to mention the sex. Perhaps his reluctance came down to a feeling that this was always going to be a short-lived affair:

In my heart, I always knew we weren't really
lovers although we went through the motions and
I liked to delude myself that we were, because
this was what I had always longed for. I think
much the same went for Mario.

By the following spring, Mario was already directing his affections elsewhere. Roger had introduced him to London's gay scene and he developed a taste for it. First, he started leaving Roger at home and arriving back late into the night. Then, increasingly, he didn't return until the next day. Nothing was said but the sex dried up and tensions grew. When Mario gave Roger a large picture book for his 29th birthday, Roger noticed immediately that the inscription inside read 'con tanto affetto', not 'con tanto amore'. This said it all, so far as he was concerned, and the two agreed it would be best for Mario to look for somewhere else to live.*

Determined not to wallow in this unhappy situation, Roger took up the offer to visit Israel with his friend Howard, who had rented an apartment in Tel Aviv ('bring your own sheets,' the invitation suggested). It was something of a daring move for Roger, further from England than he had ever travelled before. 'I have taken out insurance to cover as much as possible, and this at least ensures that my corpse is returned to England if

---

* Mario finally left London in November 1964, apparently after considering, but ultimately rejecting, an offer to become a gigolo for a rich English man living in Monte Carlo. Roger and Mario corresponded for a decade after this, but Mario returned to see Roger only once more, in 1970, when they slept together one last time.

the worst comes to the worst,' Roger wrote merrily to Lionel before departing. 'I am a little concerned, however, to see that it doesn't cover me in the event of insanity, venereal disease or childbirth.'

He reported hurriedly from Tel Aviv recounting his adventures: hitch-hiking to Caesarea, Haifa and Acre; sleeping overnight in a German convent on top of Mount Carmel; eating with workers on a Kibbutz; having Sabbath dinner in Beit Brodetsky, a hostel for new immigrants on the outskirts of Tel Aviv; and making new friends who threw him a party at Ra'anana, a small town close by.

Roger had very definitely left his problems at home, and his regrets about Mario specifically dropped away when he met a beautiful young student in a Jerusalem bus queue and fell instantly for him. Danny and Roger sat together as their bus rode through the Judaean hills, discussing history, music, architecture and politics. When they reached Tel Aviv, Danny invited Roger to his parents' home the next day, and they put on a large lunch in the garden, under the shade of their citrus trees. After lunch, Roger and Danny caught a bus to the beach, where they spent the afternoon almost completely alone, watching the Mediterranean and talking endlessly.

The two met again the following week, in one of Tel Aviv's pavement cafés, and once more when Danny amazed Roger by turning up at the beach at Eilat to see him, unannounced, on Roger's last day in Israel.

```
It was the most marvellous surprise. Together
we went out in a speedboat, racing down the
```

Gulf of Aqaba to the Egyptian border: the water
was the darkest, darkest blue, almost black,
with the vivid white foam which we churned up
spraying around us. On one side were the hazy
pink hills of Jordan, on the other the coral
reefs and the rock hills and sand of Egypt.
Overhead the sun blazing down. It was an
idyllic ending.

Oxford, 2006

Roger and I didn't ever make it to Italy.

We did take holidays together, though, all in the UK. These started off with trips of one or two nights, staying in hotels which caught Roger's interest near places he had wanted to visit. The choices of location were his, but Roger continued to enjoy a narrative that I was in charge, that I was looking after him. I suppose that once we set off, I was – in practice, more so than at Roger's house. I was to drive, to navigate, to find restaurants, to source tickets, to keep us on time and – always – to find the best Marks & Spencer on our route home so I could leave Roger with a full fridge.

Roger's passion was for country houses – stately homes, the grander the better – and the stories absorbed into them. He took me to see as many as could reasonably be squeezed into any trip. Some he knew already; some he had always wanted to visit. The classical regularity of vast palaces like Houghton Hall and Ickworth House attracted him most, but Roger was just as happy exploring the creaking staircases and romantic ruins of

ancient relics like Newstead Abbey. Roger's only disappoint-
ments were houses he said had been 'mucked around with' by
later generations. Polesden Lacey and Upton House irritated
him no end.

People sometimes asked why we bothered to tour those
places. I could stare in wonder at the intricacy of the ceiling in
the long gallery at Chastleton House or stand awestruck by the
sheer scale of Hatfield, but what did Roger get out of it? Before
losing his sight, Roger had been a fine photographer: Lionel had
declared his pictures of the villa at Massa Macinaia the best he
had seen. Roger certainly grieved his loss, feeling cheated that
he would never again have that sublime feeling of looking at
something beautiful. But, just as I'd learned from him the value
of judging a restaurant on its quiet and the quality of food rather
than the look of a space or the arrangement on a plate, he helped
me understand how to view these houses differently, to feel the
magnificence and history of a place in all the ways he did.

As we toured each house, Roger asked me to describe the
architecture and the decoration, and to point out the most interesting features of a room and pieces dotted around it. I had to
learn the language required for this – to understand the name,
the importance of this arch or that cornice. I was often corrected
by Roger, who could anticipate a space more quickly than I
could read a guidebook. And through him, I grasped how much
more there was to experiencing a house than knowing how each
room looked: the feel of thick carpets or of polished floorboards
underfoot, the sound of voices either hushed by low ceilings and
heavy curtains or swelled and repeated in high vaulted stone
hallways. Sometimes, the physical demands of squeezing into a

narrow, uneven spiral staircase would take on particular significance; sometimes it was the smell of ancient wood panelling, dusty damask or the embers from a still-functional fireplace.

Discovering these places was blissful, but never without the one peril that could ruin it all. From the first of our visits, the eager volunteer became our nemesis. An older man being guided carefully through rooms by a young person (who probably appeared ill-equipped as a guide) was a slow-moving target. Most visitors could avoid the pre-prepared talk about each room and the objects the volunteer most wanted to explain. We weren't so lucky. With a white stick added into the mix, we rarely travelled more than a few metres along our route without being accosted and told what we should notice, however much I tried to master the polite brush-off.

Even more excruciating for Roger was the encouragement that he should go with one of them past the ropes keeping the sighted population at bay and touch particular bits of furniture better to know their appearance. At times, this took the form of direction, so convinced were these helpers that any blind person must surely want to be led away and given special access in front of a jealous group of onlookers. Once, in Stratfield Saye House, Wellington's old home, Roger – conditioned by a lifetime of not wanting to be different or to stand out from a crowd – snapped hard at a volunteer who started pulling him from my arm towards another ornate sideboard. It was just too much for politeness to be sustained.

In our travels, I learned more about architecture and garden design, about the history and politics wrapped up in England's great houses and their families. But those longer trips together, in which every step we took depended in some way on me, also slowly shifted the dynamic of what we were and what I was to Roger. More and more, I was invited to, and expected at, Regent Street for extended stays. More and more, that travelling narrative – me being 'in charge' – came to infect also our time together at home. I sometimes found myself silently wondering how much more of this reliance I could manage.

It sounds selfish now, horribly so, and I felt selfish for thinking it. I understood that my help made all the difference for Roger. It had been a very long time since he had enjoyed so much freedom from worry, liberated from his daily challenges by the presence of another who could worry about them for him. But these lovely, interesting, educational experiences were also hard work. And so, too, were my visits to Regent Street, increasingly focused on Roger's domestic needs.

So, as Roger pushed for more, I became conflicted. I treasured those times, of course. Yet the need always to be available, always to offer help, always to provide a hand or arm, always to read a map, to take Roger to bathrooms, to manage any problem, any incident, any situation which didn't go to plan – living with and for someone else – was becoming too much. I was young. As Roger's confidence in his ability to rely on me grew, so the weight of that reliance began to dominate those times for me.

But what other option? I wanted to be there for him, to give him what I could, to be for him what I could.

CHAPTER 9

A Stolen Future

'I was always brought up almost, as it were, in apprehension of it, as far back as I can remember'[1]

When Roger got home from Israel in the late spring of 1964, he was met by a sharp reminder of the reality of his life – and not just the sadness of being without 'my beloved Danny', as he had begun to describe him. In the period that followed, he began to suffer increasingly acute problems with his eyes. More and more, Roger's letters to Lionel described emergency visits to Moorfields, terrifying procedures, prodding and poking, and regular measurements of eye pressure, with worrying results.

Scarcely had I finished my last letter to
you when I was stricken down with the most
devastating pain. So much so that at 1 o'clock
that morning, Barry, bless him, rushed me to
Moorfields where the porter managed to find
a nurse who ferreted out the night sister
who went and dug a doctor out of bed. This
gentleman pumped a paralysing shot of something
into my backside, filled me up with tablets and

drops, and sent me home again. None of it made
the slightest difference so that I went through
24 hours of unrivalled agony, lying alone and
physically exhausted trying to fight this pain.

The reassurance Pat Trevor-Roper offered Roger in October of 1962 had given way to an oppressive and growing anxiety, and by 1965, the doctors agreed that this persistent trouble needed some decisive action.

Roger's left eye was the real problem, so it was proposed that he have 'a little bit of surgery to take the pressure down'. His reaction was one of relief rather than apprehension, desperate to break what had begun to feel like an unending, vicious cycle:

At last something positive was to be done . . .
Anything could be tolerated if it would serve
to resolve, to settle the prolonged uncertainty.

Once the decision had been made to operate, the surgery was swiftly arranged. On 7th April, Roger made his way to Moorfields for what had been billed as a minor affair, under a local anaesthetic, which involved a small incision and a few stitches. The surgeon – a Mr Greaves, whom Pat told Roger was 'a very good man' – talked him through each aspect of the operation as he went and answered Roger's questions as the surgery progressed. The procedure itself was uneventful and Roger went to sleep that night, assured that everything seemed to have gone as planned, with his left eye covered by a pad and some surgical tape.

*

Roger woke to find his ward at Moorfields already alive with morning activity. With his uncovered eye he could just about make out a surgeon beginning his first rounds, accompanied by junior doctors – a cluster of white coats making its way, patient by patient, moving nearer to his own bedside. Roger arranged himself as best he could, moving into a seated position, propped up by pillows, and waited patiently. At last, they reached his bed.

```
The sellotape was peeled off and the pad
removed. Gingerly, I allowed the eyelid to
lift slowly, wondering if it might be sore,
and stared straight ahead to where I knew the
light of the doctor's torch must be. There
was nothing. Not the faintest glimmer. Just
utter blackness. Nothing to indicate I had
even opened the eye. 'Can you see anything?'
he asked. 'No,' I replied simply. 'Not even the
light?' he prompted. 'No.'
   And that was it. Nothing more was said. The
pad was stuck back on and the Kafka-esque little
group of silent onlookers shuffled on to the next
bed.
```

Roger's surgeon visited again later and explained something about a vitreous haemorrhage in the eye, which should drain and allow the sight to return. 'How long might this take?' Roger asked. Greaves was vague, 'Perhaps a few weeks, perhaps a few months.' Roger could tell that something had gone seriously wrong but accepted these platitudes, supposing that some sort of sight would return eventually. Even if the quality of his vision was further reduced, he was confident he could manage now the operation had resolved his pain.

A few days later, still in hospital, when another surgeon visited, Roger thought he would ask for a second opinion on how long it would take for the haemorrhage to clear. The reply came without hesitation: 'Oh, that will never clear – the sight's gone forever in that eye.'

```
This was said curtly, even with a touch of
impatience, as if contemptuous that anyone could
assume such a palpable nonsense. It seemed
that daily acquaintance with other people's
misfortunes had not done much to develop his
sensitivity. I was too taken aback to challenge
him with the source of my delusion. I think,
anyway, that I realised instinctively that he
must be right.
```

When Roger shared his life-altering news with Lionel – in a letter he dated Good Friday, 1965 – he was initially dry in his conclusion.

```
The operation, per se, was successful in that
it has relieved me from the pain I was having,
but I have lost the sight of the eye entirely.
```

But he quickly confided in Lionel that he was now scared about his right eye, which, after all, was affected by the same condition.

226

What concerns me most is how long this one will
stand up to the extra strain. Most people, if
they lose one eye, can get by quite comfortably
on the other, but in my case, this is weak
anyway so I must go incredibly carefully with
it. I can get about quite easily in familiar
surroundings, at least in the daytime, but not
at night, and crossing roads at any time is
near suicidal!

Lionel replied, disgusted at how the doctors had treated
Roger and expressing disbelief at Roger's apparent acceptance
of his fate and the crude manner of its being revealed. In fact,
Roger's reactions ricocheted. He tried to reason that he had
always been resigned to the likelihood he would lose the sight
in his left eye, and had simply never known when or how. Now,
here it was, and with that uncertainty finally resolved came a
kind of mental numbness.

Then, two days later, out with friends, everything hit him at
a pub off Piccadilly:

Suddenly, out of nothing, in the middle of
completely inconsequential chatter, a terrible
emotion welled up inside me. All in a moment I
was overwhelmed by the full realisation of what
had happened and, perhaps even more, by what it
might portend. It was a frightening experience:
I felt myself hurtling out of control. I was

```
unable to speak a word, knowing that if I
did I would break down then and there, right
in the middle of a crowded pub on a Saturday
night . . . To the bewilderment of the others I
just turned and fled without a word.
   The fact that losing this failing remnant
of sight in even one eye, which ought hardly
to have come as a surprise after all that
had gone before, could trigger off such a
histrionic reaction serves to show what a world
of difference there is between hypothetical
anticipation and the reality of the thing.
```

Decades later, Roger was still reeling. Like Lionel before him, he could only ask through bitter resignation how he could have been treated in the manner he was:

```
   Why had my surgeon misled me, given me false
   hope, not prepared me beforehand for such a
   possibility?
```

Roger's method for coping with the disorientation of his new situation was to exercise detachment in as complete a way as possible, suppressing his fears and clinging to those things which for him represented normal life. By the start of May 1965, as Roger turned 30, he returned to work and was pouring all his energies into a new project: finding a house to buy. Since his trip to Massa Macinaia, Roger had dreamed more and more about owning a home of his own, one that he loved and could fill with objects he had chosen. With his future feeling increasingly uncertain, he thought that a house would also give him greater security.

A bequest from Roger's great aunt Ethel, who had died just before he left for Israel, meant this was no longer a fantasy. Ethel was the only member of his family who Roger felt had similar tastes to his: she enjoyed classical music, visited galleries, collected art books and painted competently, with evenings spent learning languages and attending woodwork classes. Roger was convinced that Ethel was a lesbian, though they never discussed it. Her unsuccessful marriage in the mid-1920s to a furrier, of which none of the family later spoke, only affirmed his view. With her estate now liquidated, Roger was in receipt of £5,000.

In 1965, that sum was enough to buy a town house in central London, and with a little more, he could afford something bigger that would allow him to sublet a room or two. This, Roger thought, would allow him to generate additional income if he found himself unable to work. He began petitioning banks for a loan and, by July, he had found the perfect place, in a typical Fulham terrace – somewhere just waiting to be restored. He wrote to Lionel of

```
. . . large, high rooms, on the ground floor
opening by folding doors from back to
front with glass doors to a pleasant tree
shaded garden. This would give me beautiful
accommodation for myself and leave enough other
rooms to produce a comfortable £600 per annum.
```

By October, when Danny visited from Israel, Roger could proudly show him 3 Hestercombe Avenue – the house which was now his home.

Danny made four trips to England in 1965, in the wake of Roger's operation. This October trip was the longest and gave him and Roger enough time to tour the English countryside together. Roger described every day of it to Lionel, as if it were some parody of a picaresque novel.

```
We set out early on Thursday morning with a
great red sun glowing through the thick morning
mist and, after a call at Chislehurst to visit
Danny's cousins, we went on to Knole, and we
couldn't have seen it to more perfect advantage,
the sun blazed down out of a cloudless sky, the
birds sang, a dog barked and the clock chimed.
It was perfection.
```

From Knole, they went to Arundel, then Chichester, through the New Forest to see Beaulieu, then up to Bath to tour its Roman baths and Georgian assembly rooms, before heading south to Wells and across the gentle West Country hills to Longleat House near the ancient town of Warminster, ending their trip on a crisp autumn day with lunch in Frome. In among it all, they managed a detour to Broughton, Roger's favourite country house, which he was determined for Danny to see.

Roger basked in Danny's company, as they gorged themselves for a week on beautiful things. But the reprieve was temporary, and partial. Whenever Roger picked up a book or a newspaper now, it would take several seconds for his right eye to adjust to the print sufficiently for him to begin to read, 'and even then, the focus would periodically dissolve into a blur . . . it became impossible to read for more than half an hour at a stretch – sometimes not even that – without the print quivering and disintegrating beyond recall.'

He reported these concerns to Lionel, alongside happy tales of his days with Danny.

```
In some way it doesn't seem to focus as easily
as it did before and is much more erratic in
its efficiency. Some days it is quite all right,
other days I can scarcely see where I'm going.
It's hell at night time, so much so that I'm
almost afraid to go out on my own.
```

Stopping for lunch one day in Woking, Danny had crossed a road, thinking Roger was alongside him. Instead, Roger lost his nerve and became paralysed by fear at not knowing what vehicles were coming towards him from either direction.

```
A mixture of rage, frustration and embarrassment
engulfed me and I could only pace up and down
the pavement in impotent fury while Danny stood
on the other side wondering what had come over
me.
```

Within months, Roger was again feeling the tell-tale irritation that had preceded the crisis in his left eye – this time in his right. Then the eye's surface split because of high tension, engulfing him in a white fog. A friend bundled him into a taxi to Moorfields, where he spent a week resting with a patch over the eye. When the patch was removed, he found that the eye was working as it had before and he made his way to recuperate with his parents, who by now had moved to the village of Eydon, a few miles from Banbury. There, he accepted that the writing was on the wall: at the very least, another operation would be needed, with all the same risks as the last one.

```
Although I now knew what this might mean, I
felt no qualms. My position was becoming more
impossible day by day. The double strain of
trying to maintain the semblance of a normal
life under abnormal conditions, together with
this wretchedly protracted uncertainty about the
future, had become well-nigh intolerable.
```

By March 1966, Roger began to make what he called 'mental preparations for the final blackout'. High on his list of concerns was how he could continue to work, convinced he would have to leave Keith Cardale, Groves & Co. if he lost his sight completely. 'The answer, clearly, is a job which I can do at home,' he wrote to Lionel at the end of April. 'BUT WHAT? Short of becoming a bestselling novelist I can't think of a damn thing.'

He went about seeking all the advice he could:

I spent an hour at the Royal National Institute
for the Blind* yesterday: you can imagine how
depressed one has to feel to go to such an
extreme as that. I feel I'm on the razor's edge
at the moment.

Roger focused almost exclusively on practical planning.
Facing the full reality of his situation was beyond him.

By this time, I was in a peculiarly divided
state of mind: half of my consciousness
realised perfectly well and rationally that I
was holding onto this remnant of sight only
by the slenderest thread, while the other
half could not - or would not - believe that
this thread might snap at any moment. The
real difficulty lay in the impossibility of
imagining the whole remainder of a lifetime
without sight . . . It was altogether too vast
a prospect to comprehend in all its physical
and psychological, and practical and sensual
aspects.

---

* The RNIB was founded in 1868 as the British and Foreign Society for Improving
Embossed Literature of the Blind. In 2002, it became a membership organisation,
giving individual blind people more of a say within a group operating in their name.
In 2007 it renamed itself the Royal National Institute of Blind People.

Unwilling to go on like this, Roger went back to Moorfields and demanded surgery. Mr Greaves was reluctant at first but eventually agreed. 'Tell me frankly,' Roger asked him, 'and don't worry, I shan't make a fuss if it turns out for the worst. What are the chances of this preserving what's left?' 'Fifty-fifty,' was all Greaves would say.

On 5th June, Roger announced his decision to his old friend.

Now the die is cast: my fate is sealed.
Probably by the time you receive this I shall
be on my way to the operating table. I am
going back into Moorfields on Wednesday and
Greaves will operate on Friday . . . Now that
the decision has been made I feel a great deal
better: the matter is out of my hands: my fate
is decided and it is just a question of waiting
to see - either literally or metaphorically! -
what happens. At least then I will be able to
make definite plans.

    . . . my state of mind at the moment
is peculiar: I feel in a psychological
vacuum, curiously detached, almost coldly
dispassionate . . . Perhaps it's a sort of
subconscious barrier - a refusal to concede
that the worst can happen.

    . . . Think of me next Saturday morning about
10am: that will be the most dramatic, agonising
moment when they take off the bandage. I shan't
be able to breathe for those few seconds,

wondering - will there be anything there, or
NOTHING.

Ahead of the operation, Roger looked closely at everything –
his parents' village, his parents themselves, his grandmother – and
he spent the last Saturday before his surgery visiting his favourite
places in London. Wanting to etch as clear an image in his mind
as he could, of as much as he could, he focused all his energy
on this task: 'I was observing it all, carefully, as minutely as I
could, slowly registering everything. It felt like a very long time
exposure on a slow film.'

It was a bright, gusty day, perfect for walking across
Hampstead Heath, browsing books in a smart bookshop on
Haverstock Hill, and then climbing through a narrow, steep
alley between large, old houses and beyond to Fenton House.

Through the ornamental gates, and at the end
a short grassy avenue flanked by trees, I
could see the simple Mulberry brick front of
the house with its mansard roof and long white
framed windows, and in front of it a pair
of lead figures on pedestals of an arcadian
shepherd and shepherdess - about the size
of children - slightly turning towards each
other. The trees wrestled vigorously and the
brisk breeze and small clouds slid across the
rooftop. Inside the house the principal rooms
glowed with sunlight and I looked out through
the long windows at the vista in reverse.

```
Somewhere upstairs, one of the harpsichords
was being played in what otherwise appeared to
be a deserted house, in which I was the only
intruder. It hardly seemed possible that such a
setting could be barely 20 minutes journey from
Trafalgar Square.
```

The night before the surgery, nine of his closest friends threw him a send-off dinner. Then, on the morning of 8th June 1966, Roger took one last long and detailed look at the home he already loved, and which – with lodgers in place – was already providing his financial stability. He steeled himself.

```
I took a last look around . . . The morning
sunlight flooded into the front rooms with
their big windows, and into the bright little
entrance hall with its black and white tiled
floor. Then I picked up my bag, locked the
front door and walked down to the Fulham Road
to wait for a no. 14 bus.
```

Waking up from surgery, Roger let himself be carried along by routine and convention. He had some breakfast and settled down placidly to wait for the routine inspection by the registrar.

```
In my mind's eye, I could see the cluster
of humbly curious white coated figures at
the foot of the bed. Strangely, I felt just
as dispassionate myself: it was for all the
```

```
world as if my brain had been anaesthetised,
or rather, as if my emotions were still under
the anaesthetic. I felt neither optimism nor
pessimism, just a kind of static numbness, as
if I was an onlooker at myself.
```

Roger felt some fingers touch his forehead and the tug of tape at his skin as a pad was pulled away from his eye – just as one had been after his operation a year earlier.

```
With perfect calmness I let the eyelid slowly
lift, almost of its own accord, and looked
straight ahead to where I knew the light from
the doctor's torch must be. There was nothing,
of course, as in my heart I had always known
would be the case. Not even the faintest
glimmer. Just utter blackness.
```

The pad was stuck back on and the silent group of doctors, without offering any surprise, any explanation, or even any commiseration, moved on to the next patient. But Mr Greaves visited the next day and, to Roger's surprise, with a sudden burst of emotion, he took Roger's hand and held it for some time, seemingly at a loss to know what to say. Was Roger supposed to console him, he wondered – for some reason to comfort this grieving doctor, who had failed him? He mumbled something about at least knowing where he stood. The surgeon said that he really had thought the operation was going to be a success.

Roger now had 'the final answer to the miserable question which had dogged me for virtually all my life'. His feelings about it hit him in waves, often unexpectedly – including on his departure from Moorfields.

As the Sister led me through the main entrance
and out into City Road where my parents' car
was waiting, I emerged into the open air for
the first time in three weeks. I was immediately struck by a sudden warmth on my face
and realised to my surprise that it was a fine
sunny summer morning. The very next instant
came my second spontaneous reaction, this
time to my new situation of dependence and
vulnerability: I found myself involuntarily
holding back as I remembered the short flight
of steps that leads down to the pavement. My
instinct for self-preservation was stronger than
confidence in my guide. And at this moment, I
was struck by the thought that only three weeks
before I had walked out of Old Street tube
station and up this road unaided.

From his parents' house, early in July, Roger wrote to Lionel, using a battery-operated tape recorder to dictate his letter, which a friend then transcribed.

As you will have gathered by now, something
went horribly wrong after my operation: like

the other operation last year it was successful
in itself but, again like last year, this
wretchedly unpredictable haemorrhage occurred
and has now blacked me out completely. June 10th
was the fatal date; and on June 27th I became
officially a Registered Blind Person.

Oxford, 2007

One Saturday, towards the end of my doctorate, Roger suggested lunch at the pub at the end of the west Oxford street
where I was living.

Cripley Road had slightly down-at-heel, nineteenth-century
housing on one side and an unattractive row of thick brambles
and trees on the other, only partially blocking the view of the
train station behind. I had moved to a college-owned house there
two years earlier, initially with my LGB co-rep Amy (we stood
again as postgraduates). The flat was perfectly nice – two floors,
well arranged. It even had space for a spare bedroom, christened
'the room of heterosexuality', for our guests. But it was something of a comedown after so many years living in what felt
like a palace at Christ Church.

For the Victorians, this area had become defined by its location: the 'other' side of the railway line from Oxford's colleges,
so very much the bad side. I later discovered the cruel origin
of the name 'cripley' from an etching in the bathroom of the
Old Parsonage restaurant, which depicted a man with crutches

241

begging for money from a well-to-do gentleman. Amy and I announced our move there by throwing our first themed party: 'the wrong side of the tracks' (a party which set in stone a long-standing feud between us and our neighbours below).

It wasn't exactly clear why Roger was proposing to come to my part of town – and on fairly short notice. The pub at the end of the street was predictably run-down: plastic seats, shiny tables, peeling paint on ill-fitting windows, with a soullessness that the highly patterned, slightly sticky carpets couldn't mask. I wasn't keen but Roger had mentioned wanting to visit there a few times (I think it had been well thought of in a previous ownership) and it was at least an easy option for us once he'd taken a taxi from Regent Street and come for a drink in my kitchen first.

We weren't long at my house. Roger seemed distracted as I poured a fairly weak G&T for each of us from the Beefeater I now kept on hand (though it remained in the bottle at my house, not poured into a decanter like Roger's). He obviously wanted to get to the pub, so we arrived early to an empty room. Sitting by a window looking onto the busy Botley Road, I tried to be jolly and make the best of it. We ordered wine and omelettes, which, I remember, arrived suspiciously quickly. Their speedy appearance annoyed Roger – he had come with a purpose and evidently hoped to get it over with before eating.

As we ate those mediocre omelettes – by this point, neither of us particularly happy to be there – Roger told me he was ill.

Later, he claimed he'd mentioned his condition before this, but I had no memory of it. Besides, the scene-setting he'd done, the hastily arranged lunch – taken without our customary walk from Regent Street – had already suggested to me there was something out of the ordinary. Roger had, I worked out, just been for a scan and, after years of being told to 'watch and wait', he had heard something else. Something worse.

He said that, some years ago, he had been diagnosed with chronic lymphatic leukaemia which, by now, meant he was (as he called it) 'playing in extra time'. People could live for years with this condition, he told me, but he had already dispensed with more years than any doctor had suggested he might. It was inevitable that, sooner rather than later, this cancer would spread. Prostate cancer had taken his father and he imagined this would be his fate, too.

We ate our lunch and for once I asked more questions than him. How long had he known? How did he discover it? What were the symptoms? Which hospital did he visit and what were they telling him? Was there anything he could do? No doubt, unintentionally, I echoed Lionel Fielden, when Roger shared his other life-changing diagnosis half a century earlier – the unhelpful mantra that there *must* be something he could do.

Roger was always matter of fact about his health – never showing fear, regret or even a sense of injustice. He answered my questions without much emotion and without expecting me to show any.

What difference did this information make? I asked him then and there what I could do. How could I help? How could I make his life better? But I suppose I already knew the answer. Roger wanted me – nothing more, nothing less – to be with him for the time he had left. 'Stick with me, love,' he said. 'It won't be much longer and I don't know what I'd do if you didn't.'

Stick with him.

Part of me was annoyed at the implication that I wouldn't – that I might just as easily abandon this vulnerable man whose life had become so entangled with my own and whose friendship had become so important to me. But the better part of me knew the weight of what lay behind his request. Sticking with Roger meant that all those conflicting feelings which had been bubbling up for me – my sense of affection and duty to him alongside an anxiety about his growing reliance on me – now needed to be buried, or at least somehow suppressed so that they'd never emerge enough for Roger to notice.

What other option? Now I had a new perspective on those moments of feeling overwhelmed by Roger's need of me, his dependence on me to live in the way he really wanted to live. Now I understood differently the desperation to escape a restricted, difficult, lonely existence of so many years. Roger's desire to live well, and to live more, had a greater urgency – and I was his means of living.

What other option? None, then.

CHAPTER 10

Learning to be Blind

'Once you become blind it's drummed into you how hard it is to get a job and you should be jolly thankful for anything that anybody gives you'[1]

Roger's friend Peter offered to take him to Torquay, driving fast in his powerful Daimler through the fine, fresh August day, the top down all the way. Manor House, the RNIB's 'Rehabilitation Centre for the Newly Blind', was a substantial Victorian pile, vaguely Italianate in style.* When they walked in, it felt mysteriously deserted.

> Like the Castle in *The Sleeping Beauty*: there was no one about and not a sound could be heard from any part. We stood uncertainly for a minute or two, while Peter described the place in subdued tones and looked about for some means of attracting attention. He went back to

---

* Manor House closed in 2004 for lack of funding. *Conquest of the Dark*, a 1955 documentary, includes scenes from the centre and the main character has many of the same experiences as Roger.

```
the front door and found a bell push. A short
staccato ring could be heard somewhere in the
distance, after which the silence seemed even
more intense.
```

Eventually, a woman arrived and introduced herself as Mrs Drake, the Warden's wife. She led the two men up the carpeted staircase and around part of a gallery to a large room on the first floor. The room's arrangement around four beds was explained to Roger while Peter fetched some cases from the car, which he left by Roger's bedside before being ushered out. A few minutes later, Roger listened through an open window to the engine of the Daimler come to life and then fade away down the drive. He tried not to panic.

```
At that moment, I suddenly felt a pang, a
sinking feeling in the stomach: for the first
time since the onset of blindness I was alone
in a strange place, far from home and anyone
I knew. It was one's first day at a new school
all over again.
```

In 1960s Britain, prevailing attitudes treated 'the Blind' as a homogenous group: an unfortunate class of people to be directed towards a narrow range of roles they might be trained to perform in order to become productive members of society. This had been formalised by Parliament in 1914 as the guiding principle for legal and community approaches: 'the State should make provision whereby capable blind people might be made industrially self-supporting.[2] Laws passed subsequently – a Blind Persons Act after the First World War, a Disabled Persons (Employment) Act of 1944 and the National Assistance Act of 1948 – all built on this tenet, offering new ways by which blind people could be supported to work. By 1956, it could be asserted: 'The modern world is becoming increasingly conscious not only of the problems confronting its citizens of the dark but also of the potential contribution to society that can be made by the sightless.'[3]

This practical approach had mixed consequences. On the one hand, growing appreciation of the ability of blind people to work led to the expansion of opportunities for them. On the other, a unilinear focus on employment could become oppressive: organised support for blind people often neglected to ask what individuals actually wanted in order to be able to live well. Placing 'normalisation' on a pedestal also meant that people who couldn't achieve sufficient proximity to 'normal' to be employed in a recognised trade were seen as a burden which society had to bear.

In an era that continued to insist on standards and sameness, on not deviating too far from an inherited idea of what was acceptable, attitudes to blind people were not unlike those applied to homosexuals. Here was another group to be pitied and managed, with their own set of limited options, to ensure they didn't create problems for everyone else. Both 'afflictions' came complete with the well-meaning but often irritating aid of people from the dominant majority – aid with strings attached and preconceptions formed by those who had never experienced the 'afflictions' about which they now assumed themselves to be experts.

When Roger had visited the RNIB and his local authority before his failed second operation, the message he received was entirely consistent with all of this: if he were to lose his sight completely, he should find a way to re-enter work as soon as possible, with any employer willing to put up with his reduced capacities. Roger saw no reason to question this, assuming he would have to rethink his life completely. So, when one of his firm's junior partners came to see him in hospital a couple of days after his operation, Roger decided there was no point delaying the matter. 'Well, I suppose I'd better give you my notice, then,' he said. 'No no, not at all,' his visitor protested. 'Go and get yourself rehabilitated and come back and we'll see how we can place you.'

This offer of a guaranteed job was remarkable – and unlike anything he'd been warned to expect. Encouraged, Roger decided to take some early action while still sitting in his hospital bed at Moorfields. Instead of wallowing in the growing embrace of post-operative pain, he interrupted the house surgeon on his regular rounds of checks: 'It occurred to me that I might as well start to learn Braille. It would give me something to do and distract me from other problems.' The surgeon paused his note-taking, looked up and agreed: 'A good idea, it's a good mental exercise, like learning Russian. I'll see what I can arrange.'

Two hours later, a hospital social worker boomed Roger's name across the ward and marched over, bringing with her a young woman. Diane had lost her sight at 19 in a car crash, it was explained, and was doing some work experience on the ward – she would be happy to introduce Roger to the basics of Braille. The two quickly began daily lessons, which tended to dissolve after about ten minutes into general conversation about everything from telling shirt colours apart to whether it was appropriate to say 'How nice to see you.' Diane, talking about her plans for decorating her flat and a tandem holiday in France with her sister, convinced Roger 'not only that a great many more things were still possible than I might have supposed, but also that they still mattered'.

It was during this time that Roger adopted an ambition around which he could order all his decisions. Before he left the hospital, he vowed that he would restore as much of his old life – his sighted life – as possible. He would try any ways he could to become 'normal' again, to be the productive, working member of society everyone wanted him to be.

Roger contacted the RNIB as soon as he left Moorfields, telling them that he had the offer of returning to his employer – he just needed to learn the skills to get him there. This was, he knew, exactly what they wanted to hear. Having the promise of a job was 'a golden key' and he was pushed to the top of a one-year waiting list for a 'rehabilitation course'. Within five weeks of leaving hospital, alone for the first time since he lost his sight, Roger was at Torquay, about to begin this new education.

Manor House had opened its doors some twenty-five years previously as a 'specialist social and employment rehabilitation centre'. Tom Drake – himself blind, with a strong Yorkshire voice – had been instrumental in its establishment and was now its Warden. It didn't take long for Roger to work out that Drake set the tone for much of what went on there: the primary purpose of all activities was to provide elementary instruction in practical life skills.

In the bedroom that was now his for the next three months, Roger began unpacking, but Mrs Drake appeared again and put him into the care of a fellow resident, Jim, who took Roger back downstairs. As they descended, Roger noticed that the atmosphere of the place had completely changed.

```
It had suddenly come to life as people emerged
from different parts of the house, thronged
all about the hall with much babble of talk
and the calling out of names as people tried
to locate their invisible friends ... And it
was now I first began to realise one of the
more disconcerting aspects of blindness which
in my short experience, not having an occasion
to move about in a large community, had never
previously struck me. This is the way in which
a Voice suddenly springs out of the air reveal-
ing an unsuspected presence at startling close
hand. And, like the Cheshire Cat, it is liable
to vanish again just as quickly and without
warning, leaving not even a smile.
```

In just such a nonplussing fashion, Roger felt himself accosted at the foot of the stairs. 'Good afternoon,' said a dry voice from a superior height, 'my name's Broughton – I'm the Deputy Warden. Excuse me for greeting you in my shirtsleeves.'

'That's all right,' Roger joked, 'I can't see them anyway.'

Broughton's response was frosty: 'I know, that's why I mentioned it.'

Learning to be Blind

Decades later, Roger was still puzzling over this exchange.

Jim was an accountant in his forties, rapidly losing his sight because of diabetes. Much of his spare time, Roger soon learned, was spent playing Ravel on the grand piano in the lounge. He was at Manor House in a bid to gain skills that might allow him to continue to work for another twenty years, but was already resigned to taking some more menial role in an office. Any work would do, he told Roger, if only he could carry on supporting his wife and children. Roger was lucky to have a job being held open for him, he said with some envy: a comment repeated often by many of the others.

Jim and Roger moved to the dining room for the 5.45pm high tea, the last meal served of the day, where Roger's affirmative answer to the question 'Are you a beer man?' secured him an invitation to skip the evening's official entertainment plans in favour of heading to the pub with Jim and his friends.

As comfortably as he ditched the organised entertainment, Roger dodged many of the specialist classes that didn't directly help him to learn how to read and write – pottery, handicrafts, lathe operating and carpentry courses. He grudgingly agreed to basket weaving only because someone mentioned it might help make his fingers more sensitive for reading Braille (it didn't, he discovered). He was fully committed to learning this new code, but it was a gruelling process.

```
Learning the ingenious but complex formula was
child's play compared with the real problem of
actually trying to feel the wretched stuff, of
trying to distinguish those clusters of tiny
```

```
bumps on the paper one from another when they
are jammed close together and when the lines
themselves seem at first to be separated by no
more than a hair's breadth.
```

He had his breakthrough while reading *Twelve Famous Sea Stories* in grade 2, contracted Braille. Roger's school experience had made him question his intellectual capacity, but mastering Braille, he said, gave him a 'curious awakening to the knowledge that I had more ability to apply myself and a quicker aptitude for learning when the occasion required than I had ever appreciated before.'

Touch-typing came faster, but not without its own pains – a 'dragon teacher' named Mrs Turner, who was 'not inaccurately, suspicious of adult students as potential backsliders unless terrorised into unremitting effort by the good old schoolroom dread of public humiliations'. There, though, Roger enjoyed an early reward. Two months after arriving at Torquay, he could, for the first time since becoming blind, write private letters again.

```
This felt like a real liberation, perhaps
something like being released from solitary
confinement. Having to dictate personal letters
is terribly inhibiting, no matter how innocuous
the content . . . Nothing, I think, had made
me feel more constricted, more cut off, more
helpless than the inability to read and write
– strangely, not even the inability to move
```

about freely — so just becoming literate again, however imperfectly, went a long way towards restoring a sense of normality.

Of course, the first letter he typed was to the man whose correspondence had been so important to him throughout the previous decade.

> Manor House
> Middle Lincombe Road
> Torquay
> 1st October, 1966

My dear Lionel,

It is just a year ago today that Danny and I went off on that lovely week of touring. It was a perfect week in every way, and now, in a silly sort of way, it seems to me as if it was - well, Providential. There, in one, and under perfect conditions, I was able to gaze, for the last time as it turned out, at many of the places I have enjoyed most . . . One of the fears which haunts me most is that my visual memory may fade or become distorted in some weird, horrible way.

You've probably heard of the 'Talking Books', a library of tape recordings distributed by the RNIB. It's a marvellous idea and in truth has a pretty fair selection, though with some surprising omissions; but there are two of

Lettice's. Of course, the field will be widened greatly when I am able to read Braille with some degree of fluency, but this will be a year or two yet.

You ask about the training here . . . At the moment, I am too closely involved myself to be able to view it all with a proper detachment. However, this place has done for me pretty well all that I wanted: it has taught me Braille and typing (and what a joy it is to be able to write letters again - I felt almost imprisoned when I couldn't).

. . .

One odd thing is that many who come here are not completely blind, in fact there are quite a number who can see at least as well as I could before I lost my sight. The 'totals' as my category is called are in the minority. This can be rather dispiriting as it means the community tends to get split into two groups - 'them' and 'us'. And 'us' are inclined, perhaps a little unfairly, to feel out on a limb - deprived - although the staff do their best to alleviate this.

Looked at dispassionately, the attitude of the sighted general public towards the blind is interesting. The blind, inevitably, form a separate caste. So far I've been very heartened by the amount of help which people offer,

although how this will work out in the rush of
London remains to be seen. There's no getting
away from the fact that most normal sighted
people are embarrassed by blindness and there
is a degree of will-power needed to offer
help. Not only can I often sense this but I
know it to be so because that is exactly how
I felt before I lost my sight. The reason for
this, and some peculiar misconceptions about
the blind, is hard to find but it probably has
its roots very, very deep down. Blindness is
associated with darkness, and darkness with the
unknown, and therein lie all sorts of primaeval
fears . . . This is in part confirmed, and the
basic misconceptions unconsciously strengthened,
by the innumerable adjectival uses of the word
'blind' - blind-drunk, blind-fury, blind-window
(in the case of a window which has been bricked
up and so no longer admits light), or just blind
as in venetian blind, and so on and so on.
Quite interesting in a way, isn't it?

  . . .

  Enough for now. Fondest Regards,
  Roger.

Besides learning the skills necessary for reading and writing,
the chief feature of the curriculum at Torquay was called
'independent mobility'. One part of each day was dedicated
to this. The American long cane technique was only just being

introduced in England, Roger heard later, and so his instruction was in the method of 'tapping one's way along any convenient wall and never losing tangible contact for a second longer than could be helped'.

Half a dozen residents who had arrived the same day were considered Roger's cohort. Their instructor would lead them together, first around the grounds, then out in the streets and down the hill from Manor House into Torquay town, describing each stage of the route for them to memorise. The guide was a sighted person, who walked at the front of this tentative line, facing backwards to issue his instructions. Mostly, the people of Torquay were used to these classes, but to the unfamiliar it was a surprising spectacle – which created some confusion. One morning, on their regular walk into town, Roger heard footsteps running towards them and the anxious voice of a concerned stranger shouting at their guide, 'Excuse me, do you know you're walking the wrong way round?' Learning to manage the 'help' of strangers was also part of this course.

Independent mobility classes lasted for three weeks, after which Roger was observed on a solo walk into town and then signed off as competent. His speedy mastery of the technique had been helped by nightly practice with Jim and their assembled group of friends making unsupervised beer runs to the Hesketh Arms. Like the coffee shop they visited daily with their instructor, the pub had few redeeming qualities, but it was easy to reach, and a quiet place where they could sit and talk.

As their time together went on, the men boosted one another's confidence to venture further afield. This they did, as Roger put it, 'heedless of Our Lord's warning that if the blind lead the blind both shall fall into the ditch.' They undertook increasingly complicated expeditions, finally setting out for a curry house on the far side of town.

> Somehow we made our crazy way along unfamiliar
> pavements and across strange roads, perfectly
> oblivious of how many near misses we might be
> having in the way of unsuspected pitfalls, and
> checking our whereabouts whenever we could
> by accosting any passer-by whom we detected
> until eventually, a momentary, tantalising,
> unmistakable spicy whiff in the evening air
> told us that our objective could not be far
> off.

Despite his aptitude for getting around, sustaining 'independent mobility' proved traumatic when Roger returned home late in October 1966. His problem was less a lack of confidence and more an acute self-consciousness – a profound aversion to the kind of conspicuousness that came with walking as a blind person. Away from Torquay and among the general public, the white stick, the tapping, the inevitable stumbles and the offers of help brought up feelings akin to those his glasses had caused as a child, but many times worse.

> It is very repugnant to have to move about
> in what feels to be such a degrading fashion,
> aware that you are constantly the object of
> surreptitious curiosity, sometimes sympathetic,

```
sometimes embarrassed . . . the psychological
agony of public exposure, the irrational
sensitivity one felt to being observed as this
pathetic figure.
```

Roger learned a few essential routes in London, but it was obvious that something more would be needed if he were even to consider travelling from Fulham to his office in Grosvenor Square. For this, Roger would need a guide dog. That was a hard pill to swallow – perhaps the hardest in his rehabilitation.

```
I knew nothing about dogs. I had not been
brought up with one at home, I had never owned
one or ever wished to. Nowhere had they ever
featured in my life . . . I now felt it to be
one of the worst impositions of blindness that
I should have to be saddled with this unwanted
dependence and responsibility.
```

The obligatory guide dog course in the spa town of Leamington also grated on him, far more than Torquay had. Roger felt guilty about his discomfort, aware of how gushing most of the country seemed to be about 'Guide Dogs for the Blind'. 'It is not easy to speak critically – even disparagingly, it may seem – about such an admired institution,' he reflected. 'It appears too much like biting the hand that fed me.' But the whole concept made him feel patronised and he resented the distinct whiff of Victorian charity:

One was very conscious of being the recipient
of a discretionary benevolence and indeed it
was made clear that what was so given could
at any time just as easily be withdrawn if the
authorities saw fit.

After a few days of lectures in dog psychology, with an emphasis on the need for unrelenting discipline, Roger realised he was being sized up for a correct match. To his surprise, he would be given a sable and cream Alsatian bitch. 'I was even more startled, and appalled, when I learned that her name was Gay.'

When the time arrived to meet Gay, Roger was instructed to go to his room and wait, after which, in what was described to Roger almost as a sacred ritual, they would be introduced and given thirty minutes alone to play and generally make a friendly attempt to establish a connection.

I sat on my bed and waited. It was several
minutes before I heard the sound of approaching
footsteps and the quick click of claws on the
linoleum of the corridor outside. Tentatively, I
put out my hand and straight away she nuzzled
against it in an anxious to please fashion.
During the next half hour I did my best to
exhibit some genuine warmth of feeling, but I
fear it must all have seemed pretty perfunctory
to the poor creature.

Then came the dreary process of learning to walk independently – again, but this time with a dog. Every day for four weeks, morning and afternoon, Roger joined a group of students and grimly trudged up and down Warwick New Road, along the busy Parade, in and out of Woolworth's, over innumerable crossings, through heavy traffic, around endless housing estates. Soon, they were being pushed further:

> . . . to sally forth into a great threatening
> void engulfed in noise, with no reassuring walls
> to cling to - along pavements bestrewn with
> pedestrians and lamp posts and countless sundry
> hazards, startled by sudden sounds, alarmed
> by passing traffic (which always sounded much
> closer than it really was), to walk in a calm
> and natural fashion through all this relying
> for one's safety primarily on the judgement of
> an uncomprehending dog.

This was, Roger found, 'a greater test of nerve than I had supposed'. Besides the continual sense of threat, the unexpectedly jerky, uneven movement of the harness handle was itself disconcerting.

> . . . a wobbly object attached to a strange
> dog . . . anything untoward would cause me
> to start and recoil with an exaggerated
> reaction . . . With every step I expected
> to crash full-face into a post, a gate, a

```
wall - something painfully solid - or to
stumble and fall headlong over some obstacle,
or else suddenly to feel that hideous, sickening
sensation of falling as one unexpectedly steps
onto nothing.
```

Between trips out, Roger and the other students were taught to groom their dogs, practised obedience tests and negotiated deliberately contrived obstacles. All this was led by an 18-year-old trainee instructor who had the manner of a sergeant-major intent on licking his recalcitrant conscripts into shape. Roger took an instant dislike to him, perceiving 'an obnoxious little squirt with a shrill, unattractive voice and an abrasive manner'. But he had no other choice than to obey and get on with it.

London, 2008

I submitted my doctoral thesis – a technical monograph about early church law and the development of ancient theologies – late in 2007. I'd finished it a few months earlier than expected but waited until my final funding cheque had arrived before depositing the required volumes for examination. This was a characteristically Oxford process: three printed copies, hundreds of loose pages to be bound together according to prescribed specifications and taken in person to the Examination Schools. There was more to do – a viva ('oral rotisserie', as my supervisor later called it), corrections, resubmission (this time hard bound according to a different set of specifications for the Bodleian) – but none of this required me to be in Oxford, nor would it come with any further financial support.

I'd tried over the course of my final year to find opportunities to stay in the city. Junior Research Fellowships – highly competitive and highly exploitative arrangements to attract young academics to Oxford colleges without really paying them – were about all I could think of. Louise, by then freelancing as a reporter in London, helped me to find sentences to explain the minutiae of ancient ecclesiastical canons and theologies enthusiastically and comprehensibly, but she couldn't reverse the steady stream of rejection letters.

So, I left. What else was there to do? A lifetime of increasingly narrow, increasingly detailed education felt, at that point, increasingly useless when it came to employment. I all but gave up on the idea that I'd find a job which made use of my degrees. Instead, I followed some (insightful, it turned out) advice from my parents: look for a job, whatever the job, however junior, in a place you want to be, doing things you think matter.

In March 2008, as Louise left for America, I found myself hastily looking for somewhere to live in London. I'd been offered a position as a junior assistant in the offices of the Methodist Church's central administration in Marylebone, but only if I could start straight away. I lied, like most people would, and said that moving to a new city and finding a place to live in the space of a few days wouldn't be a problem.

Roger was as perplexed as ever. Theology was one thing (acceptable as an area of interest, if niche), going to church another (put it down to upbringing), but spending my days working for a church was incomprehensible (not only that, but Methodists! Not even the Anglo-Catholics with their bells and smells). He consoled himself that my six-month contract meant I would move on to something more serious soon. I never wholly have.

I wasn't completely sure myself at that point but, for the time being, I'd found some people whose work seemed worth doing, who wanted me to join them and – crucially – were willing to pay me just enough to get by. I packed up a few suitcases (most of my possessions now being either in Roger's cellar or my parents' new rectory) and moved to a college friend's spare bedroom, while I looked around London for somewhere to rent.

Londoners' stories about how and where they lived when they first came to town can be eye-rollingly nostalgic. 'Life was better back then . . .' leads into long, nauseating descriptions of crazily cheap houses in expensive neighbourhoods, often lived in by penniless intellectuals and aspiring creatives ('only oligarchs and bankers can afford to live there these days!'). My story isn't quite so grating, but I certainly landed on my feet.

Lodging near Borough Market for a few weeks, I started the new job and spent my spare time answering online adverts for available rooms, writing short descriptions to sell myself as a flatmate. I'd always somehow fit in 'you probably should know that I'm gay, in case that matters'. I remember feeling I always had to say it somewhere in that first communication – it would just be easier they know from the beginning.

After one failed visit to a gloomy Maida Vale mansion block, I was sitting in the living room of a large, three-bedroom flat in Soho, being asked to move in with Ben (a nightclub manager) and Sam (student and former Abercrombie and Fitch boy). I hadn't expected to be able to afford anything of this size or in such an astonishing location. There were downsides, they told me straight away: sometimes mice (nice, friendly ones) and the location meant the windows needed to be cleaned almost every week to wash away the pollution. Oh, and the exit onto the street behind was a quiet haven for people habitually using drugs, except during Pride when it became a staging spot for the events on Soho Square. Other than that, there wasn't much to know. I wouldn't be the only gay in the house and they were relieved that I was working in an office nine-to-five – neither of them was and it made for a good balance.

I loved the place instantly and moved in as soon as possible, trucking my bags on the tube from London Bridge to Tottenham Court Road. Flat 2, 167 Charing Cross Road was in a Victorian row of buildings, directly above Harmony – then Europe's largest sex shop, I was told, which was also our landlord (20 per cent discount for tenants). Immediately next door was the Astoria, home to the legendary G-A-Y nightclub, to which we had made regular trips by bus from Oxford. I had never imagined people actually lived there.

Just a few steps down the street was everything else Soho promised: clubs (of all kinds), a trove of gay bars, and restaurants (including the five-pound pizza and bring-your-own wine restaurant called Lorelei, which Louise and I had discovered, but turned on after it gave us both violent food poisoning). Around the corner were the famous, retro music shops of Denmark Street and the handful that remained of the Charing Cross Road's bookshops. Sitting serenely among it all was St Patrick's Church, which I looked at affectionately as I passed: Roman Catholic but known for its gay-affirming services.

Life in Flat 2 was no less singular than its location. It took me a while to adapt to the spotlights that shot beams into my bedroom from the Dominion Theatre opposite (*Thriller Live*, I think, on weekdays; a megachurch on Sunday) but they were easier to cope with than the noise. I remember just how bitterly

I was woken nightly without fail in those first couple of weeks, first by the bells of the rickshaws that loitered under Centre Point opposite and then – always – by the 3am trumpeter in the arch below my window. I did just once fall asleep in the office after an especially loud night.

A steady stream of men (Ben) and women (Sam) would arrive and depart at a rate which never stopped surprising me, the old, ill-fitting doors to their bedrooms leaving no doubt why these guests had come. And the flat was liable to fill up with visitors, piling in without any warning. The evening noise into my bedroom from the street outside would often muffle the sounds indoors, so I'd never be quite sure who and how many people I'd find in the living room, gathering at this strange home, perfectly located to start a night in town. Living in such an 'open house' reminded me a little of growing up in a vicarage – and was also absolutely nothing like growing up in a vicarage.

A short leap out of our bathroom window onto a ledge on the opposite wall gave access to a long stretch of flat roofs, all at slightly different heights, hidden behind the facades of Oxford Street. Sam showed me it first. He often spent mornings up there with his skipping rope, normally shirtless, no doubt distracting office workers in the taller buildings nearby. But the magic was at night. Walking along those roofs, looking down over the occasional low walls to the twinkling lights and bustle on the street below made for a dreamlike, rarefied experience to share with anyone, but especially people we planned to kiss under the stars.

Ben would sleep most of the day, in between visitors, and at night took me to Popstarz (over the road) or Ghetto (the basement of our building) as often as I would go. He showed me his corner of London and encouraged me to find men to take onto the roof. Buoyed up by a succession of free drinks from the smiling bar staff, there were some (I remember spotting a beautiful American in a Disney Gay Days t-shirt, uncomfortably tall under the low ceilings at Ghetto, who turned out to be called Michael Jackson), but it was never really my style.

Office hours were certainly a contrast to all this, but working at Methodist Church House was also beginning to feel as much a good decision as my choice of apartment. Each morning, I would walk there from our flat, emerging out of Soho, its pavements quiet and a little dirty from visitors the night before, into the increasingly well-heeled streets of Fitzrovia and Marylebone. I'd often intentionally cut through Harley Street, past exclusive clinics behind ornate frontages, or up to Park Square to get a brief glimpse of the stunning, white stucco Nash terraces at the south end of Regent's Park. At the end of this handsome journey, I was doing interesting things and meeting people who were kind, engaging, driven. There were, as my parents had predicted, prospects for someone like me.

My world was expanding.

It was also drifting further away from Regent Street.

CHAPTER 11

Breaking Free

'It's taken ten years but here it is, it's happened'[1]

Five years after Roger had seen Lionel and Guido carrying on with their lives in Tuscany as a same-sex couple without fear of prosecution, the law changed at home.

Sexual Offences Act 1967

An Act to amend the law of England and Wales relating to homosexual acts. 27th July 1967.

BE IT ENACTED by the Queen's most Excellent Majesty, by and with the advice and consent of the Lords Spiritual and Temporal, and Commons, in this present Parliament assembled, and by the authority of the same, as follows: –

-(1) Not withstanding any statutory or common law provision, but subject to the provisions of the next following section, a homosexual act in private shall not be an offence provided that the parties consent thereto and have attained the age of twenty-one years.[2]

The following January, Roger received an invitation from the Homosexual Law Reform Society to attend a party to celebrate the 'final success' of its work. It was a select affair, hosted by the writers J.B. Priestley and Jacquetta Hawkes, who had been among the early founders of the society. Their apartment was in the eccentric Albany complex carved out from what had been one of the last grand mansions still ornamenting the north side of London's Piccadilly. Albany was such an exclusive address that, even though Roger's job had taken him to countless grand London houses, he had never previously managed to gain access.

Approaching through the portico entrance of the eighteenth-century facade, Roger was ushered to apartment B4 and immediately found himself surrounded by the great and the good of the law reform movement. He was surprised by how warm he found Priestley to be, having always perceived him as rather a terrifying figure.* He moved on to Labour MP Leo Abse – who had been one of the loudest voices in Parliament for enacting the recommendations of the Wolfenden Report – and his wife, whom Roger found to be very affable, mostly talking about issues to do with leasehold property. But for all his love of meeting celebrities, and despite the momentous occasion the party celebrated, Roger struggled to talk much with anyone else. In truth, he didn't try hard. He couldn't bring himself to enter the spirit of the gathering.

As he had grappled with the deterioration of his sight, Roger

---

* Lionel was pleased about Roger's assessment of Priestley: 'I always found him charming and he has always been very nice to me. I like his rages about everything, and admire him very much as a writer.'

270

slipped out of the inner circle of the HLRS and by 1968, he had largely lost touch with its leadership. So, when he wrote to Lionel describing the party, Roger couldn't tell him much at all about it other than the few very familiar names that had been there. With all that had happened to him, he often found himself despondent when he was surrounded by new people or reminded of what his life had once been. The HLRS party was a difficult mix of both.

Roger's life was now unrecognisable from his activist years a decade before. It had become so difficult that homosexuality – its legal status or any other aspect of it – was neither here nor there to him in any practical sense. Two years after losing all of his sight, he could barely stay afloat. He was struggling to keep on working at the estate agency, and living under the threat of losing everything he had, after already having lost everything he had found most precious. The Sexual Offences Act wouldn't change any of that.

Roger spent much of the party sitting with his guide dog, who shared none of Roger's grief. Through it all, Gay posed grandly in the middle of the drawing room, fawned upon by all those gathered and accepting offerings of sausage and foie gras.

After Torquay and Leamington, Roger had dedicated himself to the task of going back to work and trying to resume his former way of life as if nothing had changed. Up to a point, he succeeded.

Long experience, a good memory and a helpful assistant meant that Roger was able to cope with most of the routine clerical parts of his job – correspondence, accounts and legal matters. Much of the work was done by telephone, which was as easy for Roger as anyone. But the aspects of his role Roger couldn't do were the fun parts: getting out and about, looking at interesting houses, meeting fascinating clients.

The joy seemed all to have drained away but Roger continued to remind himself (and be reminded) that he was privileged to be able to work at all. This was stable employment and he had worked hard even to be able to reach the office to conduct it. The first day Roger managed the commute alone, assisted only by Gay, the whole office at Keith Cardale, Groves & Co. applauded as he arrived. He congratulated Gay – whom he was growing to love – and his boss reiterated the promise that Roger would have a job for life.

At home, he was just about managing the day-to-day tasks of domestic life, helped by the skills he'd learned at Torquay, and the discipline to establish rigorous systems for essential tasks. He kept his spare rooms occupied with lodgers and did what he could to re-establish a social life, including throwing a party for his friends at Hestercombe Avenue when he returned from Leamington.

He had allies, too, not least Patrick Trevor-Roper. After their initial consultation in October 1962, Roger had insisted Pat send him a bill, against Pat's protestations. While writing a note alongside the payment, Roger suggested a drink 'in a non-professional capacity . . . I hope this isn't an infernal cheek.' Pat agreed that Roger should ring him and arrange to pop in to his home sometime, an invitation Roger eventually talked himself into accepting. They had subsequently become good friends.

After 1966, Pat made it his cause to build up Roger's confidence and distract him from some of the worst of what was happening, and when Roger resumed working, Pat invited him to stay and get a break from his domestic duties. Pat had a large home in one of the grand Nash terraces overlooking Regent's Park, where people wandered in and out at all times, but the fantastically busy Pat was rarely to be seen. 'I had to talk to him while he bathed,' Roger told Lionel of his week-long visit, 'in order to make the most of the time. While I reclined on a chaise longue, gin in hand, he lay in his bath with his gin balanced on the edge.' It felt too hectic and he declined Pat's offer to move permanently into the top-floor apartment.

Even from a distance Pat became one of the main sources of new friends for Roger, a buffer to the forces contracting his world. Most important of these were the composer Lennox Berkeley and his family – a friendship cemented in an instant by a remarkable love between Gay and the Berkeleys' dog. Soon after Pat's introduction, Lennox's wife Freda encouraged Roger to make himself at home in their Warwick Avenue villa whenever he wished and it became a refuge. Roger began to spend time there at weekends and as a regular guest at dinners with their group of creative and intellectual friends.

Roger came to depend on these relationships, especially as he had left behind almost all of the friends he had found in the gay pubs and clubs of London, as well as his former HLRS colleagues. As Pat had predicted, they provided new opportunities for Roger to escape London and the bounds of his life there. When the Berkeleys introduced him to John and Sheila Hill, a couple living near the Suffolk coast, in the village of Snape, he found himself invited to stay with them during the Aldeburgh

Festival, an invitation which would be repeated annually. There, Roger met Sheila's brother Heywood and his wife, Lady Anne, who had moved to Snape after years running a Mayfair society bookshop. He was immediately treated like an old friend, which meant invitations to more parties, more dinners, and more trips to Suffolk, during which he would often find himself chatting with literary and cultural figures he had long dreamed of meeting.*

But all this, wonderful as he found it, was a fantasy – and Roger's daily life in London was rapidly moving towards another crisis. He had been offered no kind of counselling or support to help him deal with the emotions of losing his sight, and his unexamined fears and anger were bubbling up in the early hours of the morning.

```
I still wake at about 4 or 5 and often can't
get back to sleep again - and it's these early
hours which are hell: that terrible feeling
in the pit of my stomach. Sheer funk. And
every so often I shudder when I realise that I
NEVER will see a damn thing ever again - ALL
THE REST OF MY LIFE. Oh, it just doesn't bear
thinking about.
```

Roger's relentless daily commute from Fulham to Grosvenor Square ground him down. It required a 6.30am start to catch

---

* Roger also made an impression on those people. In her diaries, *Ups and Downs*, Frances Partridge speculated on how Roger coped with his blindness (vol. 7, p.322).

a specific bus – the only one with accessible boarding points. Getting home at night was worse: trying to find the 74B to Earl's Court in a milling crowd, unable to see and with a large dog. It felt like an act of God when Roger finally managed to find a bus which wasn't full and then actually to get on it.

To add to this, Roger was grappling with the devastating effects of insomnia. The doctors told him it was something that would pass – a response to shock, perhaps, or anxiety – but it persisted. He continued to gulp down assorted pills with alarming regularity, but still often found himself awake in bed, rigid with tension, pyjamas clinging to him with cold sweat trickling uncomfortably down his chest.

Roger's own diagnosis was that the insomnia was closely related to his perception of light:

```
This is a curious phenomenon for which no
one has ever given me a convincing scientific
explanation, whereby on alternating days I
either see complete blackness or complete
whiteness. Pure blackness is easy enough for
a sighted person to understand. It is simply
waking up in a town at night where there is not
the faintest glimmer of light from outside. The
whiteness is less easy to imagine. It is a kind
of luminous brightness, like being enveloped in
a thick fog through which the light penetrates
but no images of substance are discernible.
```

In the normal course of events, the transition between black and white took place quickly during the night. But waking early would interrupt that transition, causing a protracted changeover and a mottled effect. This made Roger's eyes ache with tiredness, impaired his mobility and slowed down his reactions: 'One way and another it all amounted to another turn of the screw.'

Roger looked for ways to stay afloat, even going so far as to consider trying to find a woman who would marry him. After all, he had seen others like him do it. His HLRS friend David Dunhill was the first he discovered – a well-known radio broadcaster and early supporter of the movement who went on BBC television in the 1970s with his wife, Barbara Wilkins, to discuss his homosexuality. After Freda Berkeley casually dropped into conversation 'of course, Lennox is queer', and Heywood Hill suggested a dalliance during a walk in the grounds of his home at Snape, Roger began to see more fluid sexual identities all around him. Apparently, gay men, or at least men who were attracted to men, could find ways successfully to be husbands to wives, he concluded. 'The idea of marriage,' Roger wrote to Lionel, 'and a cosy domestic life daily becomes more attractive.' Eventually, he dropped the subject, deciding it could not possibly work for him, but it was a sign of quite how desperate he had become.

Instead, he struggled on alone and the months became exhausting years:

```
The remorseless daily slog continued . . . the
irksome journeying to and fro, the tedious
work, the never-ending struggle to snatch a few
minutes help from any quarter for shopping,
```

```
the unaccustomed responsibility of keeping a
dog. And all for what? It seemed as if I had
achieved nothing except perpetual bondage, that
I was even more a prisoner of circumstances
than I was before. By 8 o'clock in the evening,
when at last I could claim to be free, I
felt so utterly drained that often I just sat
vacantly listening - or rather, not listening -
to the radio, waiting to stir myself to
something more positive but unable to summon
the energy even to make up my mind.
```

Spending most of his evenings alone, too tired to make arrangements to leave the house, Roger waited mindlessly until he was engulfed by great waves of sleep. Terrified that he would wake up too early and the awful transition from black to white would be extended, he would force himself to stand up and lean against his mantelpiece in an effort to stay awake – only to be jolted awake by the sickening sensation of falling. Sometimes, he would just about manage to check himself. Other times, he wouldn't be so lucky.

```
One way and another it was altogether a quite
absurd, impossible state of affairs. What kind
of a life was this?
```

It took two years of commuting through London, to a job that now bored him, for Roger to begin to come to terms with the reality of his situation: the universal truth to which he had subscribed – that he should at all costs try to live as closely to his sighted life as possible – might not in fact be true.

> Vague, dissident, heretical thoughts were constantly floating about in my head, but all these added up to was a single rhetorical question which kept repeating itself in my mind at moments of inactivity: 'Can I continue like this for the next 30 years of my life?'

In the summer of 1968, Roger took two weeks off work to visit Lionel. The villa at Massa Macinaia had been sold early in 1967 because of Lionel's dwindling resources and he had moved to La Spinetta – a smart, smaller (though by no means small) villa near the village of Arsina. This trip was Roger's first proper break since losing his sight: 'a brief and cheerful interlude which stands out like a blaze of colour in the midst of what now appears like the prevailing greyness of those days.'

Lionel's quietly ordered and extremely secluded way of life was a complete contrast to the heaving activity of London. The visit reminded Roger just how lucky Lionel was to be leading 'a life of the most exquisite cultured ease, reflective, classical, almost Horatian.' Seeing how exhausted Roger was, Lionel made continuous petitions that it didn't need to be this way, reinforcing Roger's growing discontent.

By the time he returned to London, Roger had accepted he couldn't go on as he had, but there was no quick solution to his situation – 'I already knew what the answer must be, but it was absolutely impossible to see how it was to be accomplished.' He tried to imagine the new future Lionel had encouraged him to seek, but life seemed to be beating Roger down from all directions. In the winter of 1968, he heard that Danny had married and would be moving into a new flat in Jerusalem, expecting a baby not long after.

Roger tried a four-day monastic retreat in Prinknash Abbey, at Lennox's suggestion, as well as more trips to Suffolk, but long weekends couldn't save him. And then the panic attacks began. One night, after a dinner in London with John and Sheila Hill, Roger experienced an 'all-consuming agony . . . It was as if a steel corset had been clamped around me and screwed very tight so that I could hardly breathe.'

The attacks continued and Roger knew he had to get out of London. He took leave from work and fled to his parents in Eydon.

He caught the 5.48pm from Paddington. When the train passed Bicester, Roger and Gay had the compartment to themselves. They rattled along through flat, fertile north Oxfordshire countryside – scenery so familiar to Roger in his mind's eye – with a meandering little river, hedge-lined fields with occasional grazing cattle, leafy trees here and there. He relaxed as he felt the warmth of the evening sun strong on the side of his face. Every minute that he sped away from London, it felt as if he was being carried further and further from his problems – and the oppressive insistence that to be happy was to be some generic idea of 'normal'.

Then, as I sat savouring this prospect, an
extraordinary thing happened: I heard a voice

saying, 'You've got to chuck that job!' And with this, all the long agonising was over. It was as if a physical impediment had suddenly been removed. By the time I stepped down onto the platform at Banbury station on that beautiful summer evening, I knew beyond doubt – not in a way that I could have expressed precisely, but in my bones – that the crucial decision had been taken and that it was irrevocable.

London, 2009

Roger felt my move to London like a blow struck, full force. He told me so. A few months spent with my parents in the countryside while I planned my future was understandable, but accepting a job and taking a lease on a flat in London seemed to be decisions that closed off any future with him during the remaining time he might have. 'Stick with me, love,' he'd asked, but I hadn't. I'd left.

I'd wanted to stick with him. I felt I'd done everything I could to stay in Oxford, but without any success. How could I *not* have looked to London? At 26, after so many years of study, after so many years in one city, I couldn't just stop and stand still.

I had no other choice, I reminded myself, but I knew the hurt it caused and was desperate to find ways of being what Roger needed, despite the distance. We spoke on the telephone nearly every day and I visited Oxford whenever I could. Tuesday evenings couldn't resume, of course, but I could manage weekends, and the fast train from Paddington (or, in the worst case, a slow

X90 bus from Baker Street) could even allow for occasional weekday overnight stays at Regent Street.

On some level, Roger was also supportive of what I was doing. He had, after all, moved to London himself as a young man and spent a decade or so there exploring who he was and what he wanted to be. He understood that I needed to grow, to make something of myself – even when the result of that seemed hard to bear.

He tried to stay positive for my sake, encouraging me to make the most of what London offered. He would hear about new productions or concerts on the radio and suggest I try to get tickets and report back to him about them. In the Soho flat, I had theatres and galleries lined up along the neighbouring streets, just a short walk away, but money was an issue, of course. My rent was modest for the size and location of the flat, but what I earned only just covered it.

I was keen to do what Roger was suggesting, though, so I looked around and signed up to all the youth schemes going at the major cultural centres in my part of town. Among the best was 'Access All Arias' (I liked the name) at the English National Opera. It offered people under 30 tickets for £30 to all their shows and invited members in for special talks and tours. The spinning globe on top of ENO's Coliseum (about which I learned lots of interesting facts on one of those tours) was almost visible from my flat, so this was perfect. I booked for most things.

Roger was delighted and often recalled taking the same approach fifty years earlier. One weekend, he showed me some of his souvenirs from that time: a 1955 programme from the

Proms, signed by Malcolm Sargent, who was conducting some
Vaughan Williams; a 1957 programme for *Titus Andronicus* at
the Stoll Theatre, signed by Vivien Leigh and Laurence Olivier
in the leading roles; even a programme from the original West
End run of *Oliver Twist*, which Roger had written about in a
letter to Lionel in the early 1960s, as we'd read together. In fact,
Roger seemed to have kept the programmes from every show
he'd seen during those years. Those which weren't precious were
all stored in an old-fashioned, hard suitcase, placed in a high
cupboard in his bedroom – obviously something he'd kept from
that period, too – the two sprung clips still working perfectly
to reveal the treasure inside.

The object Roger most prized was pulled out of a special folder
when I mentioned to him that I'd been to see a new production
of Benjamin Britten's *Peter Grimes* (which I've seen many times
since). Roger showed me the programme from a 1955 'Museum
Gallery Concerts' series performance at the Victoria and Albert
Museum, which he'd attended when he was 20. It was signed
by the star performers, Benjamin Britten and Peter Pears. 'The
next time I met Pears, of course, was when Benjamin's sister
took me for tea at the Red House in Aldeburgh,' he added with
a smile. Turning to open a folder, he showed me an archive of
letters from when Roger had helped Beth Britten publish a book
about her brother.

At Regent Street, almost nothing had changed. It was, as it
always had been, a place of calm. And so those contrasting, par-
allel worlds I inhabited in London – the whirlwind of Soho and
building my career in Marylebone – were matched by another
part-life, lived with Roger as if I'd never left. In some ways,

the indulgent, peaceful atmosphere of Roger's home was only enhanced by its difference from London: an escape, of sorts, epitomised by a quickly formed habit of running a bath as soon as I arrived on a Friday evening for a weekend (baths being a luxury my London flat didn't afford). Roger would hand me a cold gin and tonic to sit on the shelf that rested on the sides of his bathtub to hold sponges, soap and the like, balanced just above the foaming bubbles, and I would start to feel like a different person.

Reading, recording, talking, drinking, trips into town, lunches out, picnics in the garden – we carried on doing all those things that Roger most enjoyed. And I did everything I could to bring my whole self to Oxford when I was with him, as often as I could. I felt then, as I do now, that it was a privilege to be with Roger while also sustaining something new in London. But being there so often, being there so fully, took effort and energy that seems unfathomable, fifteen years on.

CHAPTER 12

Coming Up

*'I thought, I might as well do what I've always
really secretly wanted to do'[1]*

The main quadrangle of Balliol College seemed to be deserted. Roger was sitting in his study-bedroom, feeling the evening chill through three sash windows that faced towards the college library and beyond to Trinity College next door. He was wondering how to begin his latest essay on a niche aspect of medieval European history when a noise startled him out of his concentration.

Directly in front of his ground-floor windows, Roger heard the opening chords of 'The Red Flag'* ringing out from a piano, which appeared to be moving at some speed from right to left. 'Then there was a burst of laughter from several young men and immediately I realised that the piano was being silently transported on a trolley with rubber tyres.'

A few of the men spotted Roger and broke away to gather

---

* 'The Red Flag' is a socialist song, normally set to the tune of 'O Christmas Tree'. Its opening lyrics 'The people's flag is deepest red, It shrouded oft our martyred dead' have been sung by generations of students, ironically and unironically.

him up and lead him to the far end of college for a meeting of the Balliol College Victorian Society. Members of the society had donned evening dress and one by one stepped up to perform Victorian songs and ballads, dramatic readings and portions of Gilbert and Sullivan operettas. Each was introduced by an impresario sitting behind a table covered with a Union Jack. The port circulated and the company became more boisterous, and as the evening drew to a climax, everyone stood to sing 'Comrades, comrades',* with their arms round each other's shoulders, ending the night with a rendition of the national anthem.

'It sounds dreadful; in fact, it was one of the very best evenings I have spent,' Roger told Lionel in a breathless letter sent during his first Christmas vacation as a university student.

The feeling of relief sweeping over Roger as he sat on the train to Eydon in September 1969 was also an acceptance that, at 34 years old, he could no longer cope with working and living in London, no longer manage to live independently. Becoming blind seemed to have robbed Roger of everything, including the freedom to enjoy any of the benefits of the change in law around homosexuality that he had helped bring about. For three years now, he had been clinging to the life he had built for himself before his operations, but he only had pain and misery to show for it. This was the lowest time he had ever experienced – quite something, given he had once woken up in hospital with the

---

* *Comrades*, for baritone and orchestra, Op. 19 (1905) was familiar to Roger – its melody was composed by Thomas Dunhill, father of Roger's friend David, broadcaster and early campaigner for homosexual law reform.

unexpected loss of sight in one eye, and then a second time with no sight at all.

By the winter of 1970, though, members of the Victorian Society would never have guessed that Roger had so recently emerged from an absolute crisis. The turnaround was amazing, but it was consistent with the same boldness Roger had shown a decade before when he refused to accept that homosexuals should stay hidden in the shadows. Then, he had taken his fate into his own hands and come out. After he arrived in Eydon, he made a decision that was just as pivotal — this time in determining the course of the rest of his life.

Roger initially decided to leave his job by Christmas, but within days of telling his boss he realised he couldn't even continue past the week. He was waved off at a farewell party put on by his co-workers, who gave him record tokens of £6 and 15 shillings, a bottle of gin and a Shetland wool sweater. And that was that. He had a very clear ambition for what he wanted to do next and, a day after the party, committed that wild idea to writing, telling Lionel:

```
So now I'm on the dole - or 'retired' as my
Mother chose to call it - or more precisely,
on sickness benefit. How it's all going to work
out financially and otherwise God alone knows.
For the next few weeks I'm going to take it as
easy as possible: try to rest and relax and
get thoroughly fit in order to start on my new
project - if all goes according to plan - in
the New Year.
```

. . .

    I want, rather belatedly, to go to university
to take a degree with a probable view, ultimately,
to some sort of teaching position. I have not
suddenly snatched this idea out of the air in
desperation: it has had a very long gestation
period - since before I became blind, I think
. . . But I couldn't seriously believe that I would
ever have the guts to really tackle it. But now
the suppressed desire has been prodded by
necessity into positive action.

For most of his life, Roger had believed that his poor sight
precluded an academic career. It was a horrible irony, of which he
was aware, that he was only pursuing the thing he most wanted
because he had become fully blind, and that it would now be
harder than ever. He also understood that there would be no
ready alternative if he suddenly decided he had made a ghastly
mistake: 'Most people can just go and get another job. I can't.
I suppose I have chosen to tackle just about the most difficult
undertaking I could have thought of.' Still, he was resolute. He
was going to find a way to do what Lionel had always encouraged – to make a life he actually wanted.

In the chain of events that made this possible, Roger had had
one lucky break already. At his guide dog course in Leamington
Spa, he was invited to dinner with one of the trainers, while
most of his classmates went out to a performance of *The Sound
of Music* at a local theatre. There Roger met a blind Scot named
Fred Reid, who had recently been made a lecturer in modern

history at the University of Warwick. The encounter transformed Roger's conception of the ambitions he could have as a blind person. 'It was a revelation to learn how he works,' Roger had written to Lionel at the time. 'Now, of course, this has revived the whole business of what can I do. I just can't stagnate in an estate agent's office for the rest of my life.'

When Roger was staying with his parents, he had remembered that meeting and contacted Fred, who suggested Roger come for a drink at his home 20 miles away in Kenilworth. For two hours, the pair talked around the subject over whisky. Fred, Roger felt, was cautious at first, weighing Roger up. But in the end, he came down firmly in favour of Roger's plan to read for a history degree.

Convinced he should proceed, Roger still had little idea of what he needed to do next, beyond assuming he might need some A levels. He didn't know much about how even schoolchildren applied to university – and there didn't seem to be any guidance available for a blind man in his mid-thirties. Hoping to find out more, he wrote to the universities of London, Sussex and Warwick.

With winter approaching, Roger took stock of his new domestic situation – and was now the one worrying about money in his correspondence with Lionel:

```
I have discovered that my financial position
is rather more precarious than I expected it
would be. The Ministry of Social Security are
coughing up only about £6. 10. 0d a week . . .
so with having to spend 30/- a week on feeding
```

```
the dog it doesn't look as if I'm going to get
very fat.
```

By the time noncommittal replies from London and Sussex arrived – and with no response from Warwick at all – Roger could only offer Lettice Cooper bacon and sausages when he invited her for dinner at Hestercombe Avenue.

Roger hadn't said anything yet to Lettice about his hopes of becoming a student, but Lionel had. That night, she was quick to intervene: 'You must go and see my cousin in Oxford. He's Chichele Professor of modern history. He's been there nearly all his life so I'm sure he'll be able to help. I'll write to him.'

Oxford University hadn't seemed to Roger to be a remotely plausible possibility and he began fretting about how a conversation with this cousin might go – an uneducated, clueless former estate agent speaking with an Oxford don. When Lettice forwarded Roger a letter from Professor Ernest Jacob of All Souls College, in which it was suggested that Roger call on him at 2.30pm on Friday 5th December, Roger felt sure that she must have given a very misleading account of his capabilities. In some consternation, he wrote to Professor Jacob directly, detailing his manifold disqualifications, saying he would greatly appreciate any advice he might be able to offer but had no wish to waste his time. The professor replied laconically that he would expect to see Roger on the fifth.

All Roger's hesitancy fell away – and a new path ahead opened up – within minutes of arriving at All Souls. The meeting was, Roger described to Lionel, like a dream, in a setting just as he might have imagined.

He has what must be some of the nicest rooms
in Oxford. We were in a big high room with
windows at each end. It was a clear, cold
afternoon, and in front the room looked over
the main quadrangle to the Radcliffe Camera,
newly restored and gleaming in the brilliant
winter sunshine. The window behind looked over
the gardens of Queen's. (You see I like to be
aware of my surroundings even though I can't
see them.) Everything was still and peaceful:
there was just the quiet voice of the old don,
and once the clock on St Mary's chimed four. I
had the impression that just such an interview
as this could have taken place exactly the same
at any time during the last 250 years since
Hawksmoor built the place.

Professor Jacob was as pleasant as his rooms. He asked Roger
a series of prepared questions, allowing him to talk in detail
about his background and circumstances. Once a full afternoon
tea had been brought in, the conversation moved on, giving
Roger the chance to pull up some obscure knowledge about
T.E. Lawrence, who had been a Fellow of All Souls in the 1920s.
It was clearly going well when the professor discussed Roger's
potential choice of college, and then called a young friend and
history don at Balliol, Maurice Keen.

Keen and Jacob agreed to another meeting with Roger in
the New Year. They asked him to send some written work in
advance, and he supplied a dense piece about the life of John

Henry Newman, and around 10,000 words about his experience of becoming blind. Roger was stunned when Keen concluded the New Year's meeting by asking if he would be willing to come to Balliol for an official admissions interview. He had a chance of entering one of Oxford's oldest, most prestigious colleges.

```
My moods vary between excitement at the
prospect of acceptance and sheer terror of
it. If it comes it will be an opportunity
more fabulous than anything I ever dreamed
possible - Balliol of all places!
```

Three historians and a lawyer met Roger for his interview in February 1970. Gay pranced into the room and greeted everyone before lying down with her back to the company and going to sleep. The panel began by asking if Roger would prefer to read law over history. This, they suggested, would be more practical. It was what most blind people study at university, he was told: more material would be available in Braille and it would offer a clearer pathway into a profession which a blind person could viably perform. The proposal was a warning of the obstacles that lay ahead for him, but Roger had never considered studying law, and the prospect of re-entering an office after his degree was a nightmarish one for him. He dismissed the idea immediately. If he was going to undertake this venture at all, he would do what he wanted to do. For too long, Roger had felt trapped in a life he had not chosen.

The law don left and the interview resumed. It seemed more casual and vague than Roger felt it should. The historians, apparently assured by Roger's work that he had interest and talent, were more concerned with questions about the practicalities of exactly how he would manage to live at Oxford as a blind person. 'All I could say was it had all been done before by others in my position which proved that it could be done.'

The interview ended sooner than Roger had anticipated, so he had an hour to kill before his father arrived to take him to Eydon for the weekend. One of the historians, Richard Cobb, told Roger to stay and have tea. He settled into the sofa and the two started chatting, ranging over topics from the inadequacy of Oxford's railway station to the Empress Eugenie (whose dates Cobb got wrong, Roger smugly noted to himself). Tea turned to sherry and when the time came for Roger and Gay to leave, Cobb shook Roger's hand enthusiastically, adding, 'I hope we shall see you here later.' Roger nervously responded, 'Well, I hope so too!' Realising Roger had missed the implication, Cobb added: 'I think we probably will.'

Days later, Roger received an offer letter, accompanied by an application form. All he had left to do, the letter informed him, was send two notes of recommendation and pass a history A level in June. He called Lettice at once to ask her to write one of the letters, and to thank her. 'As soon as it is absolutely settled – which won't be for some time yet – I am going to take her out for the best slap-up dinner I can find if I have to sell the house to do it,' he told Lionel.

Roger spent the spring cramming for his exam and dashing off intermittent letters to Italy describing his most interesting discoveries, which included encounters with Lionel's ancestor John Fielden during the passage of the Factories Act that restricted

293

the working days of women and young people in textile mills to ten hours. While he beavered away, Roger's excited friends also started to make introductions they thought might be helpful. His former colleague Angela immediately organised a dinner with her brother, Chris Patten, who had come down from Balliol in 1965. Patten's later fame as a politician almost certainly made the memory glow even brighter for Roger, and he recalled a beamingly positive guest who drove him home from Angela's Mayfair flat and dropped him off at Hestercombe Avenue with the assurance: 'You'll like Balliol, it's a very friendly college.'

Lennox Berkeley, who had provided Roger's second note of recommendation to Balliol, was just as keen to share his Oxford connections. He invited Roger to Warwick Avenue to meet Hugh Trevor-Roper, who was Regius Professor of modern history. As the two discussed Roger's plans over dinner, Roger decided the historian had none of the charm of his brother, Pat:

```
His immediate response was, 'Why Balliol?' in
a tone which implied that he didn't think much
of my choice. So I rejoined with, 'May I ask
why not Balliol?' His reply was nothing if not
direct: 'It has a renegade Master, none of
the Fellows live in and the students run the
place.'*
```

---

* After this frosty introduction, Roger and Hugh Trevor-Roper didn't remain in touch. However, when Hugh's sight began to fail him, some thirty years later, he wrote to Roger through Pat, asking for advice about how to manage as a blind person, both generally and as a scholar. The two met in the autumn of 2000 and Roger offered some helpful guidance.

Coming Up

In June, Roger finished his A level papers at home under an invigilator's supervision, and after two months of waiting he could write triumphantly to Lionel with his news.

16th August 1970

My dear Lionel,

Perhaps you'd like to make a note of my change of address. With effect from 8th October it will be: Balliol College, Oxford. So, incredibly, I've made it.

My examination results came through on Wednesday and to my amazement, I found that I had obtained an A pass in the history papers . . . I sent these results straight off to Balliol and received an enormous envelope containing about 40 pieces of paper concerning everything from the number of towels I should take to details of the rugger club (in which I anticipate being a great success).

At the moment, I can't quite think straight about my impending change of life . . . this time last year, I had no idea that I was about to cut myself completely adrift and start life again from scratch.

Roger

Roger's experience at Oxford began beautifully. The tutor for admissions had suggested he come up to Balliol a few days early to settle in before the majority of freshmen moved in on the Thursday. When he arrived with his parents at the porter's lodge, they bumped into Maurice Keen, who showed them all to Room 1 on staircase 12: Roger's new home. He soaked up the quintessential Oxford view from his windows, which he could visualise clearly.

When he was alone, Roger set about exploring, feeling meticulously down one side and up the other, examining each piece of furniture. He found a large, ugly metal wardrobe, a good bed, a re-upholstered chaise longue, a large Victorian writing table, bookshelves, sundry chairs and a handsome chest of drawers (still containing the previous occupant's belongings, for several more days before he came to get them).

```
I got myself organised as best I could and,
after about an hour, began to wonder what would
happen next. Here I had been deposited with no
indication of any other arrangements. Where and
when was I to get anything to eat? Where was
the lavatory? I could hear no one about.
```

If there was ever a moment when he ought to have felt terror, this was it. And immediate practical concerns (Roger later found the toilet was up two twisting, uneven flights of eighteenth-century stairs) were just part of it. Since receiving his offer he had worried about whether he would once again find himself an outsider, too different from the people he would meet here. Hugh Trevor-Roper's description of Balliol, he realised, had touched a nerve. But Roger was determined to be hopeful.

```
I was very conscious - had been all along -
that things might be a little sticky at first.
How difficult would it be for me to fit into
college life? For one thing, I was almost twice
the age of any of my 'contemporaries' - older
even than some of the dons. Then, being blind
and wandering about the place with a huge dog
would make a conspicuous figure (the thing
I hated most of all, but unavoidable). I was
banking on the certainty that, in a community
of some 450, there was bound to be a sufficient
number who would be congenial and who would
not be deterred by my peculiar situation from
striking up an acquaintance.
```

As these thoughts flew about his head, a sharp rap on the door brought a bright, cheery young man into Roger's rooms. Ian Davies, who lived upstairs, offered to take Roger to the college 'buttery' for a drink and then to Hall for dinner. Ian, a second-year student reading PPE – philosophy, politics and economics – initiated Roger into the mystery of how to get onto one of the long benches which might already have half a dozen young men sitting on it. Then they had their rushed three-course meal: fifteen minutes at most for soup, meat and pudding to be set down and cleared away.

A friend of Ian's came and sat down opposite Roger. He was

introduced as Michael Arthur, another second year studying PPE, and also the college music scholar.[*] Michael had characteristics which Roger soon came to associate with an elite public school education: a refined eloquence and a habit of talking very quickly, firing question after question. At the end of dinner, Ian left to play a game of Fives and Michael gave Roger his next experience of college life:

```
. . . that most tempting and time consuming of
all invitations, "Would you like to come back to
my room for a coffee?" True to form, we drank
coffee, ate biscuits and homemade fudge and
drained the last drops from a bottle of port,
talking nineteen to the dozen the whole time.
```

All the port finished, Michael walked Roger out of Balliol, across Broad Street and down to 'The Turl', one of Oxford's hidden pubs, set in part of an old coaching inn. They stayed there for the last hour before closing time. On this very first day as an Oxford undergraduate, in Michael's easy presence, Roger was thrilled by the immediate transformation of his situation.

```
I was enchanted by his exuberance, his
keen interest in everything, his breathless
enthusiasm. It was a miraculous stroke of
```

---

* Sir Michael Anthony Arthur. Michael, a British diplomat until 2010, and his wife Plaxy, remained close friends of Roger. A trip to visit Michael and Plaxy at the High Commission in New Delhi was Roger's final overseas holiday.

fortune that threw me into the path of two such
extrovert and gregarious students within barely
more than a couple of hours of my arrival.

As I lay in bed that night waiting for sleep
and listening to the flat little chimes of the
Trinity clock, I felt thoroughly at home – I
felt, in some indefinable but certain way, that
I already belonged – to a degree that would
have seemed impossible when I got up that
morning.

Those first few days were like a holiday, with the interest and
stimulation of a new place and of constantly meeting new people.
By Thursday, when the other freshmen came up, Roger was so
well settled that for a brief day or two he basked in 'that mild
smugness which goes with even the slightest seniority – with
not being the newest or the last'. He also seemed to be socially
in demand, with a heap of letters on his table waiting for him.
These included a note from the Master of Balliol, Christopher
Hill, inviting Roger to sit with him at high table for the freshmen's dinner on the first evening of term.

Roger knew very little about Hill, an eminent historian of the
seventeenth century, other than Hugh Trevor-Roper's cutting
remarks a few months before and the faint whiff of notoriety
that still clung to him from the days of his membership of the
Communist Party. But that night, Roger felt he had really,
truly arrived – not unlike how he had felt when he entered Len
Smith's living room, and walked into the Fifty Club in Soho as
a younger man.

I put on my respectable business suit and Ian
took me into Hall and left me in my place.
On my right was a South American postgraduate
and for two or three minutes we tried to make
conversation amid the babble of a couple of
hundred voices and the clatter of plates and
dishes. Then I became aware of a slight stir
around me - people were standing up - and
through the hubbub I heard someone say, 'Good
evening, Master.' A second later, Christopher
Hill introduced himself and made the usual
affable enquiry or two. This done he then said,
rather irritably, 'I suppose I'd better say
grace,' and rapped on the table for silence.
'*Benedice benedicat*,' he said perfunctorily and
smartly sat down.

During dinner, he chatted alternately with
me and with his neighbour on the left. There
was nothing remotely pontifical in his manner.
If there was any pose at all - and I suspect
there was just a little - it was the rather
negative one of deliberately playing down the
role of being The Master. At the end of dinner,
he half turned to me and muttered, 'I'm afraid
I've got to make a speech now - pray for me.'
(To whom should I pray, I wondered.) 'I heard it
was a good speech last year,' I replied. 'It'll
be the same one this year,' he answered drily
as he stood up.

Coming Up

The joy of undergraduate life that Roger felt from his first day was at odds with a painful academic experience. That duality hit him almost as quickly as the rush of settling in, when Roger noticed he had no information about when or how his studies would actually begin. By the second week of term, everyone else was writing essays and attending tutorials, and still Roger heard nothing.

> From day to day, I expected a note summoning me to meet my first tutor; or perhaps I might be accosted by a don as I walked through the quad. But nothing happened. I was at a loss to know what to do. In the meantime, I continued to plough doggedly through the very limited range of recorded history books then available, regardless of whether they were likely to have any immediate relevance. There seemed to be nothing else to do. I was becoming seriously perturbed - even embarrassed - by being so strangely ignored.

His tutors appeared to have forgotten about him entirely. In fact, this prolonged silence was a sign of worse to come, and of how little the college was prepared – or cared – about making adjustments for the first blind student of modern history they had admitted within living memory.

Dorset, 2009

Our trips started to get longer and more ambitious after I'd moved to London – I no longer had a doctoral thesis to worry about and could take vacation time from work. We took to staying in rented homes, to allow Roger more agency over the space and to avoid the need to eat too often in restaurants, for which he increasingly lacked the patience (too loud, too difficult, hardly better than what we could manage ourselves, he now said). We opted for the restored, historic buildings of the Landmark Trust – portions of abandoned gatehouses, tumbledown banqueting halls, old towers, that sort of thing – where we would spend long evenings reading books, working through Roger's papers and letters, and talking about his life.

It was on a winter trip to an ancient schoolhouse in Yorkshire, soon after I'd moved to London, that we first shared a bed. And by the time we visited a Palladian hunting lodge in West Sussex the following spring, sharing had become expected – anticipated. Just as Roger had described in that first letter in the pink folder, this was innocently intended – for

late-night reading, conversation, some warmth and companionship. Roger could, he said, always sleep better with me next to
him. When he couldn't sleep, my being there made him happy
and kept him so through the night.

Duly, when I stayed at Regent Street, I was moved to the
large, main bedroom at the front. The double bed faced a thickly
carved blanket box, on which stood a silver-framed studio portrait of Roger's mother, Doris (Roger, he told me one night, had
been the photographer). 'Just for cuddles and company' was a
narrative Roger sustained, and to which he mostly stuck. When,
on occasion, his hands wandered and a cuddle wasn't everything
he wanted, I didn't stop him. What was the harm? Why not
give him this, rather than hurting him more than I already had
by moving away?

Perhaps I had more choice than I realised, but I felt a respon-
sibility to do all those things Roger wanted – and I wanted to
give as much as I was able to a man who had spent so many years
enriching my life. I did what I could to make his remaining time
happy. In almost every other way, Roger's days were increasingly
bleak, as he spent more and more time visiting hospitals and
dealing with a growing number of medical complaints. He had
prostate problems, new lumps around his lymph nodes, pains
in his mouth – and he seemed never to get a good night of
sleep. The persistent, disorienting transition between black and
white that had stopped him sleeping ever since he lost his sight
was getting worse. On top of that, he had physical pains from
which he could rarely find relief at night. The only thing, Roger
said, that made him really, truly happy and gave him comfort

was being with me, next to me, listening to me sleeping nearby, oblivious ('purring', he called it).

Back in London, my six-month contract had been made permanent and I took on a specialist position, once again working in research. Eventually, I had to move out of 167 Charing Cross Road when the whole area was designated for demolition (I recently went to see the stage production of *Brokeback Mountain* at the theatre they built there, sitting almost exactly where my flat would have been), but I found a room in a beautiful, if crumbling, Pimlico house owned by Maria, a motherly, bohemian artist.

In many ways, I was thriving, but the pull back to Regent Street was also strengthening and, encouraged by Roger, I started to wonder whether I could spend part of each week in Oxford. Doing that would make it easier for me to turn my doctoral thesis into a book, and also enable more frequent and reliable stays with Roger, without giving up my London lodgings. I spoke with my employer about it, but fixing that kind of an arrangement wasn't proving easy. It would take more time. Roger suggested I look instead for some other work, in Oxford – a subject he brought up whenever we met. I could, he said, live with him on any basis I wanted, if I came to Oxford.

This pattern continued until one evening, while I was visiting my family in Dorset for Christmas, Roger took the conversation one step further.

During one of our daily telephone calls, he began again the discussion about how I could find a way back to Oxford. I suppose by then I was getting a little frustrated, and perhaps Roger could tell from the tone of my voice. I was trying my best to live a life of my own while also being and doing what I could for Roger – even trying to find a way to change my job. What more could I do?

'What if we get married?' he said, casually. 'It needn't be more than a quick register office job, just the two of us there. It would solve a lot of problems.'

It caught me off guard. Roger presented the idea breezily, as if it had just popped into his mind, shared almost in passing, as if marriage were nothing at all and required no further thought. Was it really a serious question, expecting an answer? It was an unromantic proposal, certainly, and as Roger continued to think out loud it became more so.

Marriage – a civil partnership, as it was for same-sex couples in 2009 – would, he said, save the house he loved from being sold off and chopped up into student flats. I could live there with him and take it on when the time came, without paying inheritance tax. His beloved possessions would have a home for another half-century. What, he speculated out loud, if we could find a way to give me some security and avoid all that dismantlement of his legacy? When he died, I could just continue in situ and take over his life at Regent Street.

I understood with total clarity, even then, in that moment, that there was more to the suggestion than Roger's prosaic description implied. Roger loved me. He wanted to find a way for us to be together for as long as he had remaining, and to make sure I was looked after when he had gone. The proposal was an act of love, but he couldn't quite bring himself to say it, and I simply did not know how to respond.

Had Roger presented the idea another way, had he asked

directly, pushed for an answer, I expect I would have given one, though I can't say now what that answer would have been. Could I just give everything up to move to Oxford, no doubt to become Roger's de facto carer as he faced the inevitable consequences of his cancer? Could I give up on the idea of having a husband at the same stage of life as me? Was Regent Street where I was meant to be for the rest of my life, as it had been for Roger when he finished his studies at Balliol?

These questions flooded my mind – impossible, unanswerable questions, they seemed – and so I flinched in the face of Roger's suggestion. I stumbled. Aware of all it meant, but unsure of how to respond, unsure of how to feel about his question, I shrugged it off as if he hadn't really meant it: 'Well, we're pretty much a married couple as it is.' I stopped at that. Treating it as breezily as Roger had brought it up seemed easier in the moment than facing the magnitude of what Roger was trying to say.

So, just as quickly as it came up, the matter was dropped. 'Think about it, love,' he said and started on some other topic, as if such a serious and devastating exchange had never occurred.

CHAPTER 13

Catching Up

*'the fulfilment of the nearest thing to an
ambition that I've ever had'*[1]

After two terms, Roger returned to Oxford from the Easter
vacation to take 'collections': college exams to test his progress.
He was given a special room, with a typewriter and an individual
invigilator, who read the questions to Roger at the start of the
allotted three hours. Roger had been given no indication of what
he would be asked to do beforehand, and to his horror he found
he had absolutely no idea how to answer.

Roger's grasp of the subject matter was so hopelessly inadequate that he did not know how to begin the three essays
expected of him. This, he found, prevented him even from being
able to type properly on the page. He started to write, driven
by the demon of desperation, but the mental effort of trying to
scrape together enough to fill a few sheets meant he had to stop
frequently to think of anything to say – as a result, forgetting
what he had written already. He was aware he was answering
flippantly and began to feel that he was only humiliating himself
by writing more. He wished that he'd just walked out at the start

instead and as he handed in the papers, he supposed his terrible performance wouldn't go unnoticed.

He was right. Roger was summoned to a meeting to discuss his 'academic progress'. Just before 2pm on the appointed day, he made his way to staircase 3 in the front quad of Balliol, up some bleak, echoing stone stairs, and along a corridor to a distant and cheerless room. There, he faced a grim trio: the senior history tutor, a research Fellow filling in for Maurice Keen, and the tutor in seventeenth-century history who appeared to Roger to be far more at home in that period than the present one.

```
Gloom enveloped the room like a November
fog, seeming to accentuate its normal deathly
stillness. I was on the defensive, recognising
from the outset that this was going to be,
if not exactly a post mortem, certainly one
of those consultations with specialists who
privately know the patient is doomed and
already have him written off in their minds.
```

The senior history tutor led the conversation, which dragged stiffly between long, uncomfortable silences. It was obvious that the three men in front of Roger were hoping he would admit defeat, do the honourable thing and leave Balliol for some more appropriate venture than his obviously failed attempt to make it as an undergraduate at Oxford.

This terrible scene was the almost inevitable conclusion of the neglect Roger had experienced during his first two terms at

Balliol. After a fortnight of waiting to be told when his academic work would begin while others busily got underway, someone finally remembered that something might need to be done – apparently even then only by chance.

```
I was on my way to dinner in Hall when
I became aware of the sound of running
footsteps - the sharp metallic clatter of steel-
tipped shoes - approaching from my left and
then the unmistakable voice of Maurice Keen -
highly refined, hesitant, every word carefully
considered and precisely articulated. 'Roger!
I'm glad to have - er, er - caught you. Perhaps
we ought to - er, er - arrange for a tutorial
within the next - er, er - day or two. How
about - er - 11 on Saturday morning?'
```

All their early tutorials – intensive, individual discussions on a subject about which Roger would be told to write an essay in advance – were in Keen's smoke-filled, hermetically sealed little room on staircase 21. The floor and chairs were strewn with books and papers, while the traffic roared outside on St Giles' street. Roger found himself incongruously thrust back to the eleventh century, to knight service, feudal land tenure, investiture crises, the *Leges Henrici Primi* and the complexities behind the Becket struggle. He was completely out of his depth.

Roger's wasn't an uncommon experience with Oxford's sink-or-swim pedagogy. Like many students who hadn't arrived fresh from public school, he was nervous that admitting he couldn't keep up was, in effect, saying he didn't belong there – and he desperately wanted to belong there.

And for Roger there was an additional challenge which made his situation close to impossible: he could not access the necessary books even to begin to learn how to keep afloat. His was a degree that revolved around reading large quantities of scholarly work each week, writing essays which drew conclusions from the assigned material and then defending his essays in tutorials against challenges posed by the experts in his field. Roger lacked the core resources for that process and yet nobody seemed to notice. Speaking up seemed out of the question, not least because he'd told his interviewers he was sure he could find a way to make things work.

Books available as audio recordings were mostly general, popular histories, and those that were offered in Braille were even more elementary and inadequate. The academic texts he really needed to read were only available in print, sometimes in libraries from which they could not be removed. To make any progress, Roger realised, he was entirely dependent on other students offering to read to him or record onto a cassette from those books, and that was nowhere near enough, he told Lionel desperately.

```
It just isn't satisfactory from any point of
view to rely entirely on people's good will.
After all, they have their own work to do and
they want to enjoy their free time, and it's
not right that I should undertake this sort
of venture on the implied basis that other
```

```
people will continually put themselves out on
my behalf. That so many do is remarkable, but I
never feel that I can ask anyone, but must wait
until help is offered. Consequently, the real
problem is getting things done in time.
```

Roger thought about paying for readers, but calculated it would cost a couple of hundred pounds a year – money he didn't have to spare.

```
In fact, I can't afford it as things are . . .
my grant is assessed to cover the six academic
months of the year and I still don't know how
I'm going to survive for the other six months,
since I'm hardly in a position to take jobs
during the vacation as most of the others here
do.
```

A lack of reading material was compounded by several other limitations. Roger couldn't look up references. He couldn't rummage through notes to find a vital quote, name or date. He couldn't see his work in front of him and reconsider whether and how to rearrange it. He did what he could to produce something to discuss at his tutorials each week, but all these hurdles made it close on impossible to write anything with academic rigour or even to have anything insightful to say to his tutors. Instead, he found himself sitting one-on-one, for an hour, unable to answer almost any of their questions.

```
It was like trying to make bricks without
straw. I managed to produce essays more or less
regularly, but these never amounted to anything.
I grieve now over all those lost tutorials. So
many valuable and irretrievable opportunities
missed because I was always so ill-prepared. I
can understand only too well how frustrating it
must have been, even for the most sympathetic
tutor - just as it was for me - to be confronted
regularly by such an unresponsive audience.
```

None of Roger's tutors had experience of working with a blind student. They might have been forgiven for not anticipating his needs, but don't appear to have asked whether he needed help once he had started, or to have considered that he was flailing for reasons he could not resolve on his own. It was taken for granted that if he had come this far, Roger ought now to be able to cope with a system designed, as it was, without him in mind. If he didn't make a fuss, everything must be all right.

Despite the intractable problems he was facing, the exhilaration Roger felt at being in Oxford beams through the letters to Lionel he dashed off in snatched moments among the activity and excitement of it all. He was struck, daily, by his good fortune and dramatic change in circumstances, and by the first Christmas vacation, he still declared:

```
I've loved every second of it. I can't imagine
ever being anywhere else. If only one didn't
```

have to sleep – and there were 48 hours in
every day!

Roger wrote with an elation similar to his descriptions of
London's gay underground a decade earlier, another time of nov-
elty and wide-eyed joy at everything unspooling before him. Just
as the HLRS had been Roger's entry to a different life, Balliol
offered him something totally new, unexpected and wonderful,
in the warm embrace of fast friends.

Roger's room was perfectly placed to ensure he built a social
life that exceeded his greatest expectations. He had a front-row
seat onto any student activity and was in the path of all who
came and went – 'a sitting duck for any passer-by with a problem
to unburden or half an hour to idle away. A tap on the door and
all work suspended.' It didn't help with his academic struggles
but he loved the easy, casual companionship of college life.

Arriving at Balliol, Roger had half expected to find himself dropped in to an ideologically charged community. Hugh
Trevor-Roper's barbed review of the college reflected how central
it had been during the student unrest of the 1960s, which was
only just petering out at the start of this new decade. Balliol had
a reputation for socialist leanings and Roger anticipated 'highly
political students, earnest and vociferous, all thoroughly versed
in their Marx and Mao, among whom I would be right out of
my depth'.

In fact, Roger found that the traditional, charmed, *Brideshead
Revisited* image of student life was dominant at Balliol (where
the idea that they might admit female students was considered
radical until they did it in 1979). He was relieved. A decade on

from the youthful bravado of his HLRS days and preoccupied by the effects of his deteriorating sight, Roger had lost most of his interest in political activism. He had also been strongly influenced by his growing circle of establishment friends in London and Suffolk, and getting to Balliol represented for him a way to be part of their world on equal terms.

Batting off approaches from enthusiastic Bible study circles and Junior Common Room politicos, Roger quickly found his people in the gentler, more romantic expressions of student life. Those included the Arnold and Brackenbury: 'one of the most exclusive of college societies', Roger noted proudly when reporting back to Lionel – an ostensible debating group to which he had been unusually invited as a freshman. Smartly printed invitation cards were sent out to members of the college who were deemed suitable, requiring them to wear a dinner jacket and bow tie. But the dress code was about the only convention that seemed to apply:

> Some attempt was made to conduct the
> proceedings with mock formality, but as the
> port and madeira circulated liberally around
> the table, the spirit of misrule soon took
> over. As far as any attempt at debating went,
> the object was to disrupt this as much as
> possible.

After a few meetings, and as he came to know more of the members, Roger began to learn the put-downs, the subtexts and the hidden jibes that were cleverly woven into each of the speeches, and even to join in the boisterous jeers and heckling. It all would have sounded ridiculous to the outsider, he knew, but Roger had found himself, for this moment, part of a group intending to take careers in the upper ranks of Britain's public institutions. These evenings, he understood, were preparation – 'a kind of training in verbally holding your own and trying never to be upstaged'. For Roger, the highlight was their gathering on the last evening of term:

```
About 40 of us sat down to dinner in Hall
and I think it must have looked rather fine.
Again, dress suits, of course, with the college
silver and only candlelight. This meant we were
a little pool of light in that great barn of
a Hall, with only the pictures dimly showing
and the high roof completely invisible in the
blackness. We had a superb six course dinner,
followed by some rather pointless speeches.
```

Every day, Roger delighted in his surroundings. In the main quad of Balliol, he could hear bells ringing out from most of the Oxford colleges, infusing each quarter hour with an atmospheric backdrop as well as helping him to order his days – telling him when to get ready for Hall, when to head to lectures and when to take Gay out for a late toilet run. And every day, he found himself surrounded by intelligent and charming men, who included Roger in their lives, were interested in his opinions, took him out for a fry-up breakfast and curry dinner on his birthday, and invited him along on all sorts of adventures.

From time to time Roger stumbled across sexual opportunities at Oxford (including a brief, highly charged encounter
with a college porter just a few days after coming up). It's
obvious from how Roger wrote about some of his closest male
companions at Balliol that for him, and perhaps for them,
some of these relationships were also infused with a spark of
sexual attraction. But that, apparently, is as far as it went with
his college friends.

```
Miles (who is enchanting, I must say) asked me
if I would like to go to a small party out at
Garsington where two or three of the chaps have
a cottage. So we all piled into a Land Rover
and off we went. Here we sat around rather
listlessly talking and drinking brandy while
John played Kurt Weill on the piano. At two
o'clock, Miles said to me, 'Would you like to go
for a walk?' And so with two or three others,
we set out across the fields to Garsington
church with Gay darting about alongside and
Miles with his arm around my shoulder (which
was very pleasant). It was a beautiful night,
clear and cold, but absolutely still. I finally
rolled back into college at half past three.
```

As Roger stood in front of his grim tribunal of history dons at
his collections, then, he was unwilling to give all this up to make
their lives easier.

```
They hoped, I was sure, that I would admit
defeat and do the gentlemanly thing - fold
my tent and quietly steal away. But I was not
disposed to be gentlemanly: I had not come
this far to give up without a struggle. If they
wanted me to go they would have to throw me out.
```

Roger knew that they had written him off in their own minds, but refused to agree that he was entirely to blame for his lack of progress. Nobody with the authority and the capacity to make a difference seemed to know what to do, and so nothing positive was achieved in that room. Presented with Roger's report, Christopher Hill simply mumbled, 'It must be bloody difficult, I don't know how you manage at all.'

After the meeting, Roger made his way straight to the rooms of Richard Cobb, the man who had entertained him after his entrance interview and who had subsequently proposed himself as Roger's 'moral tutor' – the academic designated to oversee his teaching and general welfare. Cobb had hosted Roger for several convivial dinners at his home, but the subject of his difficulties studying had never come up.

Now, Roger desperately needed his help. Cobb vowed to stop the senior tutor and others at Balliol from trying to remove Roger from college – an assurance that allowed Roger to continue into the term without fear of immediate expulsion – but Cobb didn't know how to dismantle Roger's more fundamental academic obstacles. Instead, Roger's academic salvation came completely by chance, when his third-term tutorials were scheduled with Angus Walker, lecturer in Russian thought. Walker

distinguished himself from the outset by asking to visit Roger
rather than expecting Roger to go in search of him.

He was a big man, more or less my own age I
guessed (rightly), with a vigorous, forceful,
highly-charged personality. His manner was
direct and business-like, but pleasant with it.
He sat down and straightaway began to cross-
examine me intensely with a quick succession
of plain, straight-to-the-point questions - What
was my background? Why had I embarked upon
this mad enterprise? How was I getting on? He
appeared not to be predisposed to believe that
I was bound to be an impossible case.

Walker became Roger's new champion. He began by insisting
that there was nothing intrinsically wrong with Roger's capa-
bility, merely that he was bedevilled by what Walker drily
described as 'technical difficulties'. He recognised that while
Roger was dependent on volunteers to read to him, he was also
reluctant to ask anyone for help, and decided that this must
come from a lack of practice. Not having grown up blind or
even having been blind for long before entering Balliol, Roger,
Walker concluded, hadn't learned how to fight through a world
designed for sighted people. 'Your trouble is,' he would say to
Roger, 'you're not a professional blind man – you're a sighted
man who happens not to be able to see.'
Walker designed a simple weekly time chart, divided
horizontally into the days of the week and vertically into a

certain number of working hours. Roger was to recruit a team of volunteer readers, scheduling them to read to him using the chart. This was to be placed permanently on Roger's desk so that anyone who visited his rooms could see where help was needed and commit then and there to a specific time.

It worked. Gradually, a bank of regular and reliable readers emerged, momentum built, and a smooth operation was established, meaning Roger could actually read the required materials for each week's essay. It kept him going through his second year, and a third, and to reach his goal of sitting his final examinations.

Having readers didn't solve all of Roger's problems. Note-taking remained difficult. Essays were hard to construct. There was no time to read more than the essential literature each week. He had missed much of his first year of learning. And, in the end, he had to opt out of one paper because it required too much reading, a decision that would automatically limit his end result to third class honours.

As his final exams ('Schools') began, though, Roger savoured a moment he never dreamed would be his.

```
The first morning of Schools opened crisp and
dry and perfectly still; and as I came down
the Hall steps after breakfast, the first
glint of sunshine was just breaking through
the early morning mist and touching the top of
the cupola on the Sheldonian in the distance
beyond Trinity chapel. By mid-morning the mist
```

```
had cleared completely away, and these lovely,
brilliant days - never too hot - continued
throughout the exam period and beyond. The
weather, the occasion, the activity, the
culmination of three years, the slight tinge of
danger - there was undoubtedly electricity in
the air.
```

It had been decided that Roger should not actually write his papers in the Examination Schools building with everyone else. Instead, he did them from his own room, with an invigilator present each day and an amanuensis to type as he spoke. He found this method of writing especially difficult, not least because he became self-conscious about what the invigilator might think of his answers. His invigilators also tended to cause as many problems as they solved. One day, the Dean of Balliol forgot to turn up and on another, a Miss Livingstone spent the three hours stuffing circular letters into envelopes and dropping each one onto the floor as she went. Roger tried to embrace the same traditions as the other students, most of all by dressing up in sub fusc, the required uniform for exam-taking at Oxford. He made a point of showing the obligatory dark socks to his invigilator each day before beginning.

When the exams were over, Roger allowed himself some satisfaction that he had made it: 'at least I had managed to stay the course – which was more than some of my contemporaries had done.' After a nervous wait to hear whether he would need to take a viva, Roger received notice that he had achieved his third class degree.

```
On the one hand, I was glad to have pulled it
off at all; on the other, I was maddened and
frustrated by the belief - by the knowledge
even - that I really had a much better
potential and had failed to reach it.
```

However conflicted Roger was, he kept the letters celebrating what he had accomplished, from Christopher Hill, Maurice Keen, Richard Cobb – and Angus Walker.

6th August 1973

Dear Roger

... I hope you will forgive a magisterial word as the last vestiges of my *status tutoris* slip from my shoulders and you become a senior member of the university. Your letter and your comments over the last year *a propos* of the degree breathe an air of resignation and a sort of elegiac regret for what might have been ... The point is, given time and experience, you could have got a better degree – no, that is not the point even – the point is, that, blind, inexperienced, mature student, without much help or encouragement, you got a degree from Balliol in a very distinguished year where you know that no one was your intellectual superior. I am very pleased – I do not congratulate you – I should have been very disappointed if you had let me down ... if you try and measure yourself by the ephemeral standards of the ex-Winchester undergraduates you will have a totally false impression of your own abilities and then you will not go on to blossom and exploit your talents in the way that I very earnestly hope that you will . . . So, no elegies please, start writing. I think you may be the most distinguished man of your year . . .

Yours,

Angus

Roger's vivid accounts of his time at Balliol in the regular letters he sent to Tuscany received fewer and fewer replies as those years went on. Lionel's health was deteriorating rapidly and the messy, handwritten letters he now sent were dominated by his woes. But alongside his self-pity, Lionel praised what Roger was doing: putting himself on the path to a different life from the one to which he had been born, just as Lionel had always told him to do. Roger recalled Lionel's encouragement as he wrote one more time to his friend.

The frustration of trying to work under my
conditions reduced me at times to the point
of wanting to throw things about the room,
knowing - really knowing - how much more and
how much better I really could do everything.
There, under my nose, were all the amenities
and facilities yet they were forever just out
of reach. Nevertheless, in spite of that, it's
been a tremendous experience in far more ways
than the merely academic . . .

You once rather nicely called it my 'catching
up' and, indeed, I am conscious of having
profited in umpteen different [ways] and caught

```
up a good deal . . . Above all, I've done what
I always wanted to do - I've read history at
Oxford. Not a great ambition you may think,
but most people never get the opportunity
to achieve even such a modest ambition as
that . . . There's no doubt that my last year
in Balliol was the happiest of all. Perhaps the
happiest year I've ever spent.
```

It was the Victorian Society that left Roger with the most enduring memory from that last year of his later-in-life, wholly unexpected, student days. Hours after finishing his last exam, Roger made his way with members of the society, conspicuous in evening dress, to the river: down St Aldate's, along narrow pavements abutting sandstone walls and the gothic arches of Tom Tower, past the perfect green lawns that led to Christ Church meadow and to Folly Bridge. There they embarked onto one of Salter's classic pleasure boats, which chugged gently along the Isis, past college boathouses, riverside pubs and the medieval village of Iffley.

The gathered crowd became slowly merrier as they drank port and madeira and luxuriated in the early evening sun. Performers in white tie and tails boomed out their words in voices trained in the chapels of England's public schools. Popular ballads – 'I've Been to a Marvellous Party', 'A Nightingale Sang in Berkeley Square' – were mixed with vulgar music hall ditties, accompanied by a student playing a piano wheeled up onto the boat using the same contraption that had taken it past Roger's windows a few years earlier.

The boat slid into Sandford Lock and the opening bars of 'Excelsior' were struck for the closing set-piece duet, about a young man who climbed a mountain through snow and ice, bearing a banner with a strange device. Customers of a pub nearby looked on at the spectacle in bemusement while, as the well-blended tenor and baritone voices rose to the final 'EX-CEL-SIOR', the lock gates slowly swung open and the party sailed on into the sunset.

Oxford, 2010

The winter of 2010 was bitterly cold. In the lead up to Christmas, I attended an advent carol service at the University Church with some friends (Oxford contemporaries, mostly now visiting from London), swigging miniatures in the gallery for warmth. The conductor was an ex-boyfriend of mine, whom Roger had known existed but never discussed, and we all poured into a bar across the High Street to celebrate with him when it was over.

I struggled to join in. In those last few weeks of 2010, I was staying mostly at Roger's house, trying to help him live well, trying to bring some joy into his days, while – more and more – doing my best to manage the gruesome effects of his medication. In the end, his grim predictions had been correct. Cancer had spread to his prostate, then to his bones, and by now he was in continual pain, always tired and slowly losing control of his body. So it was difficult to feel festive in the bar of the Old Bank Hotel with Roger so ill, and difficult to stay away while he suffered alone in his house, so close by. I decided to leave them to it.

As I said my farewells, one or two friends teased me for

327

still, years on, being the one to go early, yet again disappearing away to visit my mysterious blind man. It was gently done but it jarred. I was reminded how little they knew about Roger; how little I had ever really shared with anyone about who he was to me and who I was to him. But by this point, where would I start?

So, I smiled, took it on the chin and left. The buses to East Oxford were hardly running in that weather and there was too much ice on the roads to cycle, so I walked slowly back to Regent Street along pavements covered in layers of frozen snow, struggling to appreciate any beauty in this white-lined version of Oxford. As I trudged, I wondered why I had kept those friends at such a distance from the person who had shaped my life more than anyone for most of the preceding decade. I don't think I ever planned for it to be that way, but – in truth – it worked out easier for me to keep these spheres of my existence separate from one another. When I was with Roger, I realised fairly early on, I was wholly and only with him, just as he was wholly and only with me.

There were certainly never lies, but there were aspects of my life which Roger didn't want to hear about and which I knew I should avoid mentioning. Perhaps there were parts of his life he kept hidden from me, too. He was always realistic about the fact that I would have boyfriends – but ultimately, this was a benign avoidance for the sake of everyone's happiness. There could be an edge to conversations when I mentioned close friends or flatmates, men in particular, who (whatever my actual relationship to them) might represent a potential threat, draw me away from him, give me another reason not to return to Oxford. It was easier not to talk about them and to lean in to his joke that all of my friends seemed to be lesbians. Whatever else was happening in my life, Roger needed to feel he was my priority and to be reassured of that by me. Walking to Regent Street through the snow, walking away from a group of friends and towards Roger was, I suppose, a final demonstration that I was living up to that commitment. I was for Roger. And Roger was waiting for me, waiting to be cared for by me.

After a quick trip to Dorset, I shared the Christmas ritual Roger had described to me all those years earlier, before I had left for the vacation at the end of our first term together – before that first kiss. His Regency dining table was pulled out, expanded and laid. His mother's green embroidered napkins, highly starched, were taken from the chest of drawers and placed neatly down. The wine glasses we had bought together a few years before were filled. We ate sausages. We listened to the radio. We pulled crackers and wore hats.

We toasted the New Year together, drinking port Roger had sent me to find in his cellar a couple of days earlier, which he had been saving for a special occasion.

I couldn't go back to London and leave Roger, and work was understanding. I was treated sympathetically and given the time away that I needed. They were good people. Under the circumstances, they told me, I was in the right place.

We continued to read, right up to the end, in the same way we always had, me now pouring gin and tonic for us both before sitting down together and opening Roger's binders.

When the little turbo-prop plane from Milan . . .

Over the years there have been moments . . .

"You'll like Balliol" . . .

Naturally, it's depressing . . .

That awful line: it came up again and again as we navigated Roger's collection.

I shall go to my grave without ever having known the joy of a completely fulfilling relationship.

This grim summary had always been hard to hear, and became worse as our relationship grew in its complexity. As I watched Roger living out his last days, reading aloud his own dismal conclusion was almost impossibly heart-wrenching.

CHAPTER 14

Marking Time

'I'm just penned into a corner, and there I am stuck'[1]

Roger spent his last afternoon at Balliol on a wooden bench at the top of the college's main quadrangle, with a mug of tea and some peanut butter sandwiches he'd bought from the Junior Common Room. He was speaking only intermittently with the two students sitting beside him. The overcast, sultry afternoon induced a general feeling of lassitude and the few people left were drifting about the quad. The gaps in conversation lengthened, leaving Roger to his own inner thoughts.

```
Now, sitting under the chestnut tree, I reflect
on the three years that have passed. Have I
made the most of this opportunity? What have
I got out of it? Has it made any significant
difference to my way of thinking? I guess it
will need time - a measure of distance and
detachment - to get it all into perspective.
All that seems to matter at this moment is that
I've done it, simply that I've come through ...
What I wanted as much as anything when I
```

came here was simply the overall university
experience, to feel that I hadn't altogether
missed out.

So there it is. The party's over now. Time to
move on. I can hear a familiar metallic clanking
sound at the far end of the quad and Pete Long
emerges from the library passage pushing one of
the college luggage trolleys across to Staircase
12. I stand up and bid a rather perfunctory
farewell to Andrew and Duncan - we vow to keep
in touch and I walk down to join Pete. We pile
all my belongings onto the trolley, I pull the
door shut behind me for the last time on the
room which has been my home for nearly three
years and follow Pete across the front quad and
out through the Lodge to where he has parked
his car in the Broad.

Most of Roger's friends had already 'gone down' in the days
before him, scattered across the country, preparing to settle
into their bright futures. Many would be heading to London
but Roger, now approaching 40, had decided the capital was no
longer for him.

The thought of having to struggle again, day
in and day out, with all that traffic and the
distances to be covered to get anywhere was a
nightmare. What was the point?

So, with Gay perched on the back seat between Roger's luggage, Pete only had to drive for ten minutes and approximately two miles: around Longwall Street, across the Magdalen Bridge and up the Iffley Road to the top end of Regent Street, and Roger's new home.

At the beginning of his third year in college, Roger had written to Lionel explaining that he'd put in an offer on a house: 'Such is my determination to stay in Oxford that I thought I might as well get on with it.' An £11,950 freehold later, Roger took possession of 41 Regent Street in February of 1973. It was only two streets away from where the Second World War had deposited him as a child, which he thought boded well. At the end of the summer, Roger wrote again – the first letter from his new home.

```
I live in one room on the top floor with a
large table, a bookcase, a very comfortable
bed, two folding chairs and a telephone. At
the furthest point from here is a large and
rather fine kitchen leading onto the garden.
The rest is bare boards and more or less empty
rooms . . . I'm pleased to learn that the top
of Magdalen tower is just visible from the top
room - like a seaside boarding house which has
a distant glimpse of the sea.
```

Roger had perched himself in East Oxford rather than the Tuscan hills. His view was across rooftops to the bell tower, rather than across fertile fields towards the campanile of an ancient parish church. But these were variations on a theme – so changed by his experience at Massa Macinaia during the spring of 1962, Roger imagined a new home and life that would emulate Lionel's as closely as possible.

Lionel, by now, was struggling more and more, but Roger's letters continued to tell his old friend that his own best days were still ahead. His university experience had been his chance to change everything, even to become a different kind of person. At Balliol, Roger had been part of an elite establishment, joined parties reminiscent of the *fin de siècle*, and walked the ancient halls of colleges surrounded by their famous dreaming spires. He had experienced for himself, for a few brief years, the privilege and the leisure into which Lionel had been born, the rich and easy company of a cultured and educated circle, and he wanted it to continue.

Roger's decision to do everything he could to live like Lionel started with making his house a place of peace and beauty – and he had great plans for Regent Street. He spent autumn and winter decorating every room of the house in the most elegant manner it would allow (and which he could afford), until he could announce proudly to Lionel in February 1974: 'Altogether now the house is rather fine and generally admired.'

With his home established, Roger began to build up a flow of volunteer readers to come to Regent Street, in part just to help him with daily administration. Some were people who had read for him at Balliol. Others were new contacts made through them, his friends or local networks. Given how transient the Oxford population could be, the recruitment process never really stopped.

His plans were starting to come together.

```
All I need now is a congenial job and an
equally congenial boyfriend to look after me
and my new home. Not much to ask!
```

Roger's aspirations did not include building a new career. Even with an Oxford degree, he nurtured no ambitions to enter any kind of rat-race. 'I really don't fancy at all the idea of a regular, established job,' he told Lionel, adding that with the proceeds of the sale of his Fulham house, he might not need one.

```
I calculate that I can afford to jog along
without any sort of commitment until at least
the end of the year. In fact, the government,
through the beneficence of its tax laws, may
compel me out of sheer self-interest to lead a
life of happy idleness.
```

Eventually, he used his Oxford contacts for references and registered with some local tutoring agencies, taking on his first private students soon after. Whatever he thought of his academic achievement, a degree enabled Roger to coach older schoolchildren and some undergraduates – their numbers ebbing and flowing – giving him an income for the next thirty years.

In 1973, it also seemed like the last piece of the puzzle had presented itself: the boyfriend. Luke was a college friend who had travelled abroad after finishing at Balliol.

```
He wasn't bad looking, so I was led to believe,
in the English public schoolboy way, ...
```

speaking in a quiet, slightly clipped manner.
He had quite a sharp humour as well as a quick
intelligence and could put away a surprising
quantity of hard liquor with little noticeable
effect. All things considered, I was surprised,
having already been in the college for two
years, that he should suddenly have chosen to
attach himself to me. Although perfectly amiable,
he had made no other particular friend. Somehow,
we discovered an unexpected rapport and we were
soon spending much of our spare time together.

In the winter, Luke turned up on Roger's doorstep, back in
England and trying to work out what he wanted to do next.
He took a temporary job on a building site and Roger invited
him to move in. Roger's Christmas Eve letter to Lionel glowed:
'The set-up with Luke is almost too good to be true: I can
hardly believe my luck.' At Regent Street, their lives fell into a
rhythm around each other. Luke kept regular, office-type hours,
leaving the house just before nine each morning and returning
around six, when Roger would pour drinks. Roger found himself
waiting for that moment every day, 'for the only time in my life
counting the hours until I would hear his key in the lock and
feel the comfort of knowing he was back. On the face of it, we
might have been made for each other.'

I'm tempted to think that it's the best
relationship, in its way, that I've ever had –
and I only wish it could go on for ever. In

```
numerous practical ways it makes my life 100
times easier to have him around; but he is as
well the most congenial of companions.
```

Roger felt the bliss of cosy domesticity – it seemed as if they both did. Luke embraced *Mastering the Art of French Cooking* and Roger began showing him off to his friends, reporting their busy social schedule to Lionel in February 1974.

```
I do hope Lettice will manage to get here
before Easter. As often happens with such
arrangements, there was rather a congregation
in the course of one week. And it was rather
a high-powered assembly, all told. We had the
Hampshires to dinner one evening, the Halls
the next.* Then Lennox Berkeley came on his
own to lunch last Sunday as he was spending
the weekend near Thame. And finally, so far, we
had my archaeologist friends the Sinclair Hoods
from Great Milton.† Not to mention, squeezed in
between, one of Luke's many brothers. Luke has
got the whole dinner party arrangement worked
out most efficiently and we've never had a
hitch: it goes like clockwork.
```

---

* Economist Sir Noel Frederick Hall (Principal of Brasenose College, 1960–73) and his wife, Eli, were introduced to Roger through an Aldeburgh connection. They had often invited Roger to Brasenose and remained good friends.
† Roger had been introduced to archaeologist Martin Sinclair Hood and his wife, Rachel, through the socialite Lady Dorothy Lygon (generally known as 'Coote').

By April, Roger was openly gushing.

```
Last Sunday was one of those incredibly perfect
days . . . we walked down to Christ Church
meadow, right round by the river and back to
Merton. There we settled on one of the seats
set into the old stone wall, well sheltered
from the light breeze, and with the sun blazing
down full upon us. Here we sat for an hour or
more while Luke read Horace Walpole letters to
me, until we were eventually driven away by a
family with a whining child.
```

He signed off this letter by asking for an update on Lionel and his world. The following month, he repeated his plea: 'It seems to have been a long, long spell with no news of you whatever. Not a word even from Lettice.'

A week later, on 1st June 1974 – almost exactly fourteen years after they began their correspondence – Lionel died, aged 78, with Guido at his bedside.

Roger would dwell on Lionel's life for most of the rest of his own, but at the time his mental energies were so completely devoted to Luke that he did relatively little processing of the loss. Luke had decided to continue living at Regent Street for another two years while he studied for a postgraduate degree and was still almost everything Roger wanted. There was only one flaw: Luke did not see the relationship in the same way that Roger did and would not allow it to become physical.

Without Lionel to write to, Roger poured out his increasing frustrations into his diary.

```
Monday, 9th February [1975]
   I turned in fairly early but just could not
get off to sleep . . . my frustrated longing for
Luke is a real torment. I so yearn for him,
even just to sleep beside him. We are so much
together - so near yet so far. It is just like
being married (though with one aspect sadly
missing.)
```

As frustrated as he was, Roger couldn't bring things to an end. But when Luke's postgraduate degree finished, right on time, he announced to Roger that he would be leaving Oxford and taking up a teaching post at a school in the North.

Roger was resentful that Luke had not done more to stay in Oxford, then afraid of how much more difficult – and empty – life would be without him. He told Luke he would be away because he didn't want to witness his moving out – and then quietly left a day earlier than planned to avoid even having to say goodbye. He placed a note on the stairs, asking Luke not to be in touch for at least several months 'to allow everything to settle down'.

With the distance of time, Roger remained convinced that Luke wasn't straight. He blamed their lack of intimacy instead on a conservative religious attitude to sex, which he couldn't understand and which Luke had never intended to shake off.

Luke was deeply, deeply Catholic and thoroughly
screwed up about sin and sex, or so it
seemed to me. This meant that although he
was gay (I never had any doubt about this)
our relationship was doomed always to be
chaste . . . At that time, I think I was as much
in love with him as it's possible to be without
sex. I felt I wanted to keep him with me for
ever.

Each evening after dinner, he would read
to me for an hour and then he would go back
upstairs for a last hour on his studies before
retiring to his virginal bed while I pined in
half my double bed in the room below. Perhaps
he was just waiting for an overture, longing to
be seduced, wanting to be tumbled into bed and
taken by storm, but unable even by a hint to
make the first move. This is hard to imagine
but I shall never know. Even the copious dry
martinis we knocked back each evening – the gin
proportion growing greater with each one – even
these failed to unlock the last barrier between
us.

It was just my luck that one of the few
friends in my life who truly seemed to have
the potential to be an ideal partner, who came
closest to sharing my interests and lifestyle,
should have turned out to be so unresponsive,
such a non-starter.

Luke's departure was 'the end of a dream, leaving only a void'. He joined the roster of Roger's dashed hopes – after Mario and Danny – rather than giving him what Lionel had found in Guido. Roger decided there and then that he would live alone for the rest of his life. He wouldn't even take a lodger:

```
I can't bear the idea of having someone else in
my house; I feel that if I can't live with Luke
I would rather be on my own.
```

The scar Luke left was lasting. Over the decades that followed, Roger was left wondering whether he was simply unlovable:

```
Where's the problem? Have I always been
looking for the impossible? Or have I just
been unlucky? On the other hand, I can see
that it could equally well come down to a sad
inadequacy in myself, a fundamental personality
flaw.
```

When Roger slipped out of his own home to avoid participating in Luke's departure, he took his little airline suitcase and Gay straight to Wadham College to hide at the Warden's Lodge. Throughout the 1970s, his most constant friend – and the one that much of his social life revolved around – was the Warden's wife, Renée Hampshire.

Renée had spotted Roger as an undergraduate, walking with Gay on the way to the University Parks, and was enchanted by the dog. She had asked around, found another friend who knew him – Eli Hall, the wife of the Principal of Brasenose College – and then planned a dogs' tea party at Wadham for them all.

Together we walked around to the Wadham
lodgings, me with my sleek, powerful German
Shepherd marching purposefully, Eli with her
incongruous Standard Poodle tripping daintily
along in its absurd topiary. In the panelled
dining room of the lodgings, Renée had spread
a cloth on the white wool carpet and set out
two bowls of dog food side by side with water
and other dog delicacies. On the dining table,
the more orthodox afternoon tea was laid out
for the rest of us. Stuart put in a brief
appearance for the purpose of introduction on
his way to a meeting of convocation.

From then on, Roger had an open invitation to bring Gay to run in the lodgings' large gardens, while Roger and Renée would spend hours together in enthusiastic conversation.

She launched into her life history, a random
selection of details such as one doesn't expect
to be told so early in an acquaintance.
  'I'm five years older than Stuart because
I was married before to Freddie Ayer.* And

---

* Philosopher Alfred Jules 'Freddie' Ayer (1910–89) was married to Renée 1932–41. He became president of the HLRS in 1963, helping the society raise significant funds.

Marking Time

I was an heiress in my youth – I inherited Guilsborough Park in Northamptonshire but my cousin, who was a solicitor and one of my trustees, embezzled nearly all the money. I was married to Freddie at the time and we agreed that we shouldn't bring a prosecution because we were socialists and weren't supposed to believe in inherited property.'

She poured out her strange, tormented soul in a torrent – high social conscience about her upper-class privileged background and upbringing, her early relationship with Stuart (how she pretty much seduced him), above all, her passionate and thwarted love for her son, Julian. Altogether, it was an extraordinary outpouring and I just listened as I usually do without surprise or anything more than monosyllabic comment.

I was familiar with her social world up to a point – recognising her references, so to speak. This meant I soon fitted quite conveniently into the household. Often, when she had been indiscreet or unburdened some of her personal anxieties, she would flatteringly say, 'I tell you all these things because you're "family".'

Roger knew that he offered Renée a listening ear and also a 'project', for a woman who was unhappy inhabiting the traditional role of a Warden's wife and who had always previously found her purpose in voluntary social work.

> It was perhaps a pity that I didn't fall into
> the full lame duck drop-out category, destitute
> and dependent, but at least I suffered from
> a very obvious disability, which meant I was
> always obliged to rely a great deal on
> voluntary help.

Through Renée, Roger found himself regularly at events populated by the Oxford elite, becoming friendly by association with public intellectuals like the philosopher Isaiah Berlin and writers including Angus Wilson, who had written one of the groundbreaking gay novels Roger read as a young man. He would describe these moments in his diaries as confirmation that, with Renée's support, he now had a place at the table with some of the most important minds in the country.

> It was the most brilliant occasion of its kind
> I've ever been to, and, probably, am ever likely
> to go to. For four hours, I was spellbound
> by the most amusing conversation I've ever
> experienced. This was as one naively imagines
> all Oxford dinner parties are supposed to be. I
> long to be a Boswell and record it all, but the
> speed and continuity of it all simply left one
> dazed and gasping.

Roger came to consider Stuart Hampshire his intellectual guru, someone who greatly influenced his views 'on every subject under the sun during countless hours of conversation over so many years'. He especially adored the kind of airily dismissive remarks Stuart was liable to come out with in passing ('for instance, on Yeats one day, whom he once met in his youth: "He wrote about 200 lines of fine poetry, the rest is just nonsense."').

But Renée was the one who helped Roger to make his home feel as if it might fit in with her aristocratic origins and who was there at every significant moment in his years after finishing his degree. Renée had looked out for Roger as he fell for Luke, telling him sharply, 'You're on to a loser there. He's got God so he doesn't need anyone else.' And it was also Renée who adopted Gay as her own when she became too old to carry on working as Roger's guide dog, and made sure Roger was with them for Gay's final walk.

```
Somehow she got hold of a child's pushchair and
induced the obedient but no doubt bewildered
old dog to sit in this conveyance and be pushed
up the road to the University Parks, there
to alight and totter about for a few minutes
sniffing interesting odours.
```

Then Roger lost Renée, too. In January 1977, she arrived early one morning at Regent Street. Walking through to the kitchen and standing by the sink, she said quietly, 'I've just come from the hospital. I've had tests and they've found a lump.' She called him twice on 27th April, he recorded in his diary:

345

```
. . . clearly having been at the sherry or
the Sainsbury's Special - she was in that
recognisably woozy state. She insisted that I
go to tea tomorrow in order to help cope with
Lady Medawar. 'She's coming to cheer me up and
I really don't feel up to her.' Then she went
rambling on, 'I think I'm dying only no one
will tell me. Do you think I'm dying? Stuart is
being so nice. Do you think you could find out
and let me know secretly?'
```

Following a double mastectomy, a long period of invasive treatment began. In February 1980, Renée turned up unannounced at Regent Street to give Roger an old travelling desk – walnut, with brass inlay, just the kind of thing she knew would appeal to him, and one of the few remnants of her stolen inheritance. It was, she declared, an early bequest.

The following month, she drove Roger home from a brief trip into town and the two called out 'Seeya' in the mock-student fashion they liked to adopt. The next day, she took a turn for the worse and, after eight more daily updates from Stuart or Julian, Roger got the final call: she had died about an hour and a half earlier, Stuart said. Renée was cremated without any ceremony. Julian did as she had asked and brought her ashes back to the Master's Lodge and buried them in the garden, next to Gay.

Lionel was gone, Luke was gone, Gay was gone and now Renée was gone. Roger's diaries recorded the losses and changes that followed: Lennox Berkeley's increasing frailty; each of his parents' decline and death; the ageing of his Suffolk set and the decreasing frequency of his visits there; Stuart Hampshire's remarriage and the two new infants and stints in America that came with it.

He also wrote about his new guide dog Cresco's aggressive behaviour with smaller dogs and – on several occasions – her abandoning Roger. He agonised over whether to send Cresco away, 'all the more so because of my own hypersensitivity to rejection'. He wrestled too over beginning again with another dog. He knew that he lived under 'a kind of permanent house arrest' without one. But as early as 1982 he was also wondering: 'How much do I really need one in practical terms? My occupations are so concentrated here now.' And this, ultimately, decided it – there was no replacement for Cresco and Roger's life began its new phase, bounded increasingly by the walls of his home.

From early in their correspondence, Lionel Fielden encouraged Roger to think of himself as a man of letters.

> . . . it seems to me that you probably enjoy writing when you get down to it. Otherwise, you wouldn't take three hours over a letter, or recopy it, or write it so beautifully and carefully. Isn't it something to encourage? . . . I don't quite see you living your whole life in an estate office by day and pubs by night. Or is that enough for you?

Roger had always responded enthusiastically, telling Lionel repeatedly that he wished he had the time to spend writing. In one of his last letters before Lionel's death, he had told him again that to be a writer like Lionel was one of his only remaining ambitions: 'to write one really good book. Just one.' In Regent Street, Roger was without the estate agent's office or the pubs, the degree or the social whirl. When Luke and Renée had gone too, and without a dog, there were fewer trips away or interruptions to Roger's days, other than students visiting for tutorials, and his readers.

He started to work on the memoir he had been imagining since the month he became completely blind. Lettice Cooper had suggested at his bedside in Moorfields that writing about the experience could be therapeutic. That sparked Roger to begin what became his lifelong project and in letters to Lettice he said that he was writing for her. Initially, he planned to call a piece about the loss of his sight *Darkness at Noon*. Later, he expanded it into a lengthier essay that included his time at the residential course in Torquay, and used it as part of his Oxford application. This became the early basis for writing about his life from childhood up to 1973 – a memoir he called, in honour of Lionel, *Catching Up*.

The work quickly became a major undertaking, and not only because Roger wanted to include every detail and make every line perfect. Years before personal computers or voice-activated recorders, he had to go to considerable lengths just to produce it, and then to consider what he had written.

```
Writing the way I have to do is a painfully
disjointed process. The worst - most difficult -
aspect is not being able to re-read what I have
written. If you can sit down and scribble what
```

comes into your head, then go over it again
immediately, while it is still fresh in your
mind, deleting, adding, transposing, then one
can achieve a continuity and freshness which
is impossible for me. It has just taken me
six weeks to get my last passage read over to
me. I've not written a word in that time. The
trouble is, I am absurdly diffident and self-
conscious about it and I don't like to ask just
anyone to read it. The same with letters.

I begin by sketching a short section in
Braille so that I can read it back to myself,
then redraft this two or three times, making
numerous amendments all the time - adding,
cutting, rearranging - only then when complete
recording the whole lot onto cassette, again
making alterations as I go along to try to
ensure that it reads smoothly, ironing out ugly
phraseology and repetitions to the best of my
ability. I become entangled in countless jumbled
sheets of Braille and extracts on several
different cassettes which all too easily get
muddled and sometimes inadvertently eradicated.
It would all be so much easier and quicker if I
could actually see the words written on a sheet
of paper - or, I suppose, even on a screen.

I type it up from the master tape, still
making further changes when necessary,
smoothing out previously unnoticed infelicities

so far as possible. Even then, I always
afterwards think of further changes I would
like to make. No piece is ever fully and
finally satisfying.

For many years, Roger harboured an idea he might publish his efforts. He shared excerpts with his literary friends, Lettice Cooper and Heywood Hill, and his former tutors, Angus Walker and Richard Cobb – and all of them praised the quality of his work ('You are a natural writer & you simply must get published your autobiographical pieces,' Cobb wrote to Roger). But this circle of writers also pulled Roger away from his own work. They provided a ready distraction by inviting him to help them instead, and for more than two decades he became almost compulsively dedicated to helping his author friends bring their books into the world.

As early as 1973, Roger found himself giving detailed feedback to Walker on his latest book on Marxism. He spent a large part of the 1980s focusing on Beth Britten's biography, *My Brother Benjamin*, editing drafts and trying to persuade Beth to winnow down an unwieldy amount of material to something that could be printed. There were small vanity projects that never made it, like Anne Hill's attempt at a novel. Others were in an entirely different category.

After Roger left Balliol, Cobb made a habit for the rest of his life of coming to Regent Street to drink, talk and read his latest work into the early hours of the morning. He also regularly sent Roger drafts of his books by post: large bundles of small papers held together with string and rubber bands, variously covered in a mess of typed and handwritten words for Roger and his readers to try to decipher. Roger came to serve as Cobb's unofficial editor, providing comments about style, clarity, sense and focus for most of Cobb's subsequent books.

Somewhere amid all this work to help his friends publish their books, Roger lost confidence in the idea of publishing his own. Lettice sent drafts of his work to her publisher, Gollancz, and Cobb offered to do the same. Heywood volunteered to introduce Roger to publishers after reading his piece about Lionel ('How your fine awareness of atmosphere and place made me ache for Italy!' he declared). But Roger was beset by a feeling of inadequacy, seeking a form of perfection that he could not attain. In the end, he was unwilling ever to part with material until that feeling had passed – which it never did.

Even if Roger wasn't writing for anyone else to read, though, he could not bring himself to stop producing more, editing what he'd done already or considering how he might best arrange it. He wrote and wrote, so much that eventually he had enough to compile a second volume to his memoirs: he called it *Marking Time*.

And then came more. Inside Regent Street, Roger used writing as a way to inhabit the world beyond, to take himself out of the practical limits imposed on him. There was a diary tracking the activities of his life, set against world events. There were countless letters to surviving friends. There were essays about his family history, musings on his beloved Broughton House and the English stately home. There were elegies on the brilliant individuals he had known and loved, especially Lionel, Renée and Stuart, and accounts of the events in his local community (including an especially detailed one about a kidnapping trial he thought was interesting). Even when nothing happened to inspire him, Roger kept going. He simply went back to old material, always trying to make it just a little bit better, a little bit closer to perfect, again and again editing, reordering, rephrasing.

As the 1990s marched on, Roger could be found almost every day in his study on the top floor of Regent Street – the room which had once been Luke's. There, as he wrote, he lived again the times that had been – going back to days, to years when there had been more, back to Balliol, back to London, and back to the gay underground, now a world away. Back to the day when he dropped a letter in a postbox on the Charing Cross Road – a letter that changed everything.

Oxford, 2011

I was sitting at Roger's bedside when he died from the secondary cancers caused by his leukaemia, early in January 2011. A few days before, I had also been sitting at Roger's side, on his red sofa in Regent Street, when the doctor finally worked out that his body could no longer process his pain medication and that, even with constant care, he was incapable of staying at home.

I had been the one to call the doctor. Roger had become unsure of what he was doing and where he was going. He was struggling to follow what we were talking about beyond the immediate and started to repeat himself over and again. For anyone else of his age, forgetfulness might have been normal, but Roger's organised, focused mind had always remained razor sharp. I looked in the box of address cards he kept in the top of his chest of drawers (the inlaid one the gin decanter had always been placed on for our Tuesday evenings) and found the number – written clearly and neatly, no doubt by one of those North Oxford Ladies.

The doctor came, waited with Roger for a while and observed

his behaviours. Together we asked him some questions. Roger, articulate and charming to the end, didn't immediately strike her as in a critical state, but to anyone who knew him well there was no question that things were seriously wrong. In the end, I asked Roger to list the many, various pills he had to take, in what quantities and when, and where they were kept. He was unable to answer. The deed was done. When the doctor left, it was in an ambulance and Roger went with her.

I followed closely behind. In the hospice, I watched him, talked to him, read to him. What else? They took good care of Roger as his mind slipped slowly away. They were gentle when they tucked him into bed, attached clips and tubes, washed his face and pushed his hair behind his ears. I called a priest friend and asked whether he would administer last rites. It would be best not to, he said, given Roger's views on religion, but he would pray for him.

What at first had seemed like a persistent veil of mist impeding Roger from communicating became a thick fog, enveloping the person I knew, until a hard wall existed between us. Now there was silence and stillness: nothing but slow, regular breathing and the occasional swallowing reaction when I placed a sponge of water to his lips. Nurses came in and out of the room, inspecting various cables, lifting Roger's wrist to check his pulse, asking me how I was, if I wanted tea. It carried on like this until, one afternoon, with brilliant sunshine pouring into his room, Roger swallowed, opened his mouth and gasped his last breath.

I hadn't known until that moment how clearly and obviously life leaves a body, when it does. The body was there but the man had, unmistakably, gone. The nurses were kind to me, as they had been to Roger. When they'd turned off the machines, inviting a hushed peace to the room, they left me alone with him for as long as I wanted. In their experience, they said, it would help to stay. It would matter to me that I had.

I spoke a little, cried, touched his hand, pushed the hair away from his forehead. He should look neat, even now. I made one phone call and then gathered up the few things of Roger's which were there, into his small green satchel. Talking books, mostly. A comb. The special mobile phone he'd bought from the RNIB. I thanked the nurses as I passed their desk and asked if there was anything I should do. No, nothing. Not now. They would be in touch. So I left and made my way back, slowly, to Regent Street.

EPILOGUE

A Shilling Life

'as they said when they first stepped on the moon,
it was a small step for man . . . it was one more
tiny thing which did help.'[1]

As Roger spent year after year reflecting on his past and writing in minute detail of his present, there was one question that dominated everything: 'How did I rate?' He wondered how his parents had felt about him as a son. He thought about how he stacked up against his brilliant friends in London and at Balliol. He thought about their lives, their families, their contributions to history. Compared to them, what – really – had he achieved?

Lionel loomed large for Roger as he pondered this question. Roger couldn't send him letters any more but he made Lionel a dominant character in his own writing: the subject of a detailed, standalone biography and the centrepiece of reflections about his other friends. The Lionel Roger described – his published writing, his home, his long relationship with Guido – provided a constant measure for Roger's own life, and at times a reminder of the ways he had fallen short.

When Roger sent excerpts of his memoirs to Heywood Hill

for the first time, Heywood was supportive, but confused by Roger's working title:

> I was delighted to hear that you are at work on your auto-biog. If it's as good as your letters, it shall be a whizz success. I confess to being baffled by 'A Shilling Life'. The Oxford Dic. of Quotations didn't help.[2]

'A Shilling Life', Roger explained, was from the first line of W.H. Auden's poem, 'Who's Who', a sonnet in which a famous, high-achieving man who had 'climbed new mountains; named a sea' sighs as he thinks on a more ordinary man and a more ordinary life, somehow yearning for that man and that life.[3] The poem has many interpretations, but for Roger it articulated how a life of pottering, gardening, reading and writing letters, of doing small jobs around the house, might be as significant as the life of someone lauded as the 'greatest figure of his day'. Perhaps, he concluded, the ordinary man – a man like him – could be considered as worthy of a written account.

Roger continued to muse on this for years: what makes a life important? To write one's own story, is it necessary to be a great man, a notorious criminal, a celebrated artist, or a statesman?

One of the memories Roger enjoyed recounting was of the day after he'd moved the contents of his college room into 41 Regent Street. He had walked with Gay back into town for a conversation with the Oxford City Education Department and decided to pop into Balliol. He found the porter's lodge thronged with the cricket team about to set off for their summer tour, and had stopped to chat with some of them when Christopher Hill came through the gate.

'Hello,' he said looking around, 'what's going on here?'

'It's a revolution, Master,' said one of the team, making play with his favourite historical theme.

'No,' he replied, disbelieving. 'No, it can't be a revolution - not if Roger's here.'

For Roger, this was more than just an anecdote about a witty Marxist historian. It was a demonstration of the monumental change in Roger's position that took place in the early 1970s. No longer the lowly estate agent, no longer a poorly educated boy from a small town, Roger was – however playfully – being held up as a presence which assured rationality and stability, even within an ancient institution. Friendly with the sports crowd and known for being part of an establishment group by the Master of the college, Roger had arrived at the place he most wanted to be. He had managed to become in some way a reflection of Lionel Fielden. He had caught up.

The irony of Roger's Balliol vignette, though, is how thoroughly wrongly Christopher Hill judged the situation. Hill was a pioneer of the idea of 'history from below' – that what ordinary people feel and do shapes the course of events at least as much as their leaders' actions and is equally worthy of historians' attention. But he appears to have had no inkling that the Roger Butler who cheerily greeted members of the cricket team in that porter's lodge in 1973 was in fact a revolutionary.

After his letter was published in 1960, Roger never looked at it again. 'I have never re-read it,' he set down in a memoir forty years later, 'simply because I fear I would now find too much fault with it and wish I could re-write it.' As well as fears about the letter's quality, he still wished that it had been sent by someone famous. He felt it would have mattered more if it had been.

```
Obviously, such a public statement would have
attracted much more attention and carried more
weight if it had been signed by W.H. Auden,
Benjamin Britten and E.M. Forster.
```

Roger knew then that expecting any man to put his livelihood, relationships and liberty at risk in this way was unrealistic. But those risks are exactly what compelled him to take the step of placing an announcement in the national press that he was a homosexual. And that is exactly why Roger's letter is so important, even now. It matters simply because it exists at all – that one person was willing to write it.

Roger's letter is grounded in ideas that became transformational in his own lifetime, and beyond it. His goal was 'breaking through the barrier of public prejudice', and his argument was that being gay was a morally neutral identity, one equal to that of any other. He reasoned that the heterosexual majority could come to understand this by seeing homosexuals presenting themselves on their own terms, without the grubby trappings of an arrest. The criminalisation of homosexuality was more obviously irrational when it was applied to a polite, measured letter-writer, appearing without handcuffs or police officers standing by to justify it. It was easier to see that he was doing nothing wrong when he volunteered the information.

For queer people, meanwhile, Roger's letter modelled a new way to live: unashamed, unapologetic and talking about themselves, honestly and openly, to others. He started chipping away at the pitying language used by heterosexual leaders of the homosexual law reform movement, and so began the process of gay men publicly taking ownership of this cause.

A decade after Roger's letter was sent, Gay Liberation Front campaigners adopted the same theory of social change, using the first issue of the movement's newspaper, *Come Together*, to declare: 'We're Coming Out Proud'.[4] Pride events began to appear across London, with the first march in July 1972. Coming out soon became a pillar of the fight for inclusion and the expansion of ambitions beyond mere toleration.

> How can we honestly be proud of our gayness and build a gay alternative, when we accept the values that make us unable to tell straight people that we are gay? If their values are wrong, then only we can make them change, and we can only do that if they can witness what we are.[5]

The gay rights movement caught up with Roger Butler.

Today, we know that acceptance of gay men and lesbians has come as much from individual homosexual people making themselves known to their parents, their customers, their employers and their colleagues as it has from celebrity revelations. As sons and daughters, friends and neighbours, and as teachers, soldiers, plumbers – or even as estate agents – gay people have been able to extract themselves from the caricature of the malevolent, shadowy underclass and lay claim to fair, humane and equal treatment. This is why coming out is still so important for queer people and why it has also been adopted by other marginalised groups.

But Roger instinctively understood this. In December 1960, he wrote of his letter:

```
I hope so much that many more will have read
it and taken heart at the message we wanted
to get over: 'Homosexuality is nothing to be
ashamed of.'
```

It matters, then, to know that the idea and the language of coming out as a political act appeared, fully formed, in 1960 – the work of a young, otherwise unknown man living in Lewisham. It matters, too, to know that what he did was almost forgotten, because he was too busy fighting a disabling society, and it simply never occurred to him to boast about what he had done.

So it was Patrick Trevor-Roper, often overlooked himself, who saved Roger's name from absolute obscurity when he mentioned the letter during an oral history interview in 1990:

... the [Wolfenden] report came out and in the wake of that, of course, came the debate ... the next milestone, so to speak, to me, was a letter written by three young men . . . the senior Roger Butler . . . saying in effect . . . that we are homosexual, have always been, and expect always to be. Just like that. Quite a good letter.[6]

Later, when Roger learned about his brief appearance in two books about how legal change was won, it did make him think that perhaps his decision to come out had made a difference. He even acknowledged the possibility that he might really have achieved something of historical significance.

```
This probably counts as one of the opening
shots in what was much later to become the Gay
Liberation movement.
```

Ultimately, Roger did just about allow himself to speculate that his greatness might not be perceptible only through the obscure wrangling of an Auden sonnet. But on the measure which mattered to him most, Roger judged himself 'unsuccessful', even fundamentally inadequate.

In all his time at the heart of the gay scene in London, Roger had never found a partner – he had never entered into anything like a meaningful relationship. When he fell in love and got a taste of how a shared life might be, it was with a man who would not (or could not) reciprocate. When Luke left, he dealt a death blow to Roger's hopes for having more.

```
Infatuations there have been in plenty, of
course - I've seldom been without one with
```

all its pleasures and pains - but these have
usually been of a hopeless kind and always
one-sided - my sided - always unrequited. No
one has ever wanted to be my lover and life's
companion. It's rather humiliating never to have
been wanted in the fullest sense, never to have
been the exclusive object of anyone's concern
let alone desire. Somehow, I seem to have
missed out on love.

This is what brought Roger to his terrible conclusion – the one I read to him over and again, right up to his death: 'I shall go to my grave without ever having known the joy of a completely fulfilling relationship.'

Somewhere between moving into Regent Street and that first day I rang twice on his doorbell, Roger had given up on finding love. He had also given up on publishing his memoirs. Worst of all, he had become more and more penned into his home. Many of the friends he most loved had gone and he was dependent on a diminishing group of people for contact with the wider world. He was, Roger believed, simply marking time until the end.

In 2020, when I first began seriously to write about Roger, I realised that I could never do justice to him in anything I might say without hearing all the things he wanted to say to me. It was time to open the pink folder of letters again. It took a lot of courage – Dutch and otherwise – and plenty of encouragement from Louise. I did it first in small doses: four envelopes, far more than four evenings. Sitting on the small sofa in my study, often with gin in hand, I was surrounded by Roger's books, the boxes of his memoirs, his tapes, his photograph albums and – on the small desk behind me – the photograph of him as a young man, smartly dressed, reclining in an English country garden. Roger at his best.

'I would press you to keep these foolish love letters,' Roger wrote early on, 'because they relate to you and I think you may find them interesting and even entertaining in later life.' (Interesting, yes, but to find them entertaining will probably take the detachment of another decade or so.)

There was plenty in those letters to regret and to feed my fears about the role I'd played in Roger's final years. I found confirmation of precisely what had made me feel so conflicted after I'd moved to London. Leaving Oxford hadn't just reduced what I could do for Roger and the time we could spend together, it made Roger anxious, causing him to ask himself continually whether I would eventually abandon him, stop visiting and calling. Any assurances I gave didn't seem to calm his fears, which he repeated often. Hardest to read were descriptions of the pain Roger suffered in the last six months of his life. His body seemed to be falling apart, he knew he was facing the end, and I couldn't be there for him in those dark nights when his fears set in.

But gloom wasn't Roger's natural predisposition. Rather, at heart, he was a hopeful man. His favourite brand of hope was a very real belief in what he called 'flooks': moments of chance that changed his life in wonderful ways. For a man who rejected any idea of the divine, he spoke of these coincidences with a surprising reverence. They possessed a strangely magical quality,

THE LIGHT OF DAY

as if opportunities had been offered to him by a benevolent universe, just at the right time. His favourite literary quote was from Shakespeare's *Julius Caesar*, as he reminded me in one of the letters. It spoke of just such moments:

There is a tide in the affairs of men
Which, taken at the flood, leads on to fortune

Roger's memoirs identified plenty of these in his life: spotting Wildeblood's book on the Charing Cross Road and discovering who and what he was so quickly; his 1960 letter being read by Lionel Fielden, a friend who dropped into his world from a thousand miles away, who became his mentor and inspired Roger to see himself and his future in a very different way; meeting by chance Fred Reid, a blind historian who showed Roger he really could go to university; Lionel pushing into Roger's path Lettice Cooper, the woman who first encouraged Roger to write, and whose patronage enabled him to get to Oxford and 'catch up'; even the bequest of Roger's aunt Ethel, the supportive older lesbian, which gave Roger enough financial freedom to leave the horrors of commuting life in London and do what he wanted most.

Roger wrote another letter to me about them early in 2010:

```
FLOOKS! I was thinking the other day how
flooks - the flooks of chance - can profoundly
change one's life. It was flooks which have
twice brought me to Oxford in my life - the
first was Hitler, the second was Lettice
```

```
Cooper. And when Nick went to America nearly
seven years ago, it was a sheer flook that you
happened to be around at the time and that
he should have thought of suggesting that you
might like to be a stand-in reader during his
absence. The rest, as they say, is history.
```

Roger believed I was his final 'flook' – one last gift bestowed upon him by some external force – but this underestimated his own role in creating the circumstances that brought us together. I cycled to 41 Regent Street in 2003 because I'd been asked to by someone I'd met at a gathering of gay men. I'd attended that gathering at the invitation of a student LGB rep. I knew him because I'd been an LGB rep at Christ Church. I took that role because when I'd come up to Oxford in 2000, I was welcomed so warmly into the queer community. All this was only possible because I could arrive at university and live openly as a homosexual – and come out. Like all those other people, I was able to do that – in no small part – because Roger Butler had posted a letter in 1960.

Whatever he believed to be the cause, Roger wrote to me that my arrival in his life pulled him away from simply marking time and into a period when he experienced an overriding joy. And it all began with that kiss.

```
Looking back to when you first came here – and
it was brave of you to present yourself to
someone completely unknown merely on Nick's
recommendation – I remember how awkwardly formal
```

we were for the first couple of months, how
difficult it seemed to break through to the
whole gay aspect. I desperately didn't want to
frighten you off by saying anything that might
be misinterpreted as an unwelcome overture until
that magical moment when you, thank God, took
the initiative and, as you were leaving to go
home for the Christmas holiday, put your arms
around me and kissed me. You've probably never
realised how amazed and thrilled I was, and,
of course, not being able to see it took me
completely unawares. But bless you, bless you,
sweetheart. In that instant, the ice was broken.
When you came back in the New Year we were
immediately on a completely different footing.
Since then, a kind of easy, cosy familiarity has
developed - we've grown very comfortable with
each other, so it seems to me, so naturally I've
grown to love you dearly. It's been the greatest
joy of this late phase of my life.

For a good deal of time after Roger's death, I'd believed that
I was just one more disappointment. I had failed to change his
unhappy conclusion that he had never been loved or that he was
unlovable. I'd comforted myself that perhaps writing a book,
perhaps writing *his* book, was a means to make up for that –
finally to do something he wanted of me.

The letters in the pink folder told me a different story. Roger's
final writing project, at the end of a lifetime of writing, wasn't

intended to chastise, to point out my failings or regret the limits of what I'd given him. It was simply this: to tell me that he loved me and to assure me that I had given him exactly and completely what he wanted. I had shown Roger love, and this was enough.

All my life I've been lucky in having a wide range of interesting friends from the eminent to the criminal (life would have been intolerable otherwise) and of course there have been infatuations galore, always with hopeless and inappropriate men. And so, believe it or not, till now, I've never known what it is actually to be in love - sometimes I thought I was but now I see I've never really known what it meant. In fact, to be frank, I had come to believe it was something I was incapable of.

I had come to believe it must be my fault, that I was seriously deficient for some reason, incapable of emotional response and commitment. Well, sweetheart, you've cured me of that all right. It seems hardly credible and I still half fear it's too good to last. But even if this is so, God forbid, I shall still be eternally thankful for the experience, being something I thought I would go to my grave never knowing.

Roger's *Marking Time* memoir was in a completed form when he first shared it with me. After we recorded it together, he edited it occasionally, adding or changing details that occurred to him, or reflecting differently on what had happened to the people he described. But the collection was essentially fixed by the start of the new millennium. His letters to me were something different: almost an appendix to *Marking Time*, a concluding portion of Roger's memoirs. Here he was, describing the final three years of our time together and telling me that the last chapter of his life was different from the one that preceded it. He loved and knew he was loved.

> So this is the great joy – well, one of the
> many great joys – of having you in my life.
> It means that for the first time ever, I feel
> completely free – I don't need to have any
> reservations, no inhibitions with you. In fact,
> I absolutely delight in completely absorbing
> you into my life, holding nothing back, which
> doubtless has surprised you from time to
> time, though you must be used to it by now.
> Sweetheart, it's a wonderful kind of liberation
> such as I've never, NEVER known before.

Again and again, in Roger's letters to me he chanted 'if only – if only'. He wished we'd met earlier in life. He wished I could have stayed in Oxford. He wished we had more time. But even these regrets were wrapped up in happiness at the love he felt. After a lifetime of wondering whether he'd been looking for the impossible, or simply been unlucky, 'Then along came you.'

A Shilling Life

And it is wonderful to be able to relish every minute I'm with you - it's marvellous to have someone to think about all the time and care about and even to worry about a little. I just pray that you will stick with me through the relatively short time that's left - but even if not, at least I'll have had this miraculous experience that I never expected. And when I stop to think rationally for a moment I tell myself how AMAZING it is that you should be so indulgent to me <u>all things considered</u>.

All love sweetheart - we'll talk as usual tonight.

Acknowledgements

This book is only possible because Roger Butler so meticulously recorded his life and because Nick Bamforth was clever enough to introduce him to Christopher.

We are grateful to Headline Press – especially Holly Purdham for believing in the book from the moment she heard about it and Joe Thomas for making sure many more people have heard about it – and to William Morris Endeavor, our agents, and also to Liz Marvin.

We received especially important feedback on draft material from Jackie Brown, Desmond Day, Siôn Rhys Evans and Stacey Young – all of which made the book better.

Encouragement, help and advice were provided generously by many people, amongst which were Eloise Ashcroft, Daniel Baer, Isabel Benenato, John Blake, Samantha Chugh, Joanne Cox-Darling, Alexander Duma, Cara Fitzpatrick, Ben Furnival, Elena Greer, David Hogan-Hern, Anna Keighley, Gilly King,

Brian McCabe, Silvia Melchior, Sue Miller, Douglas Murray, Filippo Novelli, Joanne Ord, Polly Putnam, Caroline Radnofsky, Gulliver Ralston, Benôit Repellin, Jo Read, Christopher Rogers, Amy Russell and Rachel Telford.

We are grateful to *The Wall Street Journal* and the Southlands Methodist Trust for being supportive of our work on this project alongside our commitments to them.

Siôn, Stacey and our families have lived this book with us for years and helped us through a long, complex and at times emotional ride. Thank you.

Bibliography

C. Allen, *A Textbook of Psychosexual Disorders* (London: Oxford University Press, 1962)

C. Allen, *The Sexual Perversions and Abnormalities* (London: Oxford University Press, 1940)

C. Allen, *Modern Discoveries in Medical Psychology* (London: Macmillan, 1937)

R. Allen and Q. Guirdham (eds), *The London Spy* (London: Anthony Blond, 1971)

B. Anderson, *Edward Carpenter: A Victorian Rebel Fighting for Gay Rights* (Kibworth Beauchamp: Matador, 2021)

J. Baldwin, *Giovanni's Room* (London: Penguin, 2001)

N. Bamforth, *Sexuality, Morals and Justice. A Theory of Lesbian and Gay Rights Law* (London and Washington: Cassell, 1997)

P.K. Bandyopadhyay, *The Genesis and Growth of Broadcasting in India: From Lionel Fielden to the Present Day* (Delhi: B.R. Publishing Corporation, 2015)

R. Beachy, *Gay Berlin: Birthplace of a Modern Identity* (New York: Vintage Books, 2014)

E.J.B.D-S-M. Montagu of Beaulieu, *Wheels Within Wheels: An Unconventional Life* (London: Weidenfeld & Nicolson, 2000)

C. Berg and C. Allen, *The Problem of Homosexuality* (New York: Citadel Press, 1958)

A. Bérubé, *Coming Out Under Fire: The History of Gay Men and Women in World War II*, Twentieth Anniversary Edition. (Chapel Hill: University of North Carolina Press, 2010)

S. Brady, *John Addington Symonds and Homosexuality: A Critical Edition of Sources* (Basingstoke: Macmillan, 2012)

B. Britten, *My Brother Benjamin* (Bourne End: Kensal Press, 1986)

M. Bronski, *A Queer History of the United States* (Boston: Beacon Press, 2012)

B. Cant and S. Hemmings (eds) *Radical Records: Thirty Years of Lesbian and Gay History, 1957–1987* (London and New York: Routledge, 2010)

E. Carpenter, *My Days and Dreams: Being Autobiographical Notes* (London: George Allen & Unwin, 1916)

E. Cervini, *The Deviant's War: The Homosexual vs. the United States of America* (New York: Picador, 2021)

G. Chauncey, *Gay New York: Gender, Urban Culture, and the Making of the Gay Male World 1890–1940* (New York: Basic Books, 2019)

E. Chesser, *Live and Let Live: The Moral of the Wolfenden Report* (London: Heinemann, 1958)

D.S. Churchill, 'Transnationalism and Homophile Political Culture in the Postwar Decades', in *GLQ: A Journal of Lesbian and Gay Studies* 15.1 (2009), 31–66

R. Cobb, *Still Life: Sketches from a Tunbridge Wells Childhood* (London: Hogarth Press, 1983)

R. Cobb, *Something to Hold Onto: Autobiographical Sketches* (London: John Murray, 1988)

R. Cobb, *The End of the Line: A Memoir* (London: John Murray, 1997)

D.W. Cory, *The Homosexual in America: A Subjective Approach* (Greenburg, 1951), reprinted in the UK as *The Homosexual Outlook: A Subjective Approach* (London: Henderson and Spalding, 1953)

Bibliography

H. Daley, *This Small Cloud: A Personal Memoir* (London: Weidenfeld & Nicolson, 1986)

R. Dose, *Magnus Hirschfeld: The Origins of the Gay Liberation Movement* (New York: Monthly Review Press, 2014)

R. Duncan, 'The Homosexual in Society', originally published in *Politics*, I, 7 (August 1944)

R. Ellmann, *Oscar Wilde* (New York: Vintage Books, 1987)

E. Faas, *Young Robert Duncan: Portrait of the Poet as Homosexual in Society* (Santa Barbara: Black Sparrow Press, 1983)

L. Faderman, *The Gay Revolution: The Story of the Struggle* (New York: Simon & Schuster Paperbacks, 2016)

G. Farrell, *The Story of Blindness* (Cambridge: Harvard University Press, 1956)

D. Farson, *Soho in the Fifties* (London: Michael Joseph, 1987)

D. Farson, *Never a Normal Man: An Autobiography* (London: Harper Collins, 1997)

S. Feather, *Blowing the Lid: Gay Liberation, Sexual Revolution and Radical Queens* (Winchester and Washington: Zero Books, 2015)

L. Fielden, *Beggar My Neighbour* (London: Secker & Warburg, 1943)

L. Fielden, *The Natural Bent* (London: Andre Deutsch, 1960)

P. Flynn, *Good as You: From Prejudice to Pride: 30 Years of Gay Britain* (London: Ebury Press, 2017)

A. Grey, *Quest for Justice: Towards Homosexual Emancipation* (London: Sinclair-Stevenson, 1992)

A. Grey, *Speaking Out: Writings on Sex, Law, Politics and Society 1954–95* (London: Cassell, 1997)

M.R. Hall, *The Well of Loneliness* (London: Penguin, 2015)

H. Hardy and J. Holmes (eds), Maurice Bowra, *New Bats in Old Belfries or Some Loose Tiles* (Oxford: Robert Dugdale, 2005)

R. Hauser, *The Homosexual Society* (London: Bodley Head, 1962)

A. Herzen, *Ends and Beginnings* (Oxford: OUP, 1985)

P. Higgins, *Heterosexual Dictatorship: Male Homosexuality in Postwar Britain* (London: Fourth Estate, 1996)

H. and A. Hill, *A Bookseller's War* (Wilby: Michael Russell, 1997)

A. Hollinghurst, *The Line of Beauty* (London: Picador, 2004)

A. Horsfall, 'Battling for Wolfenden', in B. Cant and S. Hemmings, *Radical Records: Thirty Years of Lesbian and Gay History, 1957–1987* (Abingdon: Routledge Revivals, 2010), pp.15–33

M. Houlbrook, *Queer London: Perils and Pleasures in the Sexual Metropolis, 1918–1957* (London: University of Chicago Press, 2006)

J. Jackson, *Living in Arcadia: Homosexuality, Politics, and Morality in France from the Liberation to AIDS* (Chicago: University of Chicago Press, 2009)

L. Jarnot, *Robert Duncan: Ambassador from Venus* (California: University of California Press, 2012)

S. Jeffrey-Poulter, *Peers, Queers & Commons: The Struggle for Gay Law Reform from 1950 to the Present* (London and New York: Routledge, 1991)

R. Jennings, *A Lesbian History of Britain: Love and Sex Between Women Since 1500* (Oxford: Greenwood, 2007)

J.-P. Joyce, *Odd Men Out: Male Homosexuality in Britain from Wolfenden to Gay Liberation, 1954–1970* (Kibworth: The Book Guild Ltd, 2019)

H. Kennedy, *Karl Heinrich Ulrichs: Pioneer of the Modern Gay Movement*, 2nd edn (Concord, California: Peremptory, 2005)

A.C. Kinsey, C.E. Martin, W.B. Pomeroy, *Sexual Behaviour in the Human Male* (London: Saunders, 1948) (Part One of the 'Kinsey Report')

J. Kirchick, *Secret City: The Hidden History of Gay Washington* (New York: Henry Holt and Company, 2022)

D.H. Lawrence, *Lady Chatterley's Lover* (London: Penguin Classics, 2022)

A. Leland, *The Country of the Blind: A Memoir at the End of Sight* (Random House Large Print, 2023)

B. Lewis, *Wolfenden's Witnesses: Homosexuality in Postwar Britain* (London: Palgrave Macmillan, 2016)

Bibliography

B. Lewis (ed), *British Queer History: New Approaches and Perspectives* (Manchester: Manchester University Press, 2017)

M.G. Long (ed), *Gay is Good: The Life and Letters of Gay Rights Pioneer Franklin Kameny* (Syracuse: Syracuse University Press, 2014)

M.G. Long, *Martin Luther King Jr., Homosexuality, and the Early Gay Rights Movement: Keeping the Dream Straight?* (New York: Palgrave Macmillan, 2012)

L. Marhoefer, *Sex and the Weimar Republic: German Homosexual Emancipation and the Rise of the Nazis* (Toronto: University of Toronto Press, 2015)

L. Marhoefer, *Racism and the Making of Gay Rights: A Sexologist, His Student, and the Empire of Queer Love* (Toronto: University of Toronto Press, 2022)

N. McKenna, *The Secret Life of Oscar Wilde* (Random House: London, 2004)

S. Mills, *Life Unseen: A Story of Blindness* (London: Bloomsbury, 2023)

S. Morley, *John Gielgud: The Authorized Biography* (New York: Simon and Schuster, 2010)

F. Mort, *Capital Affairs: London and the Making of the Permissive Society* (London: Yale University Press, 2010)

P. Parker, *Isherwood: A Life* (London: Picador, 2004)

P. Parker (ed), *Some Men In London. Vol, 1: Queer Life 1945–1959* (London: Penguin, 2024)

F. Partridge, *Ups and Downs: Diaries 1972–1975*, vol. 7 (London: Phoenix, 2002)

D. Plummer, *Queer People: The Truth about Homosexuals* (London: W.H. Allen, 1963)

K. Porter and J. Weeks (eds), *Between the Acts: Lives of homosexual men 1885–1967* (London: Routledge, 1991)

A.K. Regis, *The Memoirs of John Addington Symonds: A Critical Edition* (London: Palgrave Macmillan, 2016)

M. Reiss, *Blind Workers against Charity: The National League of the*

Blind of Great Britain and Ireland, 1893–1970 (Basingstoke: Palgrave Macmillan, 2015)

M. Renault, *The Charioteer: a novel* (New York: Vintage Books, 2003)

R.B. Ridinger (ed), *Speaking for Our Lives: Historic Speeches and Rhetoric for Gay and Lesbian Rights (1892–2000)* (New York and London: Routledge, 2012)

G. Robb, *Strangers: Homosexual Love in the Nineteenth Century* (London: Picador, 2004)

M. Robertson, *The Last Utopians: Four Late Nineteenth-Century Visionaries and their Legacy* (Princeton: Princeton University Press, 2018)

S. Rowbotham, *Edward Carpenter: A Life of Liberty and Love* (London: Verso, 2009)

L.J. Rupp, 'The persistence of transnational organising: The case of the homophile movement' in *American Historical Review* 116:4 (2011), 1014–39

H. Ryan, *When Brooklyn Was Queer* (New York: St. Martin's Griffin, 2020)

A.C. Saguy, *Come Out, Come Out, Whoever You Are* (New York: OUP, 2020)

M. Schofield, *Sociological Aspects of Homosexuality: A comparative study of three types of homosexual* (London: Longmans, Green & Co Ltd, 1965)

E.K. Sedgwick, *Epistemology of the Closet*, 2nd edn. (London: University of California Press, 2008)

J. Saumarez Smith, *The Bookshop at 10 Curzon Street: Letters between Nancy Mitford and Heywood Hill 1952–73* (London: Frances Lincoln, 2004)

M. Signorile, *Queer in America* (New York: Random House, 1993)

M. Sturgis, *Oscar: A Life* (Croydon: Apollo, 2018)

J. Tudor Rees and H.V. Usill (eds), *They Stand Apart: A Critical Survey of the Problems of Homosexuality* (Kingswood: Windmill Press, 1955)

Bibliography

K.H. Ulrichs, *The Riddle of 'Man-Manly' Love: the Pioneering Work on Male Homosexuality* (Buffalo, NY: Prometheus Books, 1994), 2 volumes, translated by M.A. Lombardi-Nash

K. Walker, *The Physiology of Sex* (Harmondsworth: Penguin, 1965)

K. Walker and P. Fletcher, *Sex and Society* (Harmondsworth: Penguin, 1955)

A. Walter (ed), *Come Together: The Years of Gay Liberation 1970–73* (London and New York: Verso, 2018)

T. Walton (ed), *Out of the Shadows. A History of the pioneering London gay groups and organisations, 1967–2000* (London: Bona Street Press, 2011)

C. Waters, 'The homosexual as a social being in Britain 1945–68', in B. Lewis (ed), *British Queer History: New Approaches and Perspectives* (Manchester: Manchester University Press, 2017)

J. Weeks, *Coming Out: The Emergence of LGBT Identities in Britain from the 19th Century to the Present*, 3rd edn (London: Quartet, 2016)

J. Weeks, *Between the Worlds: A Queer Boy From the Valleys* (Cardigan: Partian, 2021)

D.J. West, *Homosexuality* (Harmondsworth: Penguin, 1974)

G. Westwood, *A Minority: A Report on the Life of the Male Homosexual in Great Britain* (London: Longmans, 1960)

G. Westwood, *Society and the Homosexual* (London: Gollancz, 1953)

C.J. Whisnant, *Queer Identities and Politics in Germany: A History 1880–1945* (New York: Harrington Park Press, 2016)

C. White (ed), *Nineteenth-Century Writings on Homosexuality: A Sourcebook* (Abingdon: Routledge, 1999)

O. Wilde, *De Profundis* (London: Methuen and Co., 1905)

P. Wildeblood, *Against the Law* (London: Weidenfeld & Nicolson, 2019) (originally published 1955)

P. Wildeblood, *A Way of Life* (London: Weidenfeld & Nicolson, 1956)

J. Wolfenden, *Turning Points: The Memoirs of Lord Wolfenden* (London: Bodley Head, 1976)

Reports, Interviews and Published Source Material

The Homosexual Law Reform Society, 'Report of a Public Meeting held in Caxton Hall Westminster on Thursday, May 12th 1960'

Home Office and Scottish Home Department, 'Report of the Departmental Committee on Homosexual Offences and Prostitution' (London: Her Majesty's Post Office), 4th September 1957 [the *Wolfenden Report*], reprinted in *The Wolfenden Report* (New York: Lancer Books, 1964)

Patrick Trevor-Roper interviewed by Margot Farnham, 1990, *Hall-Carpenter Oral History Project*, British Library C456/089. © The British Library

Roger Butler interviewed by Margot Farnham, 1990, *Hall-Carpenter Oral History Project*, British Library C456/091. © The British Library

Conquest of the Dark, a 1955 documentary, the central character from which has many of the same experiences as Roger (see https://player.bfi.org.uk/rentals/film/watch-conquest-of-the-dark-1955-online)

The Church of England Moral Welfare Council, 'Sexual Offenders and Social Punishment. Being the evidence submitted on behalf of the Church of England Moral Welfare Council to the Departmental Committee on Homosexual Offences and Prostitution, with other material relating thereto' (London: The Church Information Board)

Notes

Preface: *The Pink Folder*

1   Patrick Trevor-Roper interviewed by Margot Farnham, 1990, *Hall-Carpenter Oral History Project*, British Library C456/089. © The British Library.

2   Roger Butler interviewed by Margot Farnham, 1990, *Hall-Carpenter Oral History Project*, British Library C456/091. © The British Library.

3   Stephen Jeffrey-Poulter, in *Peers, Queers and Commons. The Struggle for Gay Law Reform from 1950 to the Present* (London: Routledge, 1991), identified Roger's letter as an early public gesture of coming out and 'the first small but significant step towards gay liberation' (pp.66–7). The point was re-emphasised by Nick Bamforth (whose reading slot for Roger I took in 2003) in 1997, in his *Sexuality, Morals and Justice: A Theory of Lesbian and Gay Rights Law* (London and Washington: Cassell), p.285. It was also discussed in 2019 by John-Pierre Joyce in *Odd Men Out: Male Homosexuality in Britain from Wolfenden to Gay Liberation, 1954–1970* (Kibworth: The Book Guild) pp.95–6.

4   Alexander Herzen, *Ends and Beginnings* (Oxford: Oxford University Press, 1985), p.52.

Chapter 1: *Becoming a Homosexual*

1   Roger Butler interviewed by Margot Farnham, 1990, *Hall-Carpenter Oral History Project*, British Library C456/091, Tape 1, Side 2. © The British Library.
2   P. Wildeblood, *Against the Law* (London: Weidenfeld & Nicolson, 2019), (originally published 1955), pp.2–4.
3   P. Wildeblood, *Against the Law*, p.178.
4   P. Wildeblood, *Against the Law*, p.175.

Chapter 2: *A Journey from Angel*

1   Roger Butler interviewed by Margot Farnham, 1990, *Hall-Carpenter Oral History Project*, British Library C456/091, Tape 2, Side 1. © The British Library.
2   Home Office and Scottish Home Department, *Report of the Committee on Homosexual Offences and Prostitution* (London: Her Majesty's Stationery Office, 1957), [*The Wolfenden Report*] paragraph 355.
3   J. Tudor Rees and H.V. Usill (eds), *They Stand Apart. A Critical Survey of the Problems of Homosexuality* (Kingswood: Windmill Press, 1955), p.vii.
4   J. Tudor Rees and H.V. Usill (eds), *They Stand Apart*, p.xi.

Chapter 3: *An Underground Party*

1   Roger Butler interviewed by Margot Farnham, 1990, *Hall-Carpenter Oral History Project*, British Library C456/091, Tape 2, Side 1. © The British Library.

2　R. Allen and Q. Guirdham (eds), *The London Spy* (London: Anthony Blond, 1971), p.157.

3　Cited in B. Lewis, *Wolfenden's Witnesses: Homosexuality in Postwar Britain* (London: Palgrave Macmillan, 2016), p. 219.

Chapter 4: *A Research Subject*

1　Roger Butler interviewed by Margot Farnham, 1990, *Hall-Carpenter Oral History Project*, British Library C456/091, Tape 2, Side 1. © The British Library.

2　R. Hauser, *The Homosexual Society* (London: The Bodley Head, 1962), p.9.

3　R. Hauser, *The Homosexual Society*, p.18.

4　R. Hauser, *The Homosexual Society*, p.24.

5　R. Hauser, *The Homosexual Society*, p.25.

6　A. Torrie, Review in *Mental Health* 22:1 (April 1963), p.29.

7　S. Coates, Review in *The British Journal of Criminology* 3:2 (October 1962), pp.199–200.

8　A. Horsfall, 'Battling for Wolfenden', in B. Cant and S. Hemmings, *Radical Records: Thirty Years of Lesbian and Gay History, 1957–1987* (Abingdon: Routledge Revivals, 2010), (15–33), p.18.

9　J. Mathewson, cited in T. Walton (ed), *Out of the Shadows: A History of the pioneering London gay groups and organisations, 1967–2000* (London: Bona Street Press, 2010), p.89.

10　P. Wildeblood, *A Way of Life* (London: Weidenfeld & Nicolson, 1956), p.47.

11　Cited in the pamphlet, 'Report of a Public Meeting held in Caxton Hall Westminster on Thursday, May 12th 1960', issued by The Homosexual Law Reform Society, p.1.

12　Cited by D. Plummer, *Queer People: The Truth about Homosexuals* (London: W.H. Allen, 1963), p.111.

Chapter 5: *The Letter*

1   Roger Butler interviewed by Margot Farnham, 1990, *Hall-Carpenter Oral History Project*, British Library C456/091, Tape 2, Side 1. © The British Library.

2   Roger Butler interviewed by Margot Farnham, 1990, *Hall-Carpenter Oral History Project*, British Library C456/091, Tape 2, Side 1. © The British Library.

3   *Baltimore Afro-American*, 21 March 1931. Cited in G. Chauncey, *Gay New York: Gender, Urban Culture, and the Making of the Gay Male World 1890–1940* (New York: Basic Books, 2019), p.7.

4   S. Feather, *Blowing the Lid: Gay Liberation, Sexual Revolution and Radical Queens* (Winchester and Washington: Zero Books, 2015), p.51.

5   *Come Together* 6 (May 1971), cited in A. Walter (ed), *Come Together: The Years of Gay Liberation 1970–73* (London and New York: Verso, 2018), p.88.

6   *Come Together* 4 (February 1971), cited in A. Walter (ed), *Come Together*, p.65.

7   J. Weeks, *Coming Out: The Emergence of LGBT Identities in Britain from the 19th Century to the Present*, 3rd edn (London: Quartet, 2016), p.192.

8   Roger Butler interviewed by Margot Farnham, 1990, *Hall-Carpenter Oral History Project*, British Library C456/091, Tape 2, Side 1. © The British Library.

9   The letter was not ultimately published. It is printed by Grey in his *Quest for Justice: Towards Homosexual Emancipation* (London: Sinclair-Stevenson, 1992), pp.279–82.

Notes

Chapter 6: *The Quiet Revolutionary*

1   Roger Butler interviewed by Margot Farnham, 1990, *Hall-Carpenter Oral History Project*, British Library C456/091, Tape 2, Side 1. © The British Library.
2   'The Men in the Wolfenden Report', *Sunday Pictorial*, 26 June 1960, pp.12–13.
3   'The Men in the Wolfenden Report', pp. 12–13.
4   D.J. West, *Homosexuality*, originally published in 1955 (London: Duckworth), was reprinted in 1960 (London: Pelican Books) and again multiple times in the 1960s and 1970s.
5   D. Plummer, *Queer People: The Truth about Homosexuals* (London: W.H. Allen, 1963), p.16.
6   D. Plummer, *Queer People*, pp.19, 103.
7   D. Plummer, *Queer People*, pp.113–14.
8   D. Plummer, *Queer People*, p.15.
9   *Gay News*, Issue 10, 1972, p.5.
10 P. Wildeblood, *Against the Law*, p.36.

Chapter 7: *Italy Calling*

1   Roger Butler interviewed by Margot Farnham, 1990, *Hall-Carpenter Oral History Project*, British Library C456/091, Tape 2, Side 2. © The British Library.
2   Hugh Gordon Porteus, 'Different', *Spectator*, 23 September 1960.
3   Harold Nicolson, 'The Opposition View', *Observer*, 2 October 1960.
4   Kenneth Young, 'Unofficial Mind', *Telegraph*, 1 October 1960.

Chapter 8: *A Looming Shadow*

1   Roger Butler interviewed by Margot Farnham, 1990, *Hall-Carpenter Oral History Project*, British Library C456/091, Tape 1, Side 2. © The British Library.

Chapter 9: *A Stolen Future*

1   Roger Butler interviewed by Margot Farnham, 1990, *Hall-Carpenter Oral History Project*, British Library C456/091, Tape 1, Side 2. © The British Library.

Chapter 10: *Learning to be Blind*

1   Roger Butler interviewed by Margot Farnham, 1990, *Hall-Carpenter Oral History Project*, British Library C456/091, Tape 2, Side 2. © The British Library.
2   Motion proposed by George Wardle MP and resolved in a session of Parliament on 11 March 1914. Accessed: https://assets.parliament. uk/Journals/HCJ_volume_169.pdf p.73, col. 1.
3   G. Farrell, *The Story of Blindness* (Cambridge: Harvard University Press, 1956), p.3.

Chapter 11: *Breaking Free*

1   Roger Butler interviewed by Margot Farnham, 1990, *Hall-Carpenter Oral History Project*, British Library C456/091, Tape 2, Side 1. © The British Library.
2   https://www.legislation.gov.uk/ukpga/1967/60/pdfs/ ukpga_19670060_en.pdf

Notes

Chapter 12: *Coming Up*

1   Roger Butler interviewed by Margot Farnham, 1990, *Hall-Carpenter Oral History Project*, British Library C456/091, Tape 2, Side 2. © The British Library.

Chapter 13: *Catching Up*

1   Roger Butler interviewed by Margot Farnham, 1990, *Hall-Carpenter Oral History Project*, British Library C456/091, Tape 2, Side 2. © The British Library.

Chapter 14: *Marking Time*

1   Roger Butler interviewed by Margot Farnham, 1990, *Hall-Carpenter Oral History Project*, British Library C456/091, Tape 2, Side 2. © The British Library.

Epilogue: *A Shilling Life*

1   Roger Butler interviewed by Margot Farnham, 1990, *Hall-Carpenter Oral History Project*, British Library C456/091, Tape 2, Side 1. © The British Library.
2   Heywood Hill to Roger Butler, 5 April 1982.
3   W.H. Auden, 'Who's Who' in *Collected Poems*, ed by Edward Mendelson (London: Faber & Faber, 1994).
4   *Come Together* 1, November 1970, cited in A. Walter (ed), *Come Together*, p.45.
5   *Come Together* (Camden, April 1972) cited in A. Walter (ed), *Come Together*, p.182.
6   Patrick Trevor-Roper interviewed by Margot Farnham, 1990, *Hall-Carpenter Oral History Project*, British Library C456/089, Tape 1, Side 2. © The British Library.

Christopher Stephens is an academic based in south west London. He is also CEO of an educational charity that promotes research into issues of importance to contemporary society. He has published on a range of topics, from ancient church history to language and practices relating to diversity and inclusion. Christopher met Roger Butler in 2003, as an Oxford undergraduate. He inherited Roger's extensive archive of writings and letter correspondences after Roger's death in 2011.

Louise Radnofsky is a reporter for *The Wall Street Journal* in Washington, D.C., where she has covered healthcare, the White House, immigration and, currently, sports. She holds two degrees in modern history from Oxford, where she attended University College, and one from the Columbia University Graduate School of Journalism. She and Christopher have been friends for more than 20 years.